Praise for In the Shadow of the La

"In the search for meaning and self-transformation, Jewish mysticism is one of the great spiritual resources, attracting ever-wider circles of devotees. Drs. Mark and Yedidah Cohen have made available to an English-speaking public the work of an important, though little known, master of the genre, Rabbi Yehudah Lev Ashlag. Through it, readers will discover a fascinating path to inner harmony and growth through receptivity to the Divine light that fills creation." *Rabbi Professor Jonathan Sacks, Chief Rabbi of Great Britain.*

"Here is a fresh and highly readable translation of writings by an authentic Master Kabbalist. Among the many books of Kabbalah now available, this will stand out for its unique combination of depth, authenticity, and clear, direct speech." *Rabbi Arthur Green, Professor of Jewish Thought at Brandeis University, author of "Seek My Face, Speak My Name."*

"It is a wonderful translation and introduction! You rendered perfectly that exquisite language of the Jew before the nameless: intimate, tender, simple, sweet and oh so eloquent. A real contribution." *Rabbi Don Singer, Sensei.*

"Rabbi Ashlag, in touch with the sacred, is a true mediator of that affinity with the One that enables us to remember that we are here, not for ourselves, but for the great purpose. Mark and Yedidah Cohen have translated the text with integrity and with compassion. This book is not 'about'. It will initiate you into the greater service." *Rabbi Zalman Schachter-Shalomi, ALEPH Alliance for Jewish Renewal, author of Paradigm Shift and Gate to the Heart.*

In the Shadow of the Ladder

Introductions to Kabbalah
by
Rabbi Yehudah Lev Ashlag

Translated from the Hebrew
with
additional explanatory chapters
by
Mark Cohen Ph.D. and Yedidah Cohen M.B.,B.S.

Nehora Press
Safed, Israel

Publisher:
Nehora Press, P.O.Box 2586, Har Cana'an, Safed, 13410, Israel
Tel: 972–4–6923254
email: nehora@actcom.co.il
www.nehorapress.com

The paper used in this book meets the minimum requirements of ANSI/
NISO Z39.48-1992 (R 1997) (Permanence of Paper). Printed on acid-free recycled
paper.

Publisher's Cataloging-in-Publication
(provided by Quality Books, Inc.)
Ashlag, Yehudah.
    In the shadow of the ladder : introductions to
  Kabbalah / by Rabbi Yehudah Lev Ashlag ; translated from
  the Hebrew with additional explanatory chapters by Mark
  Cohen and Yedidah Cohen. -- 1st ed.
      p. cm.
    Includes bibliographical references and index.
    ISBN 978–965–7222–08–9 (trade paper)
    1. Cabala. I. Cohen, Mark, 1951– II. Cohen,
  Yedidah. III. Title.

  BM525.A82 2002   296.1'6
                                  QB102–701547

For Chaya,
with love and thanks

Contents

Preface

The purpose of this book is to provide an authentic English translation of a small but key part of the work of Rabbi Yehudah Lev Ashlag from the original Hebrew. Our overall concern has been to maintain a fidelity to the original text whilst making the ideas of this twentieth-century Kabbalist accessible and readable in the English language.

What constitutes Kabbalah? From where does it originate? Does it fit in with philosophy or religion, or is it mysticism? These are questions asked not only by the academic doing research, but by the interested general reader. Our first chapter of this book, *Kabbalah in Context*, may be seen as a preliminary look at these questions but we make no pretence of an academic study of Kabbalah which constitutes a field of its own. Likewise chapter two, the biography of Rabbi Ashlag and his forebears, is not intended as a historical study but as an opportunity to understand with the inner eye who Rabbi Ashlag was and the tradition of which he forms a part. Nonetheless, our hope is that both the layman and the scholar may benefit from the core of this book which is the *Introductions* which Rabbi Yehudah Lev Ashlag himself wrote as preambles to his major works.

Rabbi Ashlag's thought and his use of language are specific and unique. In our, the translators' *Introduction*, we have looked at topics of faith, God, God's purpose, language and universality which are some of the more immediate issues which arise on first encountering this material. In the chapter entitled *Keywords, Definitions and Concepts*, definitions of words as used in the texts are given to enable the reader to understand the *Introductions* in as precise a way as possible. The book ends with an account of one of the translators' personal interaction with the work of Rabbi Ashlag.

As regards the *Introductions* themselves, one of their dominant features is the many quotations that Rabbi Ashlag brings from the Bible and the Talmud. As he himself explains, the same light that is invested in the Kabbalah is also manifest in these works but is dressed in different garments. Rabbi Ashlag divests the light of its outer garb and reveals the inner meaning of these quotations.

The references to biblical quotations are given in the texts; the references to all other sources may be found in the Notes at the back of the book.

The paragraph numbers given in the *Introductions* are identical to those found in the original text.

The translators are active teachers of the work of Rabbi Ashlag, and are happy to respond to questions, comments or requests for further study. They may be contacted through Nehora Press.

Acknowledgements

Nothing can compare with the beauty and power of these texts in their original language. Rabbi Ashlag's use of Hebrew is clear in style and sparse in words, yet with meanings that unfold at many levels. It is our sincere desire that the translating of these works into English will enable the reader to access some of the beauty and power of the original and allow it to touch his or her soul in the way that ours have been touched by the light within these words. We thank God for the privilege of being able to do this work and pray that it will bring benefit to many.

Our deepest, heartfelt gratitude goes to our teachers of blessed memory, Rabbi Yehudah Lev Ashlag and his firstborn son, Rabbi Baruch Shalom Halevi Ashlag. Although we were not privileged to know them in their lifetimes, we count ourselves amongst their students.

The simple word "thanks" is not adequate to express the gratitude we feel for David Baruch—teacher, neighbor and friend, whose love for the way of Kabbalah he so generously imparts to all with whom he comes into contact.

Without the loving support of Chaya, Yedidah's mother, it is hard to envisage how this project could ever have been carried through. Many, many thanks.

Thank-you also to our friends who criticized the translation and wording. At different times and in different ways, your feedback was crucial. The responsibility remains ours but our gratitude is extended to Dr. Stephen Fulder, whose detailed comments at an early stage made a very definite difference. Our thanks also go to Rami Kot-Gur,

Bracha Yanuv, Chaya Goodman, Ann Bar-Dov, Yehudit and Reuven Goldfarb and Dalit Hadassi.

Finally our gratitude and love go out to our groups who learn the work of Rabbi Ashlag together with us. Especially, we would like to mention here the Wednesday night group who first studied these *Introductions* with Mark and provided the initial inspiration for this translation. To Peter and Pamela Mond, Harriet Shrager, Phyllis Shalem, Bracha Yanuv and Yehudit Hollander goes our deepest appreciation and warmest friendship.

The publishers would like to thank Rabbi Yisroel Miller, the holder of the Hebrew copyright, for his gracious permission to use the Hebrew texts, published by Or Baruch Shalom, for the purposes of this translation.

Introduction
Mark and Yedidah Cohen

The spiritual fruit—Blessing

"Before the creation of the world, all the letters of the alphabet appeared in turn before God, each one declaring that it should be chosen to initiate the process of creation as it had just that especial attribute that would bring the whole world to its perfect resolution. Beginning with the last letter, each one presented its case; but it was found that for each letter, the positive force for good that it represented was balanced by a negative force for evil, leaving the outcome of the world uncertain.

"Then the letter ב *Bet* appeared before God and said to Him, 'Master of the Universe, You can create the world through me because I represent the attribute of blessing [Heb. *bracha*].' God replied, 'Yes, it is through you that I will create the world'" (*The Zohar*).

Rabbi Ashlag explains in his commentary on the *Zohar* that the final intended form of the world is a world filled with love. However, each force for good in the world is balanced by an opposite force for evil. Just as there are four worlds of holiness, there are four worlds of evil which oppose the worlds of holiness such that in this world there is no clear distinction between good and evil. Consequently, it is extremely hard for the world to survive as we do not know how to distinguish between the good and the evil, between the holy and the profane. However, there is one very important distinction between them. Evil is sterile and does not yield fruit. Thoughts and actions which stem from the worlds of evil do not bear spiritual fruits. These thoughts and actions do not give rise to blessing. They wither and fade and come to a dead end.

The opposite is true for those thoughts and actions that stem from the worlds of holiness. They give rise to blessing, and yield the fruit of our spiritual work. Receiving blessing is then the one and only clarification in this world which enables a person to know whether he is identifying with the holy or not. Rabbi Ashlag teaches that *bracha*—Blessing—is the only light that comes to this world directly from its source within the Infinite; untouched, unsullied and unopposed by any negative force.

But what does this blessing consist of, and how can we recognize it? Again, we need to look at the intention of the creation. "And the world will be built out of love," says the Psalmist (Ps. 89:3).

The world of love is the blessing that comes when we are doing our inner work in a way that is right for our soul. Blessing is the spiritual fruit we receive when we are on the right path. The fruit of the spiritual path is not holy visions or experiences. Rather it is the establishment of the world of love that God intends in the creation of the world.

So in our own lives, when we start to put something of our spiritual work into practice, we need to check to see whether we are experiencing and creating more love in our homes and in our relationships, more consideration in our workplace, more patience with our children and our elderly relatives and more kindness among neighbors and friends. If this is so, then we know that our work is blessed and that we are participants with God in creation.

It is only through the blessing, the spiritual fruit, that we can distinguish what is truly good and what is not.

We, the translators, have found blessing in Rabbi Ashlag's teaching and in the tradition of which it is a part. It has brought and continues to bring blessing to ourselves, to our families and to our friends. This book is our invitation to you to share in our blessing and to taste it for yourselves.

The Purpose of Creation

"God created the world in order to give pleasure to His creatures," states Rabbi Ashlag in *The Introduction to the Zohar*. This, he says, is the purpose of the creation. It is what we will experience when the world is based on love.

We all have moments when we experience these words as having a ring of truth to them, but they do not resonate within us in our ordinary consciousness. We only have to look at our own suffering and the suffering of others to know that we are not receiving much pleasure. What can Rabbi Ashlag mean? How does he know that this is the Creator's purpose? He explains in *The Introduction to the Study of the Ten Sephirot* that our perception of how the One relates to us changes as we grow in our ability to give and to serve. The study of Kabbalah and its practice teach us how to give unconditionally. As we learn how to give, our perception of how God gives to us refines, grows and changes.

The ultimate perception of Divine providence is that of the *tzaddik*, the enlightened master, who knows and experiences that God is Good and does good to all, unconditionally. It is through the perception of the *tzaddik* that Rabbi Ashlag knows the purpose of creation. Despite the fact that God as the One is, in essence, unknowable, the *tzaddik* can experience the light that emanates from God as being totally good, totally giving and totally benevolent to all that is created.

Faith

We cannot perceive God's goodness directly until we reach the stage of the *tzaddik*. Before this we need faith or belief. There is a common misconception that a religious person has faith and a secular person does not. Rabbi Ashlag points out that it is often factors of upbringing, education, family background and environment that make one person religious and another secular. None of these factors has anything to do with the deep yearning of the spirit which is the vessel for the light of faith.

This deep desire awakens in both religious and secular people. It is a yearning to transcend the world of the senses, thought and rationality. It is a desire to go beyond the polarity of our everyday existence. It is a longing for the One.

Faith manifests itself in our choices. Everyday life challenges us to respond either from faith or from habit. As the saying goes, "The righteous person renews his faith every day." It takes courage to choose to act in faith despite all the evidence of ears, eyes and even thoughts. In the face of pressure from our conditioning, our social surroundings and the media, our faith manifests itself when we choose to go beyond the clamor, choosing to believe. It is in faith that we find our truest freedom.

Language

The code in which the Kabbalah was written and handed down orally through the centuries is called "the language of the branches." Imagine a tree whose roots are in the spiritual worlds and whose branches spread out into this world. Every entity in this physical world can be considered as a separate branch, the roots of which originate in the spiritual worlds. Thus the sages, when wanting to discuss or record perceptions of spiritual realities, used words which normally signify objects or values that pertain to this physical world. Unfortunately, ordinary people, who were unaware of this use of language, then mistook the nature of Kabbalah and what it is saying. Much misconception about the Kabbalah arose. For the first time in the long history of this tradition, Rabbi Ashlag has opened this code and made it possible to learn Kabbalah without being misled in this way.

Rabbi Ashlag pays enormous attention to the precise meaning of words, and his pivotal work, *The Study of the Ten Sephirot*, is, in part, a type of spiritual dictionary. As translators, we are aware of his extremely accurate use of language and we would like to discuss certain aspects of it which have influenced our translation.

The Term "God"

Rabbi Ashlag usually uses the Hebrew word *HaShem* (the Name) as referring to God. This is the colloquial term used in Hebrew writings, as well as in spoken Hebrew, as a substitute for the holy four-letter name of God, which is not pronounced. We have translated the term *HaShem* as "God," and this is its accepted translation in the English language. But this carries its own problems. Everyone comes to this work with previous ideas and conceptions carried over from their life-experiences and cultural conditioning and these can influence our ideas of what God is and color what Rabbi Ashlag is actually saying.

The Ari states, "No thought can grasp Him." The One, in essence, is completely unknowable. No term, name or attribute that we may ascribe to "the One" can capture the essence of God in any way at all. In this sense, the term "God" does not have any meaning as such. So, if you have negative connotations or feelings associated with the term "God," as many of us may have, we suggest that you simply substitute a different term every time you come across the word "God" in this book. You may find "The Power of Love" or "The Source of All," for example, to be more comfortable.

Does God have a Gender?
Modern day sensitivity regarding not specifying a gender for God has helped us look closer at the language used in these texts which seem to be implying that God is a "He." Is Rabbi Ashlag simply using language from an older era or is a deeper meaning intended?

Male/female polarity is clearly expressed throughout the Kabbalah. The male, according to the language of the branches that we discussed above, represents the attribute of giving. This stems from the simple biological fact that male-ness is expressed in nature through its capacity of giving seed to the female. Female-ness is expressed by the ability to receive seed from the male. This is as true of the vegetable and animal kingdoms as it is of the human.

God, referred to as "He," is thus the Kabbalists' way of expressing that aspect of God as having the attribute of Giver. God as "She" is commonly termed the *Shechinah* and implies God when displaying the attribute of Receiver.

Since most of the text in this book deals with God as acting according to the attribute of Giver, Rabbi Ashlag usually refers to God as "He." When Rabbi Ashlag does use the term *Shechinah* when God is displaying the attribute of Receiver, then the female form "She" is used. It is clear that Rabbi Ashlag is not implying that God has a gender. He states more than once that the essence of the One is unknowable. God as "He," in the language of the branches, does not mean that God is a male. It refers to the One when exhibiting the quality of giving.

A person can therefore be seen as having within themselves both male-ness and female-ness, the potential for both giving and receiving. In his relationship to God as the Giver, a man may find it helpful to connect with his female-ness. A woman in her role as mother or friend may find herself activating her male aspect as she gives. *Binah*, the archetypal feminine *sephirah*, actually exhibits male-ness in her capacity of giver (*Zohar*, Vol. i, 17).

In this translation, we have therefore stayed with Rabbi Ashlag's usage of pronouns as they refer to God, feeling that they exhibit a deeper meaning than is commonly understood.

Adam, the Complete Human Being

Let us now consider his usage of the word *Adam*, meaning "Man" which occurs throughout the text. Again, before one apologizes for Rabbi Ashlag, it is worth looking at the actual use of language to see if there is a deeper meaning hidden here, in accordance with the principles of the language of the branches.

The word *Adam* really means the human being who has the potential for exhibiting the highest consciousness and thus becoming one with God. *Adam* represents the archetypal human being, male and female; the one made in God's image. The eternal soul, the highest of all the spiritual worlds, is called *Adam Kadmon*. The first soul that was created was called *Adam*, half of which was female and half, male.

So Rabbi Ashlag's usage of the term *Adam* embraces all human beings who work to fulfill their own inner consciousness and potential. Male and female, we are all called upon to do the work of Torah and *mitzvot* with full consciousness. Rabbi Ashlag taught that as regards the inner work, there is no difference between a man and a woman. So, wherever possible, we have rendered the word *Adam* as "a person," to include both men and women and have used the pronouns "he," "she" and "they" as translations for the word *Adam*.

Adam, used in the generic sense, we have translated as "Man" or "Man-kind." Gender specific man is usually rendered in Hebrew by different words such as *ish, gever* or *zachar*.

Universality

Finally, for whom is this book intended? On the one hand, the Kabbalah is the Jewish wisdom tradition and is intimately bound up with Jewish Law, Torah, Jewish ritual and Jewish legend. Equally, it is far more than this. It is beyond parochialism. Its message is truly that of love, compassion and service. Its thrust is universal and all are welcome to partake of it.

We would like to underline this by concluding with a teaching of Rabbi Ashlag's on the creation of Man.

When God made Adam, the first human, He created one eternal soul. After the eating of the fruit of the Tree of Knowledge, that one soul split into millions of souls—all the souls that make up the past, the present and the future human community. From this teaching, we see that all humanity is, in fact, one soul (*Introduction to the Panim Me'irot U'Masbirot*).

May the day come soon when we will experience ourselves as part of the One Soul.

Chapter 1

Kabbalah in Context

Mark and Yedidah Cohen

When we study the Kabbalah, we are connecting with an ancient tradition whose roots go back, perhaps even as far as the dawn of humanity. It is a teaching about what human beings are, where we come from, where we are going and how to get there.

On the one hand, Kabbalah teaches that God's ultimate purpose in creation is to give pleasure to His creatures. We are all on the way to enlightenment and in this we have no choice. God operates in instantaneous eternity and as a result we are already there—perfect and complete. On the other hand, Kabbalah also teaches the meaning of our experiences within the reality in which we all live. Our lives contain pain as well as pleasure, suffering as well as joy. The healing and repair of creation is the special work of human beings, co-creators within the framework of time and space.

This tradition has a very high degree of authenticity. It was transmitted from master to pupil, down through the millennia. Its books were written by *tzaddikim* for others of similar stature in days long before the printing press was ever thought of, in which every word and every phrase was carefully weighed and considered. The authors intended their writings to be read only by others who were themselves enlightened or well on the way to becoming so. There was no intention, for most of the history of this tradition, of publishing anything for the consumption of the general public, or of even indicating to a wider audience that such a tradition existed. For the most part it was a secret tradition, passed down privately from sage to highly qualified disciple, without any publicity whatsoever.

All this has changed today, and not because unauthorized people have got hold of material to which they should not have had access. These times are different. They are very special. This was recognized by Rabbi Abraham Isaac Kook (1865-1935). A great Kabbalist himself, he saw that in our times it is both necessary and desirable to remove this secrecy from the tradition and to make it available to everyone. The reasons why this should be so are part of the Kabbalistic teachings and are discussed in the texts presented here.

However, when something which has been secret for so long is at last made public, there are certain dangers associated with this process, which can be likened to travelling along a narrow path with a precipice to the right and another precipice to the left. The right hand danger is that as the Kabbalah moves into the public domain, anyone who has access to pen and paper or to a word processor may put out that he is a Kabbalist. Many books then appear on Kabbalah with all kinds of weird and wonderful ideas and the reader has no way of assessing what is an ego-trip and entirely fanciful, and what is an authentic teaching. The left hand danger is that, even though authentic Kabbalah books are now available to the general reader, they remain incomprehensible as they are written in a kind of code; a shorthand that needs to be unraveled and explained before it can be understood.

In this present work we have tried to avoid both of these pitfalls.

On the one hand, we have been concerned to adhere to straightforward principles of Kabbalah, not wandering off into fantasies. For this reason, we have put at the heart of this work, a translation of two Kabbalah texts by an authentic modern master, Rabbi Yehudah Lev Ashlag (1886-1955). On the other hand, we have gone to some length not just to present this material but to explain it and show how to work with it. Kabbalah was never meant to be just another body of knowledge. Its purpose was always to serve as a tool for self-transformation.

The deeper one goes into Kabbalah, the more one sees that it can be considered as a unifying principle which provides a context for many other disciplines. The sciences, mathematics, psychology, sociology, religion and the arts may be seen as having a home within Kabbalah. As science develops, more and more correlations are being found between it and the spiritual world as depicted by Kabbalah. The principles behind holograms, fractals and morphogenic fields were known to the ancient sages. Carl Jung and Roberto Assagioli are just two founders of major schools of psychotherapy who knew and were profoundly influenced by Kabbalah. The terms of reference of the Deep Ecology of Joanna Macy and Vandana Shiva are fundamental to Kabbalah. Until humankind recognizes and transmutes greed into a concern for others, no amount of "greening" is going to make much difference. The wisdom teachings of Tibetan Buddhism with their emphasis on cause and effect, the importance of selflessness, and the nature of the real enemies of the human as being the untamed mind and passions, could just as well have been written by the Kabbalists as by the Tibetan Lamas.

The Kabbalists saw themselves very much in the same way as Plato describes the philosopher who has viewed reality as it is and therefore can recognize illusion when he sees it. In *The Republic*, Plato uses the metaphor of humanity as being chained inside a dark cave, facing inwards so that all that people can see are their own shadows on the cave walls. This, for them is reality, as they know nothing else. Once in a while, however, an individual is released from his chains and ascends to the mouth of the cave where he sees the sun, which he recognizes as being reality. In the light of this understanding, he now knows that the flickering shadows on the cave wall are nothing but illusion, but the rest of humanity is not yet aware of this. The philosopher then has an ethical obligation to return once more into the darkness of the cave in order to help some of his fellow men release themselves from their chains. The true Platonic philosopher or the Master Kabbalist is someone who has had a direct perception of reality and whose teachings come straight from this perception.

Direct reality is beyond thought and beyond language. So, when reality is viewed from the highest perspective, no thought attaches to what is being perceived and no language comes naturally to label what is being viewed with a concept or name. All that is simply is. However, when a person wants to communicate what *is* to others, he or she must use some words and concepts. He or she needs to attach labels to his or her perception, otherwise one would be utterly unable to describe anything of one's experience. The Kabbalists therefore had two choices before them. They had either to invent an entirely new language to describe spiritual realities or to use our ordinary everyday language which pertains to this world but in a different way. They chose the latter course.

In Kabbalah, this is known as *The language of the branches*. Rabbi Ashlag explains the language of the branches in the following passage, taken from his major work, *The Study of the Ten Sephirot*:

"First of all we need to know that when we want to talk about spiritual entities which are beyond space, time and movement, and even more so when we refer to Divinity, we do not have the words available with which we can express ourselves or even think about such matters. All of our vocabulary is extrapolated from the world as it relates to our senses. So how can we use words taken from our everyday vocabulary in an area that cannot be experienced by the senses or even imagined by the imagination? For example, if we consider a delicate word such as "lights," even that is simulated and borrowed from the light of the sun or the light felt by satisfaction. So how can we use these words to express ourselves when dealing with matters of Divinity? The use of such a word will certainly not give the reader a true sense of what is actually being talked about.

"This is even more so in the case where we are using words to reveal in writing a complex discussion of the wisdom of Kabbalah on the printed page, in a manner similar to that of researchers of any other discipline. Then, if we were to err in our understanding of the precise meaning of even one word which is used inaccurately, the reader would become completely confused and would not understand the whole discussion.

"For this reason, the masters of Kabbalah chose a special language which can be called "the language of the branches." It is based on the premise that there is no entity or pattern of behavior in this world which is not drawn from its root in the spiritual worlds. On the contrary, the beginning of every entity in this world is in the upper worlds and only subsequently does it come down into this world. Thus the sages found a ready-made language at their disposal which they could use to communicate their perception of the upper worlds both orally between each other and in writing across generations. They simply took the names of the branches which appear in this world, such that each name, being self-explanatory, points as with a finger to its spiritual root in the higher worlds.

"This adequately explains the fact that there are to be found in most books on Kabbalah, expressions which are astonishing and which sometimes appear alien to the human spirit. Once they [the sages] had made the decision to express themselves through the language of the branches, they could not omit any one of the branches when they wanted to express a certain concept simply because it sounded odd, as they could not exchange one branch for another. Just as two hairs do not sprout from one single pore, so two branches never come from the same root. It would not be possible to omit one element of this complex spiritual reality simply on the grounds of sensitivity to the word that signifies it, as omitting a concept would cause a defect and lead to great confusion in the entire exposition of the teaching. This is because the Kabbalah—more so than any other intellectual discipline—depends on a structure of interlocking concepts which influence each other through a process of cause and effect. All of its concepts are intimately linked together from beginning to end, literally, like one long chain. Therefore one is not free to exchange words one for another. On the contrary, we must use exactly the appropriate branch, which points as with a finger to its root in the higher world. Then we must explain the term, giving an exact definition which can be understood by students.

"As long as people's eyes have not been opened so that they can directly perceive spiritual phenomena and they are still ignorant of how the branches in this world relate to their roots in the higher worlds, they are like blind men feeling their way along a wall as they are not able to understand even one word in its true meaning. Every word is the name of a branch which relates to its root. Therefore the only possibility of understanding is for them to receive an explanation from a master Kabbalist who, when he explains a concept, is really translating from one language to another; from the language of the branches to the colloquial spoken language, and thus he is able to explain a spiritual concept to some degree."

Kabbalah is a practical teaching about the process of self-transformation. One can call it a road-map of the soul, going through stage after stage until a person finally enters a state of consciousness referred to as *transformation through love of God*. This is a state of wholeness and enlightenment in which, wherever we cast our eyes, we see, through the vision of love, Divine goodness. This state, and how we arrive at it, are described in detail in the text.

The Kabbalistic texts are meant to be a tool. Through learning them, we release into ourselves the great light that is hidden within them. A constant refrain is that God is hidden within the holy texts. At the highest level, Rabbi Ashlag tells us, God and the Torah are one. There is no difference between them. As the Torah begins to descend through the worlds in a series of contractions, then the Divinity within it becomes more and more concealed but it is nevertheless still there.

Divinity, in Kabbalah, gives rise to light, which, although one and unchanging, undergoes many subtle transformations from the point of view of the vessels which contain it. Light can be "concealed" or "revealed," it can be "direct" or "returning," it can be "surrounding" or it can be "inner." Our aim is to create an appropriate vessel into which the light can enter. The whole purpose of creation, of all of history and culture, is for humanity to become a vessel which can contain the full plenitude of Divine Light. As long as this is not yet the case, much of the light remains outside as "surrounding light" which influences the vessel and waits until the vessel is properly constructed so that it can enter. Once the light has fully entered the vessel, the purpose of creation is fulfilled.

The English romantic poet William Wordsworth wrote of humanity,

"Trailing clouds of glory, we come from God who is our home." Our beginnings are within Divinity and then we forget. We move down into gross material form, no longer remembering who we are and where we have come from. Gradually, over many incarnations, we work our way up once more, in the end to return to Divinity, in perfect unity with the One.

This downwards movement, followed by a gradual return, is one of the central themes of Kabbalah. Kabbalah tells us that revelation can only occur in a place where there was, first, concealment. Consciousness is always preceded by unconsciousness. The fact is that by the time we read this material, we have long since "left" the presence of Divinity and have fallen deeply asleep. Our study is both a call and a means to awaken.

In this, the Kabbalah is optimistic. Rabbi Ashlag enthusiastically quotes Ben Haha, a Rabbi from the period of the *Mishnah*, around two thousand years ago, who said, "The reward is according to the suffering" (*Ethics of the Fathers*). There is much suffering in life, but Kabbalah insists that this suffering has meaning and pays dividends. The greater the concealment, the more light will be revealed when the transformation takes place.

Kabbalah is all about healing. The original Hebrew word for this is *tikkun*—repairing something which needs healing, which has gone a little off track. As we work on our own healing, so the world changes too. The microcosm that is a single person is part and parcel of the macrocosm. They are as alike as two drops of water. It is as if God has done a certain percentage of the work of creation and now says, "Over to you to do the rest!" This is our challenge and responsibility as human beings created in the image of God. These texts show us what to do and explain to us how to do it. When we study them, we are doing a true work of healing, for ourselves and for others.

Chapter 2

Rabbi Ashlag and his Predecessors

Mark and Yedidah Cohen

Rabbi Ashlag, in terms of his contribution to Kabbalah, may be seen as the spiritual heir to both Rabbi Shimon Bar Yochai and to Rabbi Yitshak Luria, the Ari.

Rabbi Shimon Bar Yochai

Rabbi Shimon Bar Yochai is considered by tradition to be the author of the *Zohar*, the central text of the Kabbalah. Although the exact authorship of the *Zohar* is disputed, Rabbi Ashlag himself did not enter into the academic controversy over its composition. Relying on the depth and quality he saw in it, he felt that it had to have been composed by one who was at least of the spiritual standing of Rabbi Shimon Bar Yochai. For further discussion of his perspective, see the *Introduction to the Zohar* (paragraph 59).

Rabbi Shimon Bar Yochai lived in Israel during the time of the Roman occupation around the second century. During Rabbi Shimon's lifetime, the Romans harshly tried to suppress Jewish learning and persecuted the sages. His teacher, Rabbi Akiva, died a martyr's death and Rabbi Shimon had to flee.

The following account is given in the Talmud:

"Rabbi Shimon Bar Yochai and his son went and hid themselves in the study-house. His wife would bring them bread and a jug of water. But when the decree became more severe he said to his son, 'Women are of unstable temperament. She may be tortured and expose us.' So they went and hid in a cave. A miracle occurred and a carob tree and well of water were created for them. They would strip off their garments and sit up to their necks in sand. The whole day they studied. When it was time for prayers, they robed, covered themselves, prayed and then put off their garments again, so that they would not wear them out. Thus they dwelt twelve years in the cave.

"Then Elijah came and stood at the entrance of the cave and exclaimed, 'Who will inform Rabbi Shimon Bar Yochai that the Emperor is dead and his decree is annulled?' So they emerged. Seeing a man plowing and sowing, they exclaimed, 'These people forsake eternal life and engage in temporal life!' Whatever they cast their eyes on was immediately burnt up. Thereupon a heavenly voice came forth and cried out, 'Have you emerged to destroy my world? Return to your cave!' So they returned and dwelt there twelve months saying, 'The punishment of the wicked in hell is limited to twelve months.' A heavenly voice then came forth and said, 'Go forth from your cave!' So they went out. Wherever Rabbi Eliezer [Rabbi Shimon's son] caused harm, Rabbi Shimon Bar Yochai healed. He said to him, 'My son, you and I are sufficient for this world.'"

Rabbi Shimon Bar Yochai, together with his son, received the great wisdom of the Kabbalah during their sojourn of twelve years in this cave in the form of visions and what today we might term "channelling" from Moses and from the prophet Elijah.

On their emergence from the cave, Rabbi Shimon gathered together a band of holy disciples. He taught them and together they experienced many levels of higher consciousness and angelic visions, much of which is recorded in the *Zohar*.

Rabbi Abba, one of the holy band, acted as Rabbi Shimon's scribe. He was given this task because he had a particular gift of writing in a way such that only the initiated would be able to understand. Thus the *Zohar* was locked away from the common people for centuries.

On the day that Rabbi Shimon died, he gave one of his greatest teachings to his disciples. To this day, the anniversary of his death and his ascension to the higher worlds is celebrated as a holiday in Israel with thousands of people singing and dancing as they visit the site of his grave in Meron, in the Upper Galilee.

Rabbi Yitshak Luria, the "Ari" (The Lion)

There were individual Kabbalists throughout the ages who were able to penetrate and understand the mysteries of the *Zohar*, but the first great teacher to systematize the underlying principles contained within the *Zohar* did not appear until the sixteenth century.

He was Yitshak Luria who was born in Jerusalem in the year 1534.

Shortly after his birth, his father died and his mother took him to live in Egypt with his uncle. Even as a young child, he was recognized as having great potential. His uncle supported both him and his mother. When a young man, he built himself a hut by the Nile and he would spend week after week there in seclusion, studying and meditating on the *Zohar*. His great achievement was the uncovering of the principles which underlie the *Zohar*. Like Rabbi Shimon Bar Yochai before him, he had many revelations of Elijah the prophet who taught him the higher wisdom.

In 1569 he moved to Safed in the Galilee where there was a community of Kabbalists. Even though many of them were renowned in their own right, they recognized his greatness and accepted him as their teacher. He gathered a group of disciples around him, chief of whom was Rabbi Chayim Vital [1542-1620]. The Ari's influence on this group of disciples is inestimable but he died only two years after his arrival in Safed, in the year 1572. The Ari's main work is called the *Etz Chayim*, "the Tree of Life." It was written down by Rabbi Chayim Vital and not published until many years after his death.

In the form in which it was published, the *Etz Chayim* is completely impenetrable. There is a certain code to it, and without a knowledge of this code, little sense can be made of it. This was, of course, intentional on the part of Rabbi Chayim Vital. He arranged the Ari's teachings in this way, so that only those who had reached high levels of spiritual attainment would have the key to unlock these teachings. For the rest, they would not make any sense. This is part of the old tradition of concealing the teaching of Kabbalah that originated in ancient days and continued until modern times.

It was left to Rabbi Ashlag, to finally explain the writings of the *Zohar* and of the Ari in a way that could be clearly understood by anyone, regardless of spiritual stature.

Rabbi Yehudah Lev Ashlag

Born into a Chassidic family in Warsaw in the year 1886, Yehudah Lev's interest in Kabbalah was awakened at a young age, even though he could not as yet understand it. The story is told that at the age of eleven, a book fell off a shelf and hit him on the head. His father picked it up and while replacing it, told him that it was a book for angels, not for people. But the young Yehudah decided that if it was printed, then it was certainly intended for human beings! So he started to study Kabbalah secretly and as a young man would slip pages of the Kabbalah of the Ari between the pages of his Talmud in order to study them without anybody noticing.

At the age of eleven, he began to study books of ethics and did not leave one book and go on to the next until he had fully put into practice what he had learned. At the same time he worked on his character to the extent that, by the age of fifteen, he was so attached to the truth that he was completely incapable of telling a lie. He tried to educate himself to act continuously as one who is in the presence of a great King.

By the age of eighteen, he already regarded himself as a "man", by which he meant a person who desires to resemble God in the sense of, "as He is merciful, so you be merciful." By the age of twenty-four, he had no further interest in his own desires but continued to ascend both in knowledge of Torah and in the work on his own character with an unending vigor, yet always with complete modesty. No one could have known of his inner work from the outside.

At the age of nineteen, he received ordination from the great Rabbis of Warsaw. He served as a rabbi in Warsaw for the next sixteen years. At age twenty, he married and his wife Rivkah Rosa bore him eleven children, seven of whom survived. His eldest son, Rabbi Baruch Shalom Halevi Ashlag, became his foremost pupil and later succeeded him in his work.

Already he had the habit that he was to retain all his life of rising at one o'clock in the morning to study the secrets of Torah—the Kabbalah—until daybreak. His life was totally dedicated to study and prayer. His wife took over the financing of the household, but they lived in great poverty.

His daughter tells how at the Sabbath table, her father would sit quietly, totally consumed by the holiness of the Sabbath. He took no interest in food. Even the smallest children knew not to disturb him. His students would come and then he would teach Torah, his whole person burning as if with a holy flame. His teachers were the

Chassidic Rebbes; the Rebbe of Kaloshin, the Prosover Rebbe and the Belze Rebbe.

The focus of Rabbi Ashlag's life was how to put the Divine first, over and above all worldly matters and personal needs. The service of God was his central desire. Through the years, he struggled to understand the words of the Ari and of the *Zohar*, until an extraordinary incident occurred which he related in this letter to his cousin, dated December 1928:

"I will describe to you everything that happened from beginning to end through which I merited this wisdom by virtue of the great mercy of God.

"On the twelfth day of the month of MarCheshvan, on a Friday morning, a certain man came and introduced himself to me. It became clear to me that he was wondrously wise in Kabbalah and also in many other disciplines. As soon as he started to speak, I began to sense his Divine wisdom. All his words had a wondrous quality to them, a sort of glory. I really trusted my feelings in this regard. He promised to reveal to me the true wisdom. I studied with him for three months, meeting him every night after midnight in his home. Mostly we talked about matters of holiness and purity. However, each time I would implore him to reveal to me a secret from the wisdom of Kabbalah. He began to tell me chapter headings but he never explained any concept fully. So I was left with tremendous yearnings. Then one time, after I had greatly implored him to do so, he fully explained a concept to me and my happiness knew no limits.

"However from that time I began to acquire a little ego, and as my haughtiness increased, so my holy teacher began to distance himself from me. But I did not notice this happening. This continued for around three months, in the last days of which I could no longer find him in his home at all. I searched for him but I could not find him anywhere.

"Then I truly became aware of how he had become distanced from me. I was extremely sorry and began to mend my ways. Then in the morning of the ninth day of the month of Nisan, I found him and apologized profusely for my behavior. He forgave me and related to me as before. He revealed to me a great and deep teaching on the subject of a ritual bath that is measured and found to be too small. I once more experienced tremendous joy.

"However I saw that my teacher had become weak. I stayed at his house and the next morning, the tenth day of Nisan, he passed away, may his memory shield us and all Israel. There are no words to describe the greatness of my sorrow, for my heart had been full of hope to merit this great wisdom of Kabbalah, and now I was left naked and with nothing. I even forgot for the moment all that he had taught me on account of my extreme sorrow.

"From then on, I prayed with all my heart and soul with untold longing, every moment of the day, until I found favor in the eyes of my Creator, may He be Blessed. Then, through the merit of my late teacher and his Torah, my heart was opened to the higher wisdom which from then on flowed through me like an overflowing spring. By the grace of God, I also remembered all the deep teachings that I received from my late teacher, thanks be to God. I have no way to thank God or praise Him sufficiently for the great good He has bestowed upon me.

"My late teacher was a very successful businessman and known throughout town as a fair trader but no one at all knew that he was a Master Kabbalist. He did not give me permission to reveal his name."

In the year 1922 it became clear to Rabbi Ashlag that although he was established in Warsaw as a rabbi with many pupils, his life's work was to continue in the Holy land. He and his family left Warsaw and journeyed to Israel by ship. He was thirty-six years old at the time.

At first on arrival he tried to hide his achievements in Torah and work for a living, not wishing to use the Torah for his own benefit. But his greatness was already known and he was unable to hide himself.

Rabbi Ashlag made initial contact with other Kabbalists in Jerusalem but was bitterly disappointed when he saw that they had no deep understanding of the Kabbalah and no concept of the principles underlying it.

Slowly, a small group of true and dedicated students gathered around him. The stories of these first students would make a book in itself. Each and every one of them was a *tzaddik* in his own right; men who worked on themselves unceasingly, serving God. His main lesson, or *shiur*, was given from one o'clock in the morning till nine o'clock in the morning. Then the men would go off to work to support their families.

His teaching attracted opposition, including from the wives and relatives of the men themselves. But to these men, only one thing mattered and that was their connection with one whom they increasingly saw as a holy man of God.

In the year 1924, Rabbi Ashlag moved to the neighborhood of Givat Shaul on the outskirts of Jerusalem. He was appointed Rabbi there and his house became a center of learning. His students told that in order to understand his lessons, they had to exert themselves much harder than they needed to over a page of Talmud. However Rabbi Ashlag explained each concept clearly and soon their understanding grew. His pupils would meet in the middle of the night and make their way over the then very dangerous area between the old city of Jerusalem and Givat Shaul, paying no attention to the physical danger or discomfort—the main thing for them was to unite with this holy man.

Rabbi Ashlag chose his students with great care. Only those who had a true desire to serve God and who were mature enough, did he allow into his lessons. After his main lesson of the day, he would often step outside onto the balcony of his house and carry on lecturing for a further four hours on ways to serve God. He would help his students with their inner problems and show them how to become closer to God, each one according to his own soul's needs. Otherwise Rabbi Ashlag remained hidden. His outer behavior did not reveal his own burning desire to serve God and his deep cleaving to Him. Only amongst his small chosen band did he allow his true self to emerge.

His students told that when they left his lesson, they would come out into the outer world and be amazed. "How do people waste their time on such vanity and materialism?" they would think.

In the year 1926, Rabbi Ashlag commenced writing his works. The first work, *Panim Me'irot U'Panim Masbirot* consisted of two commentaries on the *Etz Chayim* of the Ari. He would sit and write more than eighteen hours a day. But it was very difficult to publish the books. There was no money for the paper and costs of publication. His students, married with families, had scarcely enough to support themselves and he himself lived in great poverty.

He then published a short collection of articles which appeared under the name, *Matan Torah* (Gift of the Bible), the purpose of which was to explain the essence of the Kabbalah and the essence of religion in such a way that the secular world could relate to it as well.

In the year 1933, Rabbi Ashlag started his monumental work, entitled *Talmud Eser HaSephirot* (The Study of the Ten Sephirot), which encompasses all the works of the Ari. In this work he reorganized the writings of the Ari according to the flow of spiritual principles embedded within them as cause and effect. *The Talmud Eser HaSephirot* contains sixteen parts and is a major contribution to written Kabbalah. The introduction which he wrote to it is translated here and may be found in chapter four of this book.

Until the *Talmud Eser HaSephirot* was published, it is fair to say that within the Jewish tradition, Kabbalah was held to be a secret, hidden doctrine. With the publishing of this work, Rabbi Ashlag removed the secrecy and made it possible for any person of reasonable intelligence to approach this material and learn from it.

In the year 1943, Rabbi Ashlag began his commentary, the *Perush HaSulam* (The Ladder) on the *Zohar*. The commentary consists of a translation of the *Zohar* from its original Aramaic—an ancient Semitic language—into Hebrew together with his explanation of each paragraph.

Dire poverty affected Rabbi Ashlag and his students. The cost of printing, the paper and the ink were beyond their means. In many places, he was to write that due to lack of funds, he had to shorten his explanations. His students sold their belongings in order to raise the money for the printing of this work.

At the height of the writing of this commentary, he moved to Tel Aviv. Shortly afterwards he suffered two heart attacks. At first he could not move from his bed and he remained weak for many months. Unable to truly rest, his convalescence was prolonged. His son, Rabbi Baruch Ashlag, acted as his secretary until he was strong enough to write again.

Rabbi Ashlag in his lifetime achieved that which nobody before him had attempted. He penetrated to the heart of the wisdom of the Kabbalah, understanding it, teaching it and publishing it. By doing this he went against the contemporary convention which was to keep it secret. But he knew that its time had come.

The importance of the published works of Rabbi Ashlag may be considered in the following way: A person cannot move from his or her ego-centered consciousness towards one of love, of affinity with the Source without the illumination given by contact with the sacred.

By reading such works we are placing ourselves in an environment which is unfamiliar—to the extent that we are unfamiliar with our souls. Gradually, the contact with this environment starts having its effect on us, loosening our ties with our material desires, awakening in us, and bringing to our consciousness, the truer desires of our souls. Even if we read with little or no understanding of what we are reading, the surrounding lights of the Kabbalah awaken us albeit at a subtle level. In our struggles to understand such material we attract stronger, higher lights to ourselves. When we persevere, fixing a regular time for study, then these lights have the power to connect ourselves with our souls. This is what is meant by "the light of Torah which brings a person to the good way."

Rabbi Ashlag emphasizes the importance of allowing our study to affect our behavior in practice. Without the constant attention on our inner intention, our work in Torah and *mitzvot* has little meaning. He decried the misuse of Torah and the empty practice of the *mitzvot* so common among the religious establishment. Outer ritual carried out without the intention of service is the drug of death, he declared. This attitude stirred up opposition but he did not react, preferring to continue his true work of writing and teaching.

Using the same principles operative for the individual he applied them at the level of the community. He wrote about the establishment of a new society based on these same principles of love, compassion and concern for each other. He foresaw the environmental disaster towards which the world is headed and warned against it—long before such a thing was even contemplated. He spoke about the need for global economic reform in which the poorest nations should receive more of the world's resources, and the rich, less.

Rabbi Ashlag's teachings on how to work on the self, based on the principles of Kabbalah, were later expanded on by his first-born son, Rabbi Baruch Shalom Ashlag, who continued teaching and enlarging on his father's work after Rabbi Ashlag's death in 1955.

Regarding the *Introductions* brought here, Rabbi Baruch Shalom Ashlag said, "My father told me that he wrote the Introductions to his books in such a way that they appear outwardly simple. This was intentional in order that only whoever was fitting should see the true depth that lies within them."

Chapter 3

Introduction to the Zohar
Rabbi Yehudah Lev Ashlag

In this Introduction I would like to clarify some seemingly simple matters. These are issues with which everyone is, to some extent, involved and much ink has been spilt in the effort to clarify them. Despite this, we have not arrived at a sufficiently clear understanding of them.

The first question we would like to ask is, "What is our essence?"

Our second question is, "What is our role as part of the long chain of reality of which we are such little links?"

The third question concerns the paradox that when we look at ourselves, we feel that we are defective or fallen to the extent that there can be none as despicable as ourselves. But when we look at the Creator who made us, then we find that we must really be creations of such high degree that there are none more praiseworthy than ourselves, since it has to be the case that from a perfect Creator only perfect works can issue.

Our fourth question is, "According to our intellect, God must be Good and do good, there being no higher good than that which He does. How, then, could He create so many creatures who, right from the start, suffer and feel pain throughout all the days of their lives? Surely it is in the nature of the Good to do good or, at any rate, not to do so much harm!"

Our fifth question is, "How is it possible that an eternal Being, without a beginning or an end, could bring into existence creatures which are finite, die and have an end?"

2. In order to completely clarify all these matters, we first have to make some preliminary inquiries. We cannot investigate the essence of God as He is in Himself, because thought cannot conceive of Him in any way at all. We have no notion of God as He is in Himself. However, we can and should investigate God in a way that is positive and fruitful, namely by looking at His acts. As the Torah recommends, "Know the God of your father and worship Him" (1 Chron. 28:9). It is also written in the *Song of Unity*, "From Your works, we know You."

So our first inquiry is, "How can we conceive of creation as being an innovation; something entirely new that was not included in God before He created it?" After all, it must be clear, if one thinks about it, that there cannot be anything that is not included within God. Likewise, common-sense tells us that one cannot give something if one does not have it within himself or herself to give.

Second inquiry: You may argue that since God is omnipotent, He must be able to create something that is entirely new and which He does not have within Himself. Then the question may be asked, "What may this reality be, concerning which one may determine that it does not exist within God but is a completely new reality?"

Third inquiry: The Kabbalists have said that the soul of Man is part of God in the sense that there is no difference between God and the soul, except that God consists of the whole and the soul consists of a part. The Kabbalists compare this to a stone quarried from a mountain. There is no difference between the stone and the mountain except that the mountain is the whole and the stone is a part. If we look at this example, we can see that the stone is split off from the mountain by a blade which is specific for this purpose and which separates the part from the whole. But how can we conceive this as appertaining to God; that He could separate off a part of His essence to the extent that it would leave His essence and become a part which is separated from Him? How can we conceive of the soul as being only a part of God's essence?

3. Fourth inquiry: The framework of evil in the world (called "the other side" or "the shells") is so entirely estranged from God's holiness that one cannot even imagine such an extreme divergence. How is it possible for evil to issue forth and emerge from the Holy One? Not only that, but it is God, who is Holy, who sustains the framework of evil.

Fifth inquiry: This investigation concerns the revival of the dead. The body is so abject that from the moment it is born it is destined for death and burial. Not only this, but the *Zohar* tells us that until the body is completely decomposed the soul cannot ascend to its place in the Garden of Eden as long as any measure of the body still remains. If this is so, why do the dead need to be revived? Couldn't God have just given delight to the souls without the body? What is even more surprising is the statement of the sages that when the revival of the dead will take place, the bodies will be resurrected together with their blemishes, so that no one can say that this is someone else! Only subsequently will God heal their blemishes. We need to understand why it would matter to God that people might say, "This is someone else," to the extent that He would re-create these blemishes which would then require healing?

The sixth inquiry: This concerns the statement of the sages that Man is at the center of reality. All the higher worlds, together with this physical world and all that is in them, were only created for Man's sake. They also required that a person should believe that the whole world was created just for him or for her. It seems difficult to understand that God troubled to create all these worlds just for the sake of this little person who, compared with the reality of this world, has only the value of a hair—and even much less if one compares him or her with the reality of the higher worlds which are without number or limit. Furthermore, why would Man need all of this?

4. In order to understand all these questions and investigations, one strategy is to look at creation as a process and to examine its end state, which is the ultimate aim of creation. After all, it is not possible to understand any process by examining it whilst it is still developing. Only by looking at its final outcome can one understand it. It is clear that we are not dealing with a Creator who created the world without purpose. Only someone who had taken leave of their senses could conceive of a Creator who had no purpose in His creation.

I know that there are certain self-styled wise men who do not follow the path of Torah, who say that God created the whole of reality but left it to its own devices, seeing that the creatures, being so worthless, were not fitting for such an exalted Creator to oversee their petty and despicable ways. But what they say is nonsense, for it would not be reasonable to assert that we are petty and worthless unless we had already concluded that we had created ourselves with all our defective and despicable tendencies. But from the moment we decide that the Creator, who is Perfect beyond all perfection, is the craftsman who created and planned our bodies with all their positive and negative tendencies, then we also have to say that from a perfect worker can never issue an imperfect or defective work. Every work testifies to the quality of its maker. What blame may be attached to a shoddily made garment if an incompetent tailor sewed it? The story is told in the Talmud of Rabbi Eliezer, the son of Rabbi Shimon, who chanced to meet an extremely ugly man. He said to the man, "How ugly you are!" "Tell the Craftsman who made me, 'How ugly is the vessel you have made!'" replied the man.

Philosophers who claim that it is due to our own lack of worth and insignificance that it was not fitting for God to watch over us and so He abandoned us, only publicize their own ignorance. If you were to meet a person who could invent new creatures just so that they should suffer and experience pain throughout their lives as we do, and, not only that, but who would then discard them as worthless without even wanting to supervise them in order to help them a little, wouldn't you despise such a person? Is it possible even to consider such a thing about God?

5. So common sense dictates that we understand the opposite of what appears, superficially, to be the case. We are actually extremely good and supremely high beings, to the extent that there is no limit to our importance. We are entirely fitting creations for the Craftsman who made us. Any lack that you might like to raise concerning our bodies, after all the excuses one might make, must fall squarely on the Creator who created us. He created us together with all our tendencies. It is clear that He made us and we did not make ourselves. He also knows all the processes that are consequent on our nature and on the evil tendencies He planted within us.

But, as we have said, we must look to the end of the process of creation and then we will be able to understand it all. There is a proverb that says, "Don't show your work to a fool while you are still in the middle of it."

6. Our sages have taught us that **God's only purpose in creating the world was in order to give pleasure to His creatures.** It is here that

we need to put our eyes and focus our thoughts because **it is the ultimate aim and purpose of the creation of the world.** We need to consider that since the purpose of creation was in order to give His creatures pleasure, it was therefore necessary for God to create within the souls an exceedingly large desire to receive all that He planned to give them. After all, the measure of any joy or of any pleasure is commensurate with the measure of our will to receive it, to the extent that as the will to receive grows larger, in like measure the pleasure received is the greater. Similarly, if the will to receive pleasure is lessened, then, in like measure, the pleasure in its receiving is correspondingly reduced.

The very purpose of creation itself necessitates the creation within the souls of a **will to receive** that is of the most prodigious measure, compatible with the great amount of joy with which God intends to give delight; for great pleasure and a great will to receive it go together.

7. Now that we know this, we are in a position to understand our second inquiry with complete clarity. We wanted to know, "What is that aspect of reality of which we can be absolutely certain that it is not to be found within God and is not included in His essence, but of which we can say that it is an absolutely new creation, something brought into being which did not exist before?"

Now we know clearly that it was God's purpose in creation, which is to give pleasure to His creatures, that necessitated the creation of the measure of the will to receive from Him all the pleasantness and good that He planned for them. We can now see that it is this will to receive which was most definitely not included in His essence until He created it in the souls, as from whom could He Himself receive?

So God created something new that does not exist within Himself. It follows directly from the purpose of Creation that it was not necessary to create anything else besides this will to receive. This new creation is sufficient for God to fulfill His entire plan of the purpose of creation by which He intends to give us pleasure. All the content of God's purpose; all the varieties of good which He intends for us, emanate directly from God's essence. He does not create them anew but they emanate and are drawn directly from His Being into the large will to receive which is in the souls. It is thus totally clear that the only substance that pertains to the creation itself is the will to receive.

8. Now we can come to understand the insight of the Kabbalists of whom we spoke in the third inquiry. We wondered how they could say that the souls are part of God in a way which is equivalent to a stone quarried from a mountain, there being no difference between the stone and the mountain except that one is a part and the other is a whole. Even if we are to assume that the stone is separated from the mountain by the metal instrument especially designed for this purpose, still, how is it possible to say such a thing regarding God's essence? And by what instrument could the souls become separated from His essence and leave the state of being included within the Creator in order to become the created?

We are now in a position to understand the matter well. Just as a metal instrument cuts and divides a physical object, splitting it into two, so in spirituality, it is *difference of form* that divides one entity into two. For example, when two people love each other, we may say of them that they cleave to each other as if they were one body. The opposite is also true. When two people hate each other, we say that they are as far from each other as the East is from the West. We are not discussing their locality, whether near or far. Our intention is whether or not they embody *affinity of form*.

When a person enjoys affinity of form with his or her friend, each one likes what the other one likes, and dislikes what his or her friend dislikes. They love each other and are as one with each other. If, however, there is any difference of form between them, for example, one loves something even though the friend hates it, then according to the degree of this difference of form, they are removed from each other. Opposition of form occurs when everything that the one loves, the other one hates and vice versa. Then they are as far away from each other as the East is from the West, at two opposite poles.

9. Difference of form separates spiritual entities in the same way that a blade separates objects of the physical world; the degree of separation being given by the degree of opposition of form. From this you may see that since the souls have, innately, the will to receive God's pleasure which, as we have clearly shown, does not exist within God the Creator, they have acquired a difference of form from God. This acts to separate them from His essence in a way similar to that of the blade which splits the stone from the mountain. It was through this change of form that the souls emerged from the totality of the Creator and became differentiated from Him, thus becoming creatures.

However, that which the souls attain of God's light comes directly from His Being, from His essence. So from the perspective of God's light which the souls receive within their vessel—the vessel being *the will to receive*—no separation exists between the essence of God and between themselves, as the light which they receive is a direct emanation of His Being. The only difference that exists between the souls and God's essence lies in the way that the souls form a portion of His essence. In other words, the measure of light that the souls receive within the vessel which is their will to receive, already constitutes a part which has separated from God. The antipathy of form which the will to receive embodies is the vehicle which creates "the part" as opposed to "the whole." Through it, the souls left the aspect of the whole and embodied the aspect of the part. And so we see that there is no difference between God and the souls except that one constitutes a whole and the other constitutes a part just as in the case of a stone quarried from a mountain. Understand this well as there is nothing more to be said in this very high place!

10. Now a doorway has opened for us to understand the fourth inquiry. We asked, "How is it possible that from God's holiness the whole framework of uncleanness and the shells (the evil) could arise, given that they are absolutely at the opposite pole from God's holiness? How could He possibly support and sustain them?"

First of all, we need to understand the essential nature of the framework of uncleanness and the shells. These are the great wills to receive that, as we have said, are the substance of the souls' essence inasmuch as they are created. For it is only through their will to receive that the souls are able to receive all the content of the purpose of creation. However, the will to receive does not remain in this form within the souls, for, were it to do so, the souls would, of necessity, be permanently separated from God because the antipathy of form which is within them would separate them from Him.

In order to remedy the matter of this separation which is laid upon the vessels of the souls, God created all the worlds and divided them into two frameworks; according to the inner meaning of the verse, "One opposed to the other, God made them" (Eccles. 7:14). This refers to the four worlds, *Atzilut, Briyah, Yetsirah* and *Assiyah* of holiness and opposed to them are the four worlds, *Atzilut, Briyah, Yetsirah* and *Assiyah* of uncleanness. He stamped the *will to give benefit* within the framework of the four worlds of holiness, removing from them *the will to receive for oneself alone*, which He placed within the framework of the four worlds of uncleanness, through which they became separated from the Creator and from all the worlds of holiness.

For this reason, the shells are referred to as "dead" as in the verse from the Psalms, "They ate the sacrifices of the dead" (Ps. 106:28). The wicked who are attracted to the shells are referred to as "dead" in the same way. The sages say that the wicked in their lifetime are called "dead" as the will to receive for themselves which has been stamped within the framework of uncleanness is in opposition of form to God's holiness, thus separating them from the "Life of All Lives." The framework of uncleanness is at the opposite extreme from Him. God, having no aspect of receiving within Himself, is only giving. The shells, having no aspect of giving, only receive for themselves for their own pleasure. There can be no greater opposition of form than this. We have already seen that spiritual distance starts with a measure of difference of form and ends with opposition of form which is the ultimate in spiritual distance.

11. The worlds unfold until we arrive at the reality of this physical world where body and soul exist, and likewise a time of spoiling and a time of healing. Our body, which is formed from the will to receive for itself alone, comes forth from its root within the purpose of Creation but it passes via the framework of the worlds of uncleanness, as Scripture says, "A man is born like a wild ass" (Job 1:12). It remains subject to this framework until a person reaches thirteen years of age. This period is designated "the time of spoiling." Then, from the age of thirteen onwards, through performing *mitzvot* which he or she does in order to give benefit to others and pleasure to the Creator, the person begins to purify the will to receive for oneself which is inherent within them. The person gradually transforms the will to receive for oneself alone into a will to give benefit. By this means, a person progressively attracts to themselves a holy soul from its root within the purpose of Creation. This soul passes through the framework of the worlds of holiness and enclothes itself within the body, and this is the time of healing.

So the person carries on, continuing to acquire and attain higher levels of holiness drawn from the purpose of Creation within the *Ein Sof* [Infinite]. These higher levels of holiness help the person to transform the will to receive for oneself alone until it has entirely transformed into the will to receive in order to give pleasure to the Creator without including their own self-benefit. It is by this means, that the individual acquires affinity of form with the Creator. For receiving only for the purpose of giving to others or to God is considered as having exactly the same form as pure giving. Thus the person acquires complete unity with God, because spiritual unity is none other than affinity of form. How could a person become united with Him except by becoming one with His qualities? It is by this means that a person becomes fit to receive all the good, the pleasantness and the tenderness that is implicit in the purpose of Creation.

12. So now we have clarified the healing of the will to receive that is inherent in the souls as a consequence of the purpose of Creation. For the sake of the souls, God created the two frameworks described above, one opposed to the other, which the souls traverse, dividing into two aspects, body and soul, that enclothe one another.

Through the practice of Torah and *mitzvot*, the will to receive is eventually transformed into the will to give. Then the souls are able to receive all the Good that is implicit in the thought of Creation. With this, they merit to a wondrous unity with God, since they have earned affinity of form with their Creator through their work in Torah and *mitzvot*. This state is designated as the end of the healing process.

Then, since there will no longer be any need for the other side, the unclean side, it will disappear from the earth and death will be swallowed up forever. The work of Torah and *mitzvot* which is given to the totality of the world during the time period of its existence, and likewise, to each individual during the years of his or her life, has as its only purpose to bring us all to this final healing in which we come into affinity of form with the Divine.

Now we have also explained how the framework of the shells and uncleanness are created and emerge from God's holiness. We have seen that this was necessary so as to allow the creation of the body which a person can subsequently heal through the work of Torah and *mitzvot*. If we did not have such bodies which contain within them the defective will to receive provided by the framework of uncleanness, we would never be able to heal it as one cannot heal anything that one does not have within oneself.

13. However, we have yet to understand how it could be that the will to receive for oneself alone, since it is so defective and distorted, could possibly have issued forth from the thought of Creation in the *Ein Sof* (Infinite), whose unity is so wondrous that no thought or word can express it.

The truth of the matter is, that at the very moment that God had the thought to create the souls, His thoughts completed Creation instantly, God having no need of physical action as we do. Immediately, all the souls, together with all the worlds that were yet to be created, emerged, filled with all the goodness, delight and tenderness that God planned for them, in the same complete and total perfection that the souls are destined to receive at the end of the healing time. This will come about when the will to receive which is within the souls has received all its healing to completion and transformed into pure giving, in total affinity of form with the Creator.

In the eternity of God, the past, present and future function as one. The future functions as the present, as God does not require time. It is for this reason that the defective will to receive that manifests in the form which is separated from God, never existed at all in the *Ein Sof*. On the contrary, it is the very same affinity of form with God, destined to be revealed in the future at the very end of the healing process, that appeared instantaneously in God's eternity. It was concerning this that the sages said, "Before the world was created, He and His Name were One" ["His Name" being the will to receive]. The defective form of the will to receive did not manifest in any way in the souls' reality as they emanated according to the thought of Creation, but they were one with Him in affinity of form, according to the inner meaning of, "He and His Name are One."

14. Therefore we find that the souls have three overall states of being. The first state is their existence within the *Ein Sof*, according to the thought of Creation, where they already possess their future form which belongs to the completion of their healing. The second state is their reality during their worldly state in which they are divided by the two frameworks of uncleanliness and holiness into body and soul. Here, they are given the work of Torah and *mitzvot* in order to transform the will to receive which is within them and to convert it into the will to give pleasure to their Creator, not using it for themselves at all. During the period of this state, the healing work is done on the souls alone, not on the bodies. That is to say, the souls need to remove every element of receiving for themselves which is the characteristic of the body, remaining only with a will to give benefit. This is the form of the will as expressed by the soul. It is taught that even the souls of the righteous cannot enjoy the delights of the Garden of Eden after their death until their bodies have completely finished disintegrating into dust.

The third state is the completion of the healing of the souls after the revival of the dead, when a complete healing will come to the bodies as well. Then the receiving itself, which is the form of the body, comes under the influence of pure giving, and the souls thus become fit to receive all the good, delight and pleasantness implied in the thought of Creation. Additionally, they merit oneness with God through their affinity of form with their Creator. All this they receive, not with their will to receive for themselves alone, but only through their will to give pleasure to their Creator, as God takes delight when we receive from Him.

From now on, for the sake of brevity, I will refer to these states of the souls as state one, state two and state three. You must remember everything that has been explained here, every time we use these terms.

15. When we look at these three states, we see that the existence of every one of them implies the existence of each of the others with total certainty. If you could imagine any aspect of one of these states not existing, then none of these states could exist.

For example, state three represents the complete transformation of the form of receiving into the form of giving. If this state were not to become manifest, then state one, which is in the *Ein Sof*, could not have come into being. This is because all the perfection, which, in the future, will be expressed by state three, already functions as the present within the eternity of God. Thus, all the perfection implied in state one is like a copy taken from the future into the present of the *Ein Sof*, such that if it were possible that the future were to be abolished, then there could not be a reality within the present of the *Ein Sof*. Thus state three implies the existence of all that is in state one.

This is equally true if something were to be abolished from state two. State two is the reality of the work which is destined to be completed in the third state. This is the work of the spoiling and of the healing and of the bringing forth into incarnation the various levels of the soul. How could the third state come into being if the second state were left incomplete? Thus the second state implies the third state. Likewise, the existence of the first state, which is in the

Ein Sof, wherein already operates all the perfection of the third state, thus requires that state two and state three should become manifest with exactly the same degree of perfection that exists in the *Ein Sof,* no more and no less.

So it is the first state itself that obligates the emergence of the two frameworks of holiness and of uncleanness, one opposed to the other within the second state. It is thus the first state itself which allows the existence of the body, with its defective will to receive, to develop via the framework of uncleanness, in order that we may repair it. If this framework of the worlds of uncleanness did not exist, then we would not have this will to receive and we would not be able to heal it and arrive at stage three, since one cannot heal something unless it is within one. You might want to ask—but it would not be a good question—"How is it that the framework of uncleanness is created from the first state?" On the contrary, it is the first state itself that requires that the framework of uncleanness should exist and be sustained during the second state.

16. We might feel that according to the above, free will is negated, since we are obliged to come to our perfection in the third state as this third state already exists within the first state.

However the matter is as follows: God prepared two pathways within the context of state two with which to bring us to state three. The first path lies through the practice of Torah and *mitzvot* in the way that we have explained above, and the second path is via the path of suffering. Suffering in itself cleanses the body and forces us finally to transform the will to receive which is within us and to accept the form of the will to give, bringing us to cleave to God. This is according to the saying of the sages, "If you reform, that is good, and if not I will set a king like Haman over you who will force you to reform."

The rabbis further commented on the Scripture "In its time I will hasten it" (Isa. 60:22), saying, "If they are worthy, I will hasten it, and if not, it will come in its due time." In other words, if we merit to travel on the first path which is the path of the practice of Torah and *mitzvot*, then we hasten our healing. We do not then need hard and bitter suffering and the longer time required for suffering to transform us against our will. If we take the way of suffering, healing will come, but in its own time. That is, only at the time when the suffering has completed our healing, and we arrive at this healing against our will.

The choice is ours. Whichever way we choose, the final healing which is state three, must most certainly come about because its existence is implied by state one and the only choice that we have is whether to take the path of suffering or the path of Torah and *mitzvot*. So now we have clarified how these three states of the souls are connected to each other and obligate each other's existence.

17. On the basis of what we have now explained, we are able to answer the third question that we asked above (paragraph 1). We noted that when we look at ourselves, we feel that we are defective and fallen to the extent that there can be none as despicable as ourselves. But when we look at our Creator who made us, we find that we must really be creations of such a high degree that there are none more praiseworthy than ourselves, as is fitting for the Creator who created us. It is in the nature of a perfect Creator that His works should be perfect.

From what we have learnt, it can now be understood that our present body with all its occurrences and insignificant acquisitions is not our true body at all. Our true body, that is to say our eternal body, which is perfect with all manner of perfections, is already available, existing and established within the *Ein Sof* in its aspect of state one. There, it is already receiving its perfected form, taken from the future yet to be manifest in state three. Its receiving is in the form of giving, and thus it is in affinity of form with the *Ein Sof*, blessed be He.

So if our first state itself necessitates that in the second state we should be given the shell of our body in its contemptible and spoiled form of the will to receive for ourselves alone, which causes separation from the *Ein Sof*, we should not complain. It is to enable us to repair it and to make it possible for us to receive our eternal body in the third state in all actuality. We do not need to complain about this at all, as our work can only be carried out whilst in this temporal and worthless body, as one cannot heal anything that is not within one.

So, even in this, our state two, we do in fact exist in the measure of total perfection which is fitting and appropriate to the perfect Creator who made us. This body does not damage us in any way as it is destined to die and to be negated. We only have it for the limited time which is necessary to nullify it and to receive our eternal form.

18. Together with this, we have now settled the fifth question that we asked (paragraph 1). We wanted to know, "How is it possible that from an Eternal Being could issue forth creatures that are transient, destructive and harmful?" From the explanations we have already given, we can understand that the truth is that we have already come forth from God as eternal creatures in all perfection in a way that is fitting to His Eternity. Our eternal state necessitates that the shell of the body that is given to us only for the purpose of work should be temporal and worthless. For if it were to remain in eternity, then we would forever remain separated from the Source of our Life, God forbid! We have already stated (in paragraph 13) that the present form of our body, that is the will to receive for oneself alone, is not found at all in the eternal thought of Creation, for there we exist in our form which pertains to state three. But we need to have a body here in this reality of state two in order to enable us to heal it. Regarding the situation of the creatures of the world other than Man, we do not

need to consider them in any different way. As we will see further on (paragraph 39), mankind is the center of creation. The other creatures help to bring Man to his perfection and thus go up and down together with him, rather than in an autonomous fashion.

19. Now we can answer the fourth question that we asked. Since it is in the nature of the Good to do good, how is it that God could create creatures that suffer and feel pain all their lives? As we have already said, all these sufferings necessarily follow from our state one, in which our complete and eternal perfection is received from our future state three. This perfection compels us either to follow the path of Torah and *mitzvot* or the path of suffering in order to arrive at our eternal form in state three in actuality (paragraph 15).

All these sufferings prevail only over our shell of a body which was created only for death and burial. This teaches us that the will to receive for oneself alone that is in the body was likewise only created in order for us to blot it out, remove it from the world and transform it into the will to give. The sufferings that we undergo are simply disclosures that reveal to us the futility and damage that overlies the will to receive for oneself alone.

Let us see what it will be like when all humanity agrees unanimously to nullify and completely remove the will to receive for themselves alone which is within them, and they will then have no other will than that of giving to their companions. Then all our worries and all that is injurious to us will vanish from the earth and all beings will be certain of healthy and full lives, since each one of us will have a whole world looking out for us and fulfilling our needs.

It is from the fact that all are chasing after their own will to receive for themselves that all the sufferings and the wars, the slaughters and the holocausts from which we have no refuge, originate. Our bodies become weakened with all kinds of illnesses and pains. Yet all the sufferings of our world are only warning lights to push us into doing this work of nullifying the evil shell of the body and receiving the perfected form of the will to give. As we have said, the way of suffering itself has the capacity to bring us to the desired form of the body.

You should know that the commandments in the Torah that deal with the relationship of a person to his or her fellow human being take precedence over the *mitzvot* that are between Man and God, as acting benevolently towards our fellow leads us to act towards God in a similar way.

20. In the light of what we have already explained, we have resolved our first question, which was "What is our essence?"

Our essence, like that of all of the created world, is neither more nor less than the will to receive. However, not in the form that it manifests in state two, which is the will to receive for ourselves alone, but in its true form that exists in state one in the *Ein Sof*; in its eternal form, which is of receiving, only in order to give satisfaction to our Creator. Even though we have not yet arrived in practice at the third state and our work is still incomplete, nevertheless this does not damage our essence in any sense as the third state is already ours with complete certainty as it is implicit in state one.

There is a principle in the Talmud that states: If anyone is owed money that he or she are sure to collect, it is as if he or she has already collected it. That this has not yet occurred in practice is only considered a defect if there is even the smallest doubt as to whether or not it will happen. The fact that state three is not yet manifest to our consciousness would only be a problem if there were any doubt as to whether state three was going to happen or not. But since it is certainly going to come about, it is as if we had already come into the third state. Likewise, the body in its present form does not damage our essence in any way since it and all its acquisitions will be completely nullified together with the entire framework of uncleanness that is its source. We learn [from the Talmud that] anything which is about to be burned can be considered as if it were burned already. Thus the body is considered as if it never came into being.

The essence of the soul that is enclothed within the body is also that of will, however its essence is that of the will to give. It is drawn to us from the framework of the four worlds, *Atzilut, Briyah, Yetsirah* and *Assiyah*, of holiness. The souls exist eternally, since the form of the will to give is in complete affinity of form with the Life of all Life and is not at all exchangeable (see paragraph 32 for completion of this discussion).

21. You should not be led astray in this matter by the opinion of certain philosophers who say that the essence of the soul consists of the intellect and it exists only because of the knowledge it acquires and through which it grows and has all its being. They maintain that what remains of the soul after the death of the body completely depends on the measure of intellectual learning a person achieves within his or her lifetime, to the extent that if a person lived his or her life without having acquired any intellectual learning, then nothing would survive the death of the body. This is not the view of Torah. Also, it does not speak to our hearts which intuitively know a deeper truth. Anyone who has ever tried to learn anything intellectually knows and feels that such knowledge is something acquired and not an integral part of a person's essence.

The only material that is actually created, whether we are dealing with spiritual entities or physical entities, is no more and no less than the will to receive. The way we discriminate between one entity and another is only via its will alone. The will which is in every entity gives birth to needs, and needs give birth to thoughts and to intellectual considerations in the appropriate measure required to bring about the fulfillment of these needs, all of which are generated by the will to receive.

In so far as people's desires differ from one another, so their needs, their thoughts and their intellectual worlds are different from each other. For example, there are those whose will to receive is limited to animal lusts alone. As a result, their needs, their thoughts and even their intellectual worlds are devoted to fulfilling this animal will. Even though they are using their intellect and their experience as human beings, nevertheless these are subjugated to the purpose of fulfilling their animal needs. Other people's will to receive predominantly takes the form of human appetites which are, for example, issues of honor or of control over others, which are not desires found within the animal species. All their needs, thoughts and intellectual designs are dedicated to fulfilling this will in every possible way. Then there are people whose will to receive is directed towards scholarship and acquiring intellectual knowledge. Their needs, thoughts and intellectual world are directed towards fulfilling this end.

22. These three types of will are to be found, for the most part, in varying degrees throughout the entire human species, but combined in each person in differing amounts, which thus accounts for the variations that exist between one person and another. From this consideration of materialistic attributes, one can extrapolate to a like consideration of the attributes of spiritual entities according to their spiritual value.

23. One can also regard the human soul in this way. Human souls are spiritual entities which, through the garments of the specific type of light they receive from the higher spiritual worlds from which they have come, have only the will to give pleasure to God. This will is the essential nature of the soul. Thus, when the soul is enclothed within the body of the human being, it begets within the person

needs, thoughts and intellectual designs which are directed towards fulfilling its will to give to its full capacity, in other words, according to the measure of the will within that particular soul.

24. The substance and essence of the body is only the will to receive for itself alone. All that happens to it and its acquisitions are only fulfillments of this defective will to receive. It was only created right from the start in order for us to remove it entirely from the world so that we may come to the third state, a state of perfection which manifests at the end of the time of healing. Therefore the body, together with all its acquisitions, is mortal, transitory and worthless, like a passing shadow that leaves no trace behind it.

In contrast, the being and essence of the soul consists only of the will to give. All that happens to it and its acquisitions are fullfilments of that will to give that already exists in the first eternal state, and in the third state that has yet to come. Therefore, it is not at all mortal or exchangeable; it itself and all that it has acquired exist forever in life eternal. At the time of the death of the body, no lack occurs to the soul and all it has acquired. On the contrary, the absence of the body in its defective form strengthens the soul greatly and enables it to then ascend to the higher spiritual worlds, to the Garden of Eden.

Now we have properly explained that the immortality of the soul is in no way dependent on what knowledge it acquired, as those philosophers suggested. On the contrary, its immortality is part of its very essence which is the will to give. The knowledge that it acquires is its reward, not its essence.

25. Now we can offer a complete solution to our fifth inquiry (para. 3) in which we asked the following question: Seeing that the body is so defective that the soul cannot manifest its full purity until the body has completely disintegrated, why then, does the body have to

return in the revival of the dead? The question is compounded by the statement of the sages which tells us that when the bodies return to life they will have all the blemishes that they acquired during their lifetimes so that no one will be able to claim that this is someone else.

We can understand this very well in the light of the thought of Creation, that is, from state one. Since the thought of Creation is to give pleasure to created beings, this of necessity requires the creation of a massive will to receive all the bounty which is contained in the thought of Creation. Immense pleasure and immense will to receive [the pleasure] go together. We have already said that this immense will to receive is the only raw material of creation. One needs nothing more in order to fulfill the thought of Creation. The nature of a perfect Creator implies that nothing superfluous would be created. As it is said in the *Song of Unity*, "In all Your work, You have forgotten nothing. You did nothing less than what was necessary and nothing more."

This prodigious will to receive was removed from the framework of holiness and was given over to the framework of uncleanness from which springs the existence of the bodies, their sustenance and their acquisitions in this world.

This is the case until a person reaches thirteen years of age. Then, through the practice of Torah, he or she begins to attain a soul of holiness, which then gets its sustenance from the framework of the worlds of holiness according to the measure of the holy soul which they have attained.

We have also said above, that no healing comes for the body during the course of the period of the world's existence which is given to us for the work of Torah and *mitzvot*. That is to say, no healing comes to this massive will to receive that is contained within the body. All healing that comes through our work only affects the soul which ascends, through this healing, to higher levels of holiness and purity, ever increasing the soul's will to give. It is for this reason that the destiny of the body is to die, to be buried and to disintegrate as it itself receives no healing.

However it cannot remain like this because, in the final analysis, if this massive will to receive were to be permanently lost from the world, the thought of Creation could not be carried out. The purpose of creation is that we should receive all the great delights with which God planned to give joy to His creatures. Great will to receive and great pleasure go together. If the will to receive were to be reduced in any measure, then in accordance with that reduced measure, the joy and pleasure received would be correspondingly lessened.

26. Now, we have already seen that state one absolutely obliges that state three should issue forth in all the full measure of the thought of Creation just as it is in state one, with not even the smallest detail missing. Therefore it is state one which necessitates the resurrection of the dead bodies. That is to say, it necessitates the resurrection of the body's prodigious will to receive for oneself, which has already been wiped out, lost and rotted in state two, and must then come and be revived again in all its most exaggerated measure with no straits placed upon it, in other words, with all the blemishes that it had. Then the work begins anew of transforming this enormous will to receive so it will only be used as the *will to receive in order to give benefit.*

From this we profit in two ways: a) Firstly, we now have a vessel of sufficient capacity to receive all the good, the delight and the tenderness that is implied in the thought of Creation inasmuch as we already have a body with a fantastically large desire to receive those pleasures, and the measure of the desire and the measure of the pleasure received go together. Secondly, since our receiving in this manner will only occur according to the measure with which we can give satisfaction to our Creator, and, furthermore, this type of receiving is considered as complete giving, we find that we have also come to complete affinity of form which is oneness with God. This is our form in state three. Thus we can see that state one definitely requires the revival of the dead.

27. The revival of the dead can only come about close to the end of the healing process, which is to say, near the completion of state two. For once we have merited to negate our prodigious will to receive for ourselves and received the will only of giving, and once we have merited all the wonderful degrees of the soul which are called *Nefesh, Ruach, Neshamah, Chayah* and *Yechidah* through our work in negating this will to receive, we will then have reached a most supreme perfection. At this point, it is possible to revive the body with all its prodigious will to receive but now we are no longer damaged by it as it does not separate us from our unity with God. On the contrary, we overcome it and give to it the form of giving.

Actually, this is the accepted way of dealing with any personal negative trait we wish to work on. At first, we need to completely disassociate from it to the absolute extreme so that nothing is left of it at all. Afterwards we can allow it to come back when we can then accept it and deal with it in the middle way. But as long as we have not first removed it from ourselves, it is not at all possible to deal with it in the desired and balanced manner.

28. We have already seen that the sages said that in the future the dead will come back to life with all their blemishes and after that they will be healed. What this means is that in the first instance, the body, which is the prodigious will to receive, is revived without any limits at all. It re-appears exactly in the way it grew whilst under the subjugation of the worlds of uncleanness, before we merited to purify

it somewhat through the practice of Torah and *mitzvot*. This is what is meant by the expression, "with all its blemishes."

At this point, we begin a new work which is to bring all this massive will to receive into the form of the will to give. Then the will to receive will be healed, as it too will have attained affinity of form with God. The sages' remark "that no one should say that it is another," means that the will to receive should not manifest in any other form than that which it takes in the thought of Creation. For there it stands, this enormous will to receive, ready to receive all the good that is implied in the thought of Creation, except that in the meantime, it has been given to the shells [framework of uncleanness] and then given over for purification. But in the final analysis, it may not be a different will to receive, because if it were to exist in any lesser measure, it would be considered as other than itself and not fitting at all for use as a vessel for all the good that is implied in the thought of Creation. Indeed it is already receiving there in the aspect of state one. Understand this well.

29. Now the door has been opened for us to settle the second question (paragraph 1) that we asked above. We wanted to know, "What is our role in the long chain of reality of which we constitute but tiny links during our short lives?"

You should know that the work of the years of our life is divided into four parts:

Part one: In this period a person attains the massive will to receive in its full measure, without limits placed on its spoiled nature under the influence of the framework of the four worlds of uncleanness. If we were not to have this spoiled will to receive within us, we would not be able to heal it in any way as we cannot heal anything that is not within us. The measure of the will to receive that is inherent in our bodies simply by virtue of being born into this world is not suffi-ciently large, so the will to receive needs to be a vehicle for the unclean shells for at least thirteen years. During this period, the shells dominate it and give it satisfaction from their lights. But the effect of these lights is to keep increasing and amplifying the will to receive because the satisfaction that the shells supply to the will to receive only serves to amplify its demands.

For example, when a person is born, he or she only desires one unit and no more. But when the *sitra achra* (the evil side) supplies this unit, this straightaway enlarges his or her will to receive so that now the desire has grown to two hundred units. Then, when the *sitra achra* satisfies these two hundred units, the will to receive expands once again and now the desire is for four hundred units. If he or she fails to deal with this process through practising Torah and *mitzvot* and thus purifying the will to receive and transforming it into the will to give, then the will to receive just carries on expanding throughout the person's life until he or she dies with half of their cravings unfulfilled. In this case all their life was lived within the domain of the shells whose function is to increase and expand the will to receive and to amplify it beyond any limits. The purpose of the framework of the shells is to provide a person with all the raw material he or she needs to work on, in order to correct it.

30. Part two: This takes place from the age of thirteen years and onwards, when strength is given to a point within the person's heart, the hitherto inactive part of the *Nefesh* of holiness [the smallest of the lights pertaining to the soul]. This point, which was enclothed within the will to receive at the time of birth, only begins to awaken from the age of thirteen years. From this time onwards, the person begins to enter into the domain of the framework of the worlds of holiness, according to the degree with which he or she involves themselves with Torah and *mitzvot*.

A person's main purpose during this period is to attain and enlarge his or her spiritual will to receive. From birth until the age of thirteen years, he or she acquires a will to receive which relates only to the physical world. Therefore, even though one has acquired a massive will to receive before the age of thirteen, this does not in fact spell the end of the growth of one's will to receive. Actually, the major part of the will to receive becomes manifest when it is applied to the realm of spirituality.

For example, the will to receive before the age of thirteen desires to swallow up all the riches and glory that exist in this physical world when it is obvious to all that this world is only temporary, like a shadow that passes and leaves no trace. But when a person acquires the enormous will to receive that appertains to spirituality, then he or she wants to swallow up all the good and richness of the next world for his or her own pleasure. The person wants to acquire an everlasting possession. He or she desires to acquire eternity!

So the major part of the massive will to receive only becomes complete when the person acquires a will to receive in spirituality.

31. The *Tikkunei haZohar* explains the Scripture, "The leech has two daughters crying, 'Give! Give!'" (Prov. 30:15) as follows: The meaning of "the leech" is hell. The wicked who are trapped in this hell are crying, "Give! Give! Give me this world! Give me the world to come!"

Still, despite this, part two is inestimably more important than part one. Not only is it the stage where the person acquires the true measure of the will to receive, giving him or her all the material that is needed to work with, but it is the step that brings the person to practise Torah and *mitzvot, for its own sake.* As the sages taught, "A person should practise Torah and *mitzvot* even if it is *not for its own sake,* because through practising *not for its own sake* he will eventually come to practise *for its own sake.*"

Therefore, this part that develops after the age of thirteen is nonetheless considered as belonging to the realm of holiness, according to the inner meaning of the phrase, "The holy maidservant who serves her Mistress" (Prov. 30:23), the Mistress here being a metaphor for the *Shechinah*. For it is the maidservant [who represents the practice of Torah not for its own sake] who brings a person to the practice of Torah for its own sake, thus enabling him or her to merit the inspirational presence of the *Shechinah*.

However, a person must use all the necessary means in focusing his or her **intention** to come to the stage of practising Torah for its own sake. If this effort is not made, then the person will not come to the stage of practising Torah for its own sake, but will fall straight into the trap of the unclean maidservant who is the opposite number to the maidservant of the side of holiness. The purpose of the unclean maidservant is to confuse a person so the work of Torah that is practised not for its own sake will never lead them to Torah that is practised for its own sake. About this maidservant it is said, "And the maidservant will disinherit her Mistress" (Prov. 30:23). She will not allow the person to get close to the Mistress, to the Holy *Shechinah*.

The final level of this second part is that a person should fall in love with God with a great lust similar to the way a man of large appetite lusts after something in the physical world. This desire should grow in the person until it never leaves his or her awareness, by day or by night. Just as the poet says, "When I remember Him, I just cannot sleep." Then, it is said of such a person, "Desire fulfilled is a tree of life" (Prov. 13:13), the tree of life here being a metaphor for the five levels of the soul, which are described below.

32. Part three: This part applies to the work with Torah and *mitzvot* which is done for its own sake, that is in order to give pleasure to God and not for the sake of a reward. This work purifies the will

to receive for oneself alone and transforms it into the will to give, whereby, according to the measure of purification of the will to receive, it now becomes a suitable and fitting vessel to receive the five parts of the soul which are called, "*Nefesh, Ruach, Neshamah, Chayah* and *Yechidah*" (see paragraph 42).

These aspects, which belong to the will to give, cannot be enclothed within a person's body as long as the will to receive for oneself alone dominates it, as the soul is in opposition of form to the body. Even if it is in some difference of form, the soul still cannot be enclothed within the body. For the light to be enclothed within a vessel, there must be affinity of form between them.

At the very moment when the person merits to be wholly concerned only with the will to give and has no aspect left of the will to receive for oneself, then the person is in complete affinity of form with the five parts of the soul, the *Nefesh, Ruach, Neshamah, Chayah* and *Yechidah*. These originate in their source in the *Ein Sof* in state one, come through the worlds of holiness and are straightaway drawn to the person who enclothes them, one by one.

Part four: This part applies to the work we do after the revival of the dead. The will to receive, after it had already disappeared through death and burial, now returns and comes back to life in its most prodigious form. This is the inner meaning of the saying of the sages, "In the future the dead will come to life again with all their blemishes." At this stage, we transform the will to receive for oneself alone into the will to receive in order to give. However there are a few special people who are already doing this work during their lives in this world.

33. Now all that is left for us to explain is the sixth inquiry. Its subject was the statement of the sages that all the worlds—the higher worlds as well as the lower worlds—were only created for the sake of Man. On the surface, it seems to be rather astonishing that for the sake of this little Man, the Creator, Blessed be He, should create all this!

When one compares the value of a man or a woman with the whole of the reality of this world, not to mention the higher spiritual worlds, one cannot say that he or she has the value of even a tiny hair! Yet God created all this for us.

An even more astonishing question is: What need does Man have for all these many and splendid spiritual worlds?

Now you need to know that all the satisfaction God has in giving pleasure to His creatures depends upon the measure to which the creatures can feel that it is God who is their benefactor and it is God who gives them their enjoyment. Then God takes great delight in them, like a father who delights in playing with his dear child. His pleasure increases according to the degree that the child can feel and recognize the greatness and the noble qualities of the father. Then the child's father shows the child all the treasure houses that he has prepared for the child. Just as Scripture says, "'What a dear son Ephrayim is! He is my darling child! For whenever I speak of him, I earnestly remember him. My compassion is stirred for him. I will surely have mercy on him,' says the Lord" (Jer. 31:19). Look carefully at this sentence and you will understand and know the great delight that God enjoys with those people who have reached their wholeness. They have merited to sense His presence and to recognize His greatness in all the ways that He has prepared for them. God relates to them as a father relates to his dear child, as a father with the child of his delight. As we meditate on this description, we can understand that for the sake of the pleasure and delight God takes in these people who have come to their wholeness, it was worth it to God to create all these worlds, the upper as well as the lower, as we will further explain.

34. In order to prepare His creatures, so that they would be able to reach this high and elevated state, God works through four stages which develop naturally one from the other and which are called the **inanimate**, the **vegetable**, the **animal** and the **speaking**. These are

actually four levels of the will to receive. Every single world amongst all the higher worlds [and also our physical world] is divided into these four categories. The greatest aspect of desire is contained in the fourth level of the will to receive, but it is not possible for this fourth level to emerge without the prior existence of the three previous levels. The will to receive is revealed and developed gradually through the three previous levels before reaching its final completed form in the fourth level.

35. The first level of the will to receive is called **inanimate**. It is the beginning of the manifestation of the will to receive in this physical world. The inanimate is characterized by having only a general capacity for movement. Individual objects within the realm of the inanimate have no perceptible capacity to move of their own. The will to receive gives birth to needs and these needs give birth to movements sufficient to attain these needs. Since here the will to receive is very minimal, its effect is only apparent as causing a general movement but its effect is not apparent on the individual parts.

36. The next and second aspect of the will to receive is the **plant** world. This is already a much greater manifestation of the will to receive than is attributed to the inanimate. Here the will to receive influences each and every individual separately. As we see in the plant world each individual has its own particular capacity for movement. Plants turn and move to face the sun. Plants, too, can "eat" and "drink" and rid themselves of waste products. This is a capacity that each individual plant has. However plants do not have any capacity for free motion that is peculiar to each individual plant.

37. Now we can add the **animal** kingdom, which is the third aspect of the will to receive. This is a much more advanced level of the will to receive. Here, the will to receive endows every single animal with the

capacity of feeling itself to be an individual. Each animal has its own particular life, different from that of other animals. However animals, generally speaking, lack the capacity to feel the feelings of other animals. They have no capacity to feel the pain of their fellow animals' misfortune or to rejoice in their fellow animals' happiness and suchlike.

38. Finally we come to the **speaking,** which is the fourth level of the will to receive. This is the will to receive in its completed and final form. At this human level of the will to receive, the capacity exists to feel the pain of others as well as our own.

If you want to know exactly how great the difference is between the third level of the will to receive, the animal level, and the fourth level of the will to receive, the human level, I tell you that it is exactly that of one element of creation as compared to the totality of creation! The will to receive as it exists in the animal kingdom, lacking the capacity to feel the other's feelings, is only able to give birth to the lacks and needs of that one individual animal. This is not so in the human kingdom in which the capacity to feel other people's feelings gives rise to lacks that were not originally the person's own, but are born from seeing that which his fellow possesses. The person fills with jealousy and he or she desires to own everything that another owns. A person's wants and needs become greatly multiplied until they want to swallow up the substance of the whole world.

39. Now it has been explained that the desired purpose of the Creator in carrying out the creation is only to give pleasure to His creatures in order that His creatures should recognize His truth and His greatness. They should receive from Him all the good and the pleasantness that He has prepared for them. Its measure is indicated in the quotation, "'What a dear son Ephrayim is! He is my darling child!

For whenever I speak of him, I earnestly remember him. My compassion is stirred for him. I will surely have mercy on him,' says the Lord" (Jer. 31:19).

It is clear that this purpose cannot be fulfilled by the inanimate realm, not even by the great spheres, the earth, the moon or the sun, no matter how brightly they shine. Nor can it be fulfilled by the plant or the animal kingdoms, which lack the capacity to feel the feelings of the other, even those of one from the same species. How could they possibly feel appreciation for the Divine and His goodness? Only the human species has the required potential to appreciate God through the capacity to feel the feelings of one's fellow human beings. Once a human being completes his or her work in Torah and *mitzvot* and transmutes the will to receive for oneself into the will to give to others, then he or she comes into affinity of form with the Creator. The person then receives all the levels that are prepared for them in the upper worlds, which are called *Nefesh, Ruach, Neshamah, Chayah* and *Yechidah* through which he or she becomes fitted to receive all the content implicit in the thought of Creation. Thus we see that all the worlds were only created for the sake of Man.

40. I know that this view is not acceptable to some philosophers who believe that human beings are so negligible and worthless that they could not possibly lie at the center of such a great and exalted creation. But they, the philosophers, are like a worm that is born in a radish which sits there and thinks that the whole of God's world is dark, bitter and small, just like the radish within which it was born. But the moment that the worm breaks through the skin of the radish and looks outside it, it is astonished and says, "I thought that the whole world was just like the radish in which I was born. But now I see before me a big, bright and wondrously beautiful world."

It is the same with people who are immersed in the shells of the will to receive with which they were born and who have never tried to use the special healing spices, which are the practical work in Torah and *mitzvot*, which have the power to penetrate this hard shell, transforming it into the will of giving pleasure to one's Creator. Such a person, just like the worm in the radish, would have no choice but to believe that human life is empty and meaningless because this is his or her perceived reality. He or she would not be able to entertain even the thought that the whole universe was created for them. But if such a person would practise Torah and *mitzvot* with the intention of giving pleasure to God in all purity, then he or she would split the shell of the will to receive for oneself alone with which they were born. In place of this the person would receive the will to give. Straightaway, their eyes would be opened to see and they would attain for themselves all the stages of wisdom, understanding and clear intimate knowledge that await them in the spiritual worlds and which are delightful to such a degree that the soul loses itself in ecstasy. Then such a person would themselves say, as in the words of the sages, "What does a good guest say? He says that all the trouble which the Master of the house took, he took for me!"

41. Yet we still have not got completely to the bottom of the question as to why Man needs all these higher worlds that God created for him.

You must know that the whole spiritual universe is divided, generally speaking, into five worlds which are called 1) *Adam Kadmon*, 2) *Atzilut*, 3) *Briyah*, 4) *Yetsirah* and 5) *Assiyah*, each one of them being composed of endless sub-worlds. These worlds correspond to the five principle *sephirot* (see table 1). The world of *Adam Kadmon* corresponds to the *sephirah* of *Keter*. The world of *Atzilut* corresponds to the *sephirah* of *Chochmah*. The world of *Briyah* corresponds to the *sephirah* of *Binah*. The world of *Yetsirah* corresponds to the *sephirah* of *Tipheret* and the world of *Assiyah* corresponds to the *sephirah* of

Malchut. The lights that are enclothed within these five worlds are called *Yechidah, Chayah, Neshamah, Ruach* and *Nefesh.* The light of *Yechidah* shines in the world of *Adam Kadmon.* The light of *Chayah* shines in the world of *Atzilut.* The light of *Neshamah* shines in the world of *Briyah.* The light of *Ruach* shines in the world of *Yetsirah* and the light of *Nefesh* shines in the world of *Assiyah.* All these worlds and everything in them are implied in the holy four-letter name of God, which is י׳ה׳ו׳ה YHVH, together with the tip of the first letter, י (See table 1).

We have no way to apprehend the first world of *Adam Kadmon* on account of its elevation, so we only hint at it through the tip of the י (the *yud*) of the four-letter name. This realm being so exalted, we often do not mention it at all and refer only to the four worlds of *Atzilut, Briyah, Yetsirah* and *Assiyah.* The י itself connotes the world of *Atzilut.* The first ה signifies the world of *Briyah.* The ו connotes the world of *Yetsirah* and the final ה refers to the world of *Assiyah.*

42. These five worlds contain all the spiritual reality originating at the level of the *Ein Sof* and continuing right down to this world. Now each is included within the others such that each world contains within it all the aspects of each of the five worlds. That is to say that the five *sephirot* of *Keter, Chochmah, Binah, Tipheret* and *Malchut* in which are enclothed the lights *Yechidah, Chayah, Neshamah, Ruach* and *Nefesh* relating to each of the five worlds respectively, are also to be found within every world.

Besides the five *sephirot: Keter, Chochmah, Binah, Tipheret* and *Malchut*, that are present in every world, there are also to be found the four aspects of the spiritual will to receive—inanimate, vegetable, animal and speaking, in each world. The speaking aspect of the will to receive in these worlds is the soul of Man. The animal aspects of each world are the angels of that particular world. The vegetable aspects of each world are called its garments and the inanimate aspects of the spiritual will to receive are called its houses (table 2).

Table 1

Worlds	Sephirot	Lights	God's Name	wills to receive
Adam Kadmon	Keter	Yechidah	Tip of Yud י	
Atzilut	Chochmah	Chayah	Yud י	speaking
Briyah	Binah	Neshamah	Hay ה	animal
Yetsirah	Tiferet	Ruach	Vav ו	vegetable
Assiyah	Malchut	Nefesh	Hay ה	inanimate

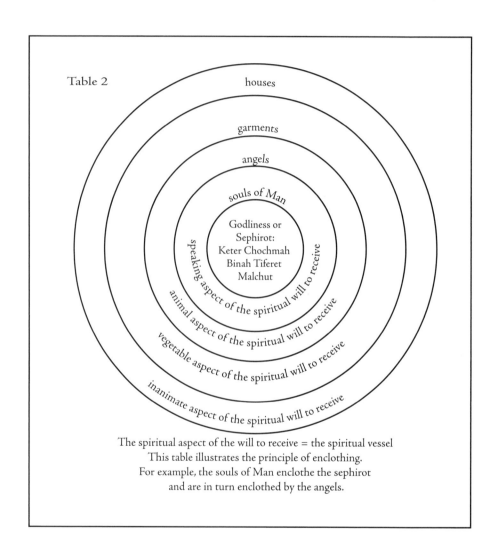

Table 2

houses

garments

angels

souls of Man

Godliness or
Sephirot:
Keter Chochmah
Binah Tiferet
Malchut

speaking aspect of the spiritual will to receive

animal aspect of the spiritual will to receive

vegetable aspect of the spiritual will to receive

inanimate aspect of the spiritual will to receive

The spiritual aspect of the will to receive = the spiritual vessel
This table illustrates the principle of enclothing.
For example, the souls of Man enclothe the sephirot
and are in turn enclothed by the angels.

These aspects enclothe one another. The speaking aspect, being the soul of Man, enclothes the *sephirot: Keter, Chochmah, Binah, Tipheret* and *Malchut* which are the godliness of each world. The animal aspects, the angels, enclothe the souls of Man. The vegetable aspects, being the garments, enclothe the angels, and the inanimate aspects, the houses, enclothe and surround all of them (see table 2). The concept of "enclothing" means that when one aspect enclothes another it serves and supports it and allows the development of one aspect into another.

This is just the same, by analogy, as occurs in the relationship of the inanimate, vegetable, animal and human to each other in this physical world. We have already pointed out how the inanimate, vegetable and animal kingdoms on the physical plane did not come into existence for themselves but, rather, their purpose was to open up and expand the fourth aspect of the will to receive, the speaking aspect, which is the human species. Their only purpose, therefore, is to serve and help mankind. This is also true of all the spiritual worlds. The three aspects of inanimate, vegetable and animal in the spiritual worlds are only there to serve and assist the speaking aspect in the spiritual worlds, which is the human soul. Therefore, they all enclothe the soul of Man for the person's benefit.

43. A person, the moment he or she is born, has a soul of holiness. But this is not a realized soul. It is, rather, an inactive soul or a soul in potential; the least aspect of the soul. Since it is still small, this aspect of soul is considered as a point which is enclothed within a person's heart, that is to say that it is enclothed within his or her will to receive, which reveals itself chiefly through the heart.

You may be familiar with the concept that whatever applies to the whole of reality applies equally in each individual world and to every particular particle in that world however tiny it may be. So, just as there are five worlds within the whole of reality which correspond to the five *sephirot: Keter, Chochmah, Binah, Tipheret* and *Malchut*, so there are five *sephirot: Keter, Chochmah, Binah, Tipheret* and *Malchut* within each world. Likewise there are five *sephirot* in every particle in every world. As we have said, our world is divided up into the inanimate, vegetable, animal and human aspects. These correspond to the four *sephirot* of *Chochmah, Binah, Tipheret* and *Malchut*, the inanimate corresponding to *Malchut*, the vegetable corresponding to *Tipheret*, the animal corresponding to *Binah*, the speaking corresponding to *Chochmah* and the highest root of all of them corresponding to *Keter* (see table 1).

However as we have stated, one individual entity from any of the inanimate, vegetable, animal or human species, also has within it all the four aspects pertaining to the inanimate, the vegetable, the animal and the speaking. So, for example, within any person lie the inanimate, vegetable, animal and speaking aspects which are the four aspects of his or her will to receive, that enclothe the point of his or her holy soul (table 2).

44. Before the age of thirteen, there is no outer manifestation of this point of the holy soul within the heart. After the age of thirteen, if a person begins to practise Torah and *mitzvot*, even if this is as yet without any inner intention; that is to say without any degree of love or awareness of serving God, nevertheless, this causes the point of the soul within his or her heart to enlarge and to show its action. Even without positive intention, the act of doing these *mitzvot* purifies the will to receive for oneself, but only at its first level which is called the inanimate.

As he or she purifies the inanimate part of the will to receive, the person constructs the 613 limbs of the point of the soul within the heart, which is the inanimate aspect of the holy *Nefesh*. When he or she has completed all the 613 commandments from the practical aspect, then all the 613 limbs of the point within the heart which comprise the inanimate aspect of his or her holy *Nefesh*, are completed. The 248 spiritual organs are built up by performing the 248 positive commandments and the 365 spiritual sinews are built up by refraining from transgressing the 365 negative commands. Then the inanimate aspect of the holy *Nefesh* becomes a complete spiritual entity and the *Nefesh* then ascends and enclothes the *sephirah* of *Malchut* which is in the spiritual world of *Assiyah*.

All the spiritual units, the inanimate, vegetable, and animal, which are to be found in the world of *Assiyah* that relate to the *sephirah* of *Malchut* of *Assiyah*, help and assist that person's soul-entity of *Nefesh* that ascends to the *sephirah* of *Malchut* of *Assiyah* according to the measure that the soul (*Nefesh*) is enlightened to receive them. This enlightenment becomes spiritual nourishment for the *Nefesh*, which gives it strength to grow and increase in capacity until it can draw towards itself the light of the *sephirah* of *Malchut* of *Assiyah* in all its complete perfection, which then gives its light within the body of the person. This perfect light helps a person to increase his or her work in Torah and *mitzvot* so that they may go on to receive other levels.

We have already stated that when a person is born, a point source of the light of *Nefesh* enclothes itself within their will to receive. Similarly here, when he or she has given birth to the spiritual entity which is the *Nefesh* of holiness, there is born together with it a point source which originates from the stage above. That is to say that there arises a point source from the inactive aspect of the light of *Ruach* of *Assiyah*, which enclothes itself within the inmost aspect of the entity of *Nefesh*, in a similar way to that above. The process proceeds in this way throughout all the stages. Whenever one stage is born, the point source of the inactive aspect of the next stage above it is born within it. This makes the connection between the higher stage and the stage below it, and this process continues up to the very highest stages. Thus through the assistance of the point of the higher level, enclothing itself within the lower, the soul is enabled to ascend each time to a higher stage.

45. The light of *Nefesh* is the light of the inanimate aspect of the holy world of *Assiyah* and it corresponds to the purification of the inanimate aspect of the will to receive as it exists within the body of Man, as we have explained above. The action of its illumination in spiritual terms can be compared to that of the inanimate in the physical world, which does not manifest individuation of its particular parts but only a general movement of all its parts together. Similarly, the illumination which comes from the entity of *Nefesh* of *Assiyah* is a general illumination. Even though it contains within it 613 limbs, which are 613 different ways of receiving God's bounty, still, at this stage, they are not distinguishable from each other, but the light illuminates them all equally as a general illumination, so that individual parts are not recognizable as such.

46. Know that the *sephirot* are Divine. There is absolutely no difference between the *Keter* of *Adam Kadmon* [the very highest] and the *Malchut* of *Assiyah* [the very lowest]. Nonetheless, from the point of view of the receiver, there is a great difference. The *sephirot* consist of lights and vessels. The light within the *sephirot* is pure Divinity, but the vessels, which are called *Keter, Chochmah, Binah, Tipheret* and *Malchut*, that exist in each of the three lower worlds, *Briyah, Yetsirah and Assiyah*, are not Divine as such. Rather, they are covers that hide the light of the *Ein Sof*, blessed be He, within them. They limit and put a measure on this light for those who receive it, in order that a person may only receive light according to the degree of his or her own purity. From this point of view, even though the light, in its essence, is one, nevertheless, when it enters the different vessels, we call it by different names according to the characteristics of these vessels. These

names are *Nefesh, Ruach, Neshamah, Chayah* and *Yechidah*.

Malchut consists of the thickest of the coverings that hide the light of the *Ein Sof*, blessed be He. It only allows a very small amount of light from God through to the receiver, in a measure which is proportionate to the purification of the inanimate aspect of the will to receive in Man and thus it is called *Nefesh* (at rest).

The vessel of *Tipheret* is clearer than that of *Malchut* and the light which it allows to pass through it from the *Ein Sof* relates to the purification of the vegetable aspect of the will to receive for oneself. It is more active than that of the light of *Nefesh* and is called the light of *Ruach* (wind).

The vessel of *Binah* is clearer than that of *Tipheret* and the light that passes through it from the *Ein Sof* relates to the purification of the animal aspect of Man's will to receive for oneself and is called the light of *Neshamah* (breath).

The vessel of *Chochmah* is the clearest of all. The light which it allows to pass through it from the *Ein Sof*, may He be blessed, is specifically related to the purification of the speaking part of Man's will to receive for oneself and is called the light of *Chayah* (life). There is no limit to its action as we shall see below (table 1).

47. As we have already said, within the spiritual entity of *Nefesh*, which a person has acquired through the practice of Torah and *mitzvot*, even without proper intention, there is already to be found enclothed the point source belonging to the light of *Ruach*.

As the person strengthens himself or herself through Torah and *mitzvot*, gradually refining his or her motivation, that part of the vegetable aspect of the will to receive which is within him or her becomes purified and in like measure gradually builds up the point of *Ruach* into a spiritual entity. Through the person carrying out the 248 positive commandments with intention, the point expands into 248 spiritual organs. And by refraining from transgressing the 365 negative commands, the point of light expands into 365 spiritual sinews. When all the 613 spiritual limbs are complete, then the entity ascends and enclothes the *sephirah* of *Tipheret* which pertains to the spiritual world of *Assiyah*. This transfers to the person a clearer light from the *Ein Sof*, the light of *Ruach*, corresponding to the purification of the vegetable aspect of the will to receive within the body of Man. All the particular items which relate to the inanimate, the vegetable and the animal of the world of *Assiyah* which are related to this stage of *Tipheret* help the person's spiritual entity of *Ruach* to receive all the lights from the *sephirah* of *Tipheret* in all their entirety. The spiritual entity, the *Ruach*, is considered as the vegetable aspect of holiness. And indeed the nature of its illumination is equivalent to that of a plant in the physical world, in that all individual elements have their own particular ability to move. So the light of this spiritual entity already has great power and illuminates each specific pathway of each separate limb of the 613 limbs which are in the spiritual entity of *Ruach*, each one showing the different action related to that specific spiritual limb.

As the spiritual entity of *Ruach* emerges, there is born within it a point source from the stage higher than itself which is the point of the light of *Neshamah*, which it enclothes within its innermost part.

48. Through studying the innermost parts of Torah and practising the *mitzvot* with a deep understanding of their true nature and purpose, a person purifies the animal part of the will to receive. To the degree that he or she does this, the point of *Neshamah* which is enclothed within the person develops into an entire soul-entity of 248 organs and 365 sinews and it then ascends and enclothes the *sephirah* of *Binah* of the spiritual world of *Assiyah*. This vessel is immeasurably purer than that of *Tipheret* or of *Malchut*. This vessel is fitted to

receive a much greater light from the *Ein Sof* which is called the light of *Neshamah*. All the aspects of inanimate, vegetable and animal in the world of *Assiyah*, which are related to the level of *Binah*, function to assist the person in developing this soul-entity of *Neshamah* until he or she can fully receive the light emanating from the *sephirah* of *Binah*, in exactly the same way we described for the light of *Nefesh*. This soul entity is also referred to as the animal aspect of holiness since it comes about through the purification of the animal aspect of the will to receive for oneself.

The nature of its illumination is similar to that of the animal kingdom in the physical world. It gives an individual feeling to each and every limb of the 613 limbs of the spiritual entity. Each limb feels itself free and alive, independent of all the other limbs, without dependency on the entity as a whole, until the 613 limbs become 613 spiritual entities, each one illumined with its own spiritual light. The superiority of this light over that of *Ruach* in the spiritual world can be likened to the difference in consciousness of the animal kingdom over the plant and mineral kingdoms in the physical world. Likewise a point source from the light of *Chayah* of holiness, which is the light pertaining to the *sephirah* of *Chochmah*, emanates together with the spiritual entity of *Neshamah* and is enclothed within its innermost aspect.

49. Once the person has merited this great light of *Neshamah* and each one of the 613 limbs of this spiritual entity is already giving forth a perfect and clear light, specific to each limb as if each limb is a spiritual entity in its own right, then a doorway is opened for him or for her to perform each and every *mitzvah* according to the true intention which is within it. For every limb of the soul world of *Neshamah* illuminates for the person the inner wisdom of the particular *mitzvah* that is associated with that limb. With the great power of these lights, he or she is able to go on and purify the speaking aspect of the will to

receive for oneself alone, transforming it into the will to give. As the person does this, the point of the light of *Chayah* enclothed within his or her soul gradually acquires its 248 spiritual organs and 365 spiritual limbs until it becomes a complete soul entity. Then the soul ascends and enclothes the *sephirah* of *Chochmah* in the spiritual world of *Assiyah*.

There is no end to the purity of this vessel and so it draws down to itself a great and mighty light from the *Ein Sof*, Blessed be He, which is called the light of *Chayah*. All the individual aspects of the world of *Assiyah*, the inanimate, the vegetable and the animal aspects of the world of *Assiyah* which are related to the *sephirah* of *Chochmah* help the person to receive the light of the *sephirah* of *Chochmah* in its entirety. This is called the speaking aspect of holiness, as it corresponds to the purification of Man's speaking aspect of the will to receive for oneself. The importance of this light over the previous lights within Divinity is comparable to the place of the human being with respect to the animal, vegetable and inanimate in the physical domain, in that this light has the quality of being able to feel another's feelings. The great measure of this light as compared to the measure of the inanimate, vegetable, animal and spiritual entities is as vast as the measure of the speaking aspect in the physical world is over its inanimate, vegetable and animal aspects. The aspect of the light of the *Ein Sof* which is enclothed within this soul-entity is called the light of *Yechidah* (unity).

50. However you should know that all these five aspects of light; *Nefesh, Ruach, Neshamah, Chayah* and *Yechidah*, which are received from the world of *Assiyah*, are, however, only the *Nefesh, Ruach, Neshamah, Chayah and Yechidah* of the light of *Nefesh* [which is the light associated with the world of *Assiyah*] (see table 3). They do not yet have anything of the light of *Ruach*, which has its place in the world

Table 3 The Worlds and their Subdivisions

World.................................. Assiyah
Sephirah............................. Malchut
Purification of the will to receive.... Inanimate
Light.................................. Nefesh

Subdivisions of Assiyah

Will to receive	Sephirot	Lights
	Keter of Assiyah	Yechidah of Assiyah
speaking	Chochmah of Assiyah	Chayah of Assiyah
animal	Binah of Assiyah	Neshamah of Assiyah
vegetable	Tiferet of Assiyah	Ruach of Assiyah
inanimate	Malchut of Assiyah	Nefesh of Assiyah

World.................................. Yetsirah
Sephirah............................. Tiferet
Purification of the will to receive.... Vegetable
Light.................................. Ruach

Subdivisions of Yetsirah

Will to receive	Sephirot	Lights
	Keter of Yetsirah	Yechidah of Yetsirah
speaking	Chochmah of Yetsirah	Chayah of Yetsirah
animal	Binah of Yetsirah	Neshamah of Yetsirah
vegetable	Tiferet of Yetsirah	Ruach of Yetsirah
inanimate	Malchut of Yetsirah	Nefesh of Yetsirah

World.................................. Briyah
Sephirah............................. Binah
Purification of the will to receive.... Animal
Light.................................. Neshamah

Subdivisions of Briyah

Will to receive	Sephirot	Lights
	Keter of Briyah	Yechidah of Briyah
speaking	Chochmah of Briyah	Chayah of Briyah
animal	Binah of Briyah	Neshamah of Briyah
vegetable	Tiferet of Briyah	Ruach of Briyah
inanimate	Malchut of Briyah	Nefesh of Briyah

World.................................. Atzilut
Sephirah............................. Chochmah
Purification of the will to receive.... Speaking
Light.................................. Chayah

Subdivisions of Atzilut

Will to receive	Sephirot	Lights
	Keter of Atzilut	Yechidah of Atzilut
speaking	Chochmah of Atzilut	Chayah of Atzilut
animal	Binah of Atzilut	Neshamah of Atzilut
vegetable	Tiferet of Atzilut	Ruach of Atzilut
inanimate	Malchut of Atzilut	Nefesh of Atzilut

of *Yetsirah*. Similarly, the light of *Neshamah* has its home in the world of *Briyah*, the light of *Chayah* in the world of *Atzilut* and that of *Yechidah* in the world of *Adam Kadmon*.

However, as we have already mentioned, every aspect of reality that exists in the macrocosm, also manifests in the microcosm. This is true right down to the tiniest unit that it is possible to describe. Therefore all five aspects, *Nefesh, Ruach, Neshamah, Chayah* and *Yechidah*, are found in the world of *Assiyah* in the way we have described them, but here they are only the *Nefesh, Ruach, Neshamah, Chayah* and *Yechidah* of *Nefesh*. In exactly the same way, *Nefesh, Ruach, Neshamah, Chayah* and *Yechidah* are found within the world of *Yetsirah* and they are the five parts of *Ruach*. Similarly, there are the five aspects, *Nefesh, Ruach, Neshamah, Chayah* and *Yechidah* within the world of *Briyah* and they constitute the five parts of *Neshamah*. Likewise in the world of *Atzilut*, the five aspects, *Nefesh, Ruach, Neshamah, Chayah* and *Yechidah*, constitute the five aspects of the light of *Chayah* (see table 3). Indeed, it is the same for the world of *Adam Kadmon* where they constitute the five parts of the light of *Yechidah*.

The way each world relates to the worlds which are higher or lower than it, is the same as the way the five levels of illumination, *Nefesh, Ruach, Neshamah, Chayah* and *Yechidah* relate to each other within the world of *Assiyah*.

51. You should know that the process of healing and purification of the will to receive for oneself alone only receives its full light when it is permanent and we no longer go back to our foolish ways. The sages asked, "What constitutes the full healing [of the defective will to receive for oneself alone]?" and they answered, "When God Himself testifies that the person will never return to his foolishness."

We said that when a person purifies the inanimate part of the will to receive for oneself alone, he or she merits the soul-entity of *Nefesh* which then ascends and enclothes the *sephirah* of *Malchut* of *Assiyah*. This implies that the purification of the inanimate aspect is completely permanent and he or she will never return to their foolishness again. Now the person can ascend to the level of the spiritual world of *Assiyah* as he or she enjoys purity and complete similarity of form with that world. However the other stages that we mentioned, namely, *Ruach, Neshamah, Chayah* and *Yechidah* of *Assiyah* require purification of their corresponding parts of the will to receive for oneself, namely the vegetable, animal and speaking aspects of the will to receive for oneself, in order that they may enclothe and receive these lights. Here however, the purification does not need to be completely permanent to the extent that "God Himself testifies that he or she will never return to their foolish ways." The reason is that the whole world of *Assiyah*, with its five component *sephirot* of *Keter, Chochmah, Binah, Tipheret* and *Malchut*, really only constitutes the *sephirah* of *Malchut* which relates solely to the purification of the inanimate aspect alone, the five *sephirot* here being merely the five components of *Malchut*. Thus, since the person has already merited to purify at least the inanimate aspect of his or her will to receive on a permanent basis, then he or she has already attained affinity of form with the whole world of *Assiyah*.

However every *sephirah* in the world of *Assiyah* draws its sustenance from that aspect in the higher worlds that corresponds to it. For example, the *sephirah* of *Tipheret* in *Assiyah* receives its sustenance from the world of *Yetsirah* which, in its essence, is entirely *Tipheret* and whose light is that of *Ruach*. The *sephirah* of *Binah* in the world of *Assiyah* receives its sustenance from the world of *Briyah* whose light is

Neshamah. Likewise the *sephirah* of *Chochmah* of *Assiyah* receives its sustenance from the world of *Atzilut* whose essence is *Chochmah* and whose light is *Chayah.*

Therefore, even though a person has only purified the inanimate aspect of the will to receive for oneself in an irreversible way, and has worked on the vegetable, animal and human aspects of the will to receive, but has not completely and irreversibly transformed them, nonetheless he or she can still receive the *Ruach, Neshamah* and *Chayah* from *Tipheret, Binah* and *Chochmah* of the world of *Assiyah,* but not on a permanent basis. The moment one of these three levels of will to receive for oneself alone wakes up again, these lights are immediately lost.

52. Once a person has purified the vegetable aspect of the will to receive for oneself alone in an immutable way, he or she may then ascend to the world of *Yetsirah.* There the person receives the light of *Ruach* permanently. He or she is able, at that level, to attain the lights of *Neshamah* and *Chayah* associated with the *sephirot* of *Binah* and *Chochmah* in the world of *Yetsirah,* which are *Neshamah* of *Ruach* and *Chayah* of *Ruach* respectively (see table 3). The person attains these lights in an intermittent way even before they have transformed the animal and human aspects on a permanent basis in the same way as we explained for the world of *Assiyah.* Once he or she has completely purified the vegetable aspect of the will to receive for oneself alone on an enduring basis then he or she is in affinity of form with the whole world of *Yetsirah,* even with its highest aspects.

53. Then the person purifies the animal aspect of the will to receive for oneself alone and transforms it into the will to give to such an extent that "God testifies that he or she will never again return to their foolishness." The person is now in affinity of form with the world of

Briyah. There one can receive all the lights up to and including the light of *Neshamah* permanently. Now, through working on the speaking aspect of the will to receive, a person is able to ascend to the *sephirah* of *Chochmah* and receive its light of *Chayah*. This is so even if the person has not purified it in a permanent way. However as long as the process is incomplete, the light that illuminates him or her is similarly not permanent.

54. When the person has merited to purify the speaking component of the will to receive for oneself alone irreversibly, he or she comes into similarity of form with the world of *Atzilut* and then he or she receives its light of *Chayah* for good. When the person becomes even more purified, he or she merits to receive the light of the *Ein Sof* and the light of *Yechidah* which is enclothed within the light of *Chayah*. There is nothing more to add here.

55. Now we have given a full and complete answer to the question, "Why does a person require all the higher worlds that God created for him or for her? What need does he or she have of them?" (paragraph 41). We see now that it would be completely impossible for a person to perform any acts in order to give pleasure to the Creator, were it not for the help of all these worlds. For according to the degree to which the person has purified the will to receive for oneself alone, he or she attains the lights and ascensions of the soul which are called *Nefesh, Ruach, Neshamah, Chayah* and *Yechidah*. At every level that the person attains, the lights of that level help him or her in the process of purification. The person ascends up the levels until he or she merits and attains all the delights which constitute the ultimate purpose of the thought of Creation (as above paragraph 33).

The *Zohar* discusses the expression of the sages, "When someone tries to purify themselves, they get help." And asks, "How do they get help?" The *Zohar* answers, "Through the holy soul." For it is impossible to arrive at the purification that is required for the thought of Creation to be carried out except through the help of all the stages of the soul which are *Nefesh*, *Ruach*, *Neshamah*, *Chayah* and *Yechidah* of the soul, as we have described above.

56. Now, one needs to know that these five aspects, *Nefesh*, *Ruach*, *Neshamah*, *Chayah* and *Yechidah*, of which we have spoken, are five parts into which the whole of reality may be subdivided. Furthermore, everything that is present in the macrocosm behaves in the same way even in the smallest possible subdivision of reality. So, for example, even within the inanimate aspect of the spiritual world of *Assiyah*, one needs to attain the five aspects of *Nefesh*, *Ruach*, *Neshamah*, *Chayah* and *Yechidah* of that level which are related to the macroscopic divisions of *Nefesh*, *Ruach*, *Neshamah*, *Chayah* and *Yechidah*. This implies that it is impossible to attain even the light of *Nefesh* of *Assiyah* except through working on all of the four parts of the will to receive as we mentioned above.

It follows that no one can exempt themselves from dealing with all of the four parts of the will to receive, according to their capacity. It is necessary for a person to involve himself or herself in Torah and *mitzvot* with intention, in order to receive the light of *Ruach*, according to their capacity. Likewise it is necessary for the person to deal with the innermost aspect of Torah according to his or her capacity so that they may receive the light of *Neshamah* at their level. The same follows as regards the reasons of the *mitzvot*. Even the smallest light in the reality of holiness cannot be completed without their involvement.

57. From here you will understand the nature of the dryness and the darkness which is to be found in the Judaism of our generation. There

was nothing like it at all in previous generations. This is because even those people who take their religious life seriously, have abandoned the study of the secrets of the Torah, that is to say, the Kabbalah. Maimonides gives a true example of this. He asks us to imagine a line of a thousand blind people going on a journey who are led at the head of the line by at least one person who can see. They can still be sure that they are going in the right direction. They will not fall into any snares or traps in their path since they are following the one who can see. But if the one person who can see is missing, they will undoubtedly stumble over every obstacle laid in their path and they will all fall into a dark pit. This is exactly our situation. If at least the people who are the spiritual leaders of our generation would occupy themselves with the innermost aspect of Torah that is the Kabbalah, they would draw to themselves a complete light from the *Ein Sof*, Blessed be He. As a consequence, the whole generation would be able to follow after them; everyone would be sure of their way and would not stumble. But if the spiritual leaders of our generation have removed themselves from this wisdom, then it is little wonder that the whole generation stumbles on account of them. From the great sorrow that I feel, I cannot write any more on this.

58. I know that the reason that this has arisen is mainly due to a lessening of faith in general and, in particular, a weakening of faith in the great *Tzaddikim* and Masters of previous generations. The books of Kabbalah and the *Zohar* are full of images drawn from the physical world and so people became afraid that they might not understand this imagery in the correct way and fall into a form of idolatry.

This is what has inspired me to undertake the task of properly explaining the work of the Ari and of the holy *Zohar*. I have completely removed this fear because I have explained and clearly demonstrated the spiritual analogue that exists for every entity, stripped of any material image, not connected to space and time. Those who are interested can see this for themselves.

I have made it possible for everyone in the House of Israel to study the holy *Zohar* and warm themselves by its holy light. I have called my commentary, *The Ladder*, to illustrate the fact that the purpose of my explanation is the same as that of any other ladder. If you have an attic full of bounty, all you need is a ladder to go up and then all the good of the world is within your reach.

However, the ladder is not a goal in itself. If you were to rest on the steps of the ladder and not enter the attic, then you would not have fulfilled your intention.

So it is with my explanation of the *Zohar*. Its words are unfathomably deep. The means by which to express its depth have yet to be created. However my explanation at any rate constitutes a path and an introduction which any person can use to ascend and to look deeply into the book of the *Zohar* itself. Only then would my intention in writing this explanation be fulfilled.

59. All serious students who have studied the holy *Zohar*—that is those who understand its contents—universally agree that its author is the holy *Tanna*, Rabbi Shimon Bar Yochai. Only those who are far from a true understanding of this wisdom have doubts about its authorship. On the basis of external evidence they claim that its author was the noted Kabbalist, Rabbi Moshe De Leon or one of his period.

60. As for myself, from the day that I merited through the light of God to understand a little in this holy book, it never occurred to me to question its authorship for the simple reason that from the content of the book, there came to my heart a sense of the holiness of the *Tanna*, Rabbi Shimon Bar Yochai which was immeasurably greater

than that of the other holy *Tannaim*. If it was completely clear to me that the author was someone else such as Rabbi Moshe De Leon, then I would think of him as having attained a level far beyond that of the *Tannaim* and even greater than that of Rabbi Shimon Bar Yochai. Actually, the book reaches such a depth of wisdom that if it turned out that its author was one of the ancient prophets of the Bible, I would find that even more reasonable than ascribing its authorship to one of the *Tannaim*. Even were it to be proved that Moses, our Teacher, received it straight from God at Mount Sinai, I would have no difficulty accepting this fact, so deep is the wisdom I see in it.

Therefore, since I have been privileged to write an explanation of this book in such a way that anyone who is interested can understand something of it, I feel myself discharged from the need to research the identity of its author. When the reader begins to appreciate the depth of this work, he or she will themselves feel satisfied that it must have been written by someone who has attained at the very least the spiritual level of the Holy Rabbi Shimon Bar Yochai.

61. We both can and should ask at this point why the *Zohar* was not revealed to earlier generations. They were, undoubtedly, higher souls than the later generations and more suited to it. We can also ask why the explanation of the *Zohar* was only revealed at the time of the Ari and not to the Kabbalists who preceded him. The most astonishing puzzle of all, however, is why the explanation of the words of the Ari and of the *Zohar* have only been openly revealed in this generation and not prior to it?

The answer to these questions is that the world is one spiritual entity, which divides up into three parts within the time period of its existence. There is a head part, a body part and a tail part, which divides in accordance with the *sephirot* as follows: *Chochmah, Binah* and *Da'at* being the head; *Chesed, Gevurah* and *Tipheret* being the body; *Netzach, Hod* and *Yesod* being the tail part. According to the sages, the head part of the spiritual entity corresponds to the stage of chaos; the body part corresponds to the stage of Torah, and the tail part corresponds to the days of the Messiah.

In the first time period of the world's existence, namely the head part, the lights were few and considered only as potential lights. They were of the quality of *Nefesh*.

In any spiritual entity, the growth of the vessels of that entity always occurs in the opposite order when compared with the incarnation of the lights, the general rule being that the **highest vessels** grow first, whereas, for the lights, the opposite applies. The **lowest lights** enter the spiritual entity initially. Thus, so long as only the highest vessels are present—that is those related to the *sephirot* of *Chochmah, Binah* and *Da'at*, only the lights of *Nefesh*—the lowest lights—can come down to be enclothed within these vessels. Thus the first time period of the world is designated by the sages as the stage of chaos.

Then came the second time period of the world. The vessels that evolved at that time relate to the *sephirot* of *Chesed, Gevurah* and *Tipheret*. The vessels enclothed the light of *Ruach* in the world which is the Torah. Thus the sages designated this time period as the stage of Torah.

In the final period of the world's existence, the last vessels of *Netzach, Hod, Yesod* and *Malchut* come in and then the light of *Neshamah* is enclothed in the world. *Neshamah* is a greater light and thus this period is called the days of the Messiah.

This process applies for any spiritual entity. When the highest vessels, *Chochmah, Binah, Da'at*, together with *Chesed, Gevurah* and *Tipheret* are in the entity, that is from the head until the level of the chest, then the lights are still covered and they do not begin to shine with the revealed illumination of the light of God until the lower vessels are ready. These are *Netzach, Hod, Yesod* and *Malchut* which belong in the spiritual entity from the level of the chest and downwards.

So, therefore, concerning the spiritual entity that constitutes the world, before its vessels of *Netzach, Hod, Yesod* and *Malchut* began to emerge—which is to say in the last period of its existence—the wisdom of the Kabbalah in general and of the *Zohar* in particular was hidden from the world. However during the time of the Ari, in which the lower vessels were forming, the higher light became revealed through the Divine soul of Rabbi Yitshak Luria [the Ari] who was able to receive this great light. He was able to reveal the underlying principles of the book of the *Zohar* and of the wisdom of the Kabbalah to the extent that he superseded all those who had preceded him.

Since, however, the vessels were not yet completed in his time, the world was still not ready for his words and thus his teachings remained available only to a few very special individuals of great attainment who did not have permission [from Above] to reveal their understanding to the world.

However in this, our generation, we are close to the completion of the last period of the world. Therefore, we have been permitted to reveal the teachings of the Ari and those of the *Zohar* in a most significant measure to the world. From our generation onwards, the words of the *Zohar* will begin to be revealed more and more until their whole measure is revealed according to the will of God.

62. Now we can see in actual fact that the souls of the earlier generations were immeasurably higher than those of the later generations. The rule for all spiritual entities, both pertaining to worlds and to souls, is that the purest vessels always incarnate first in the spiritual entity.

Thus, the vessels pertaining to *Chochmah*, *Binah* and *Da'at*, both of the world and of the souls, incarnated first, making the souls that incarnated during the head period of the world incomparably higher than those who came after them.

Despite their tremendous elevation, they could not receive the full amount of light due both to the lack of lower souls in the world and to the lack of their own lower components which are the *sephirot* of *Chesed, Gevurah, Tipheret, Netzach, Hod, Yesod* and *Malchut*.

Even during the middle period, when the vessels of the world and of the souls that emerged were of the *sephirot* of *Chesed, Gevurah* and *Tipheret*, then the souls were still extremely pure, seeing that the vessels of *Chesed, Gevurah* and *Tipheret* are close to the vessels of *Chochmah, Binah* and *Da'at*. At this stage, the higher lights were still concealed from the world due to the lack of incarnation of vessels from the level of the chest and below, both in the world and in the souls themselves.

In our generation, the souls that are incarnating are from the very lowest *sephirot*. However, they complete both the spiritual entity that consists of the world, and the spiritual entity which consists of all the souls. They are the last of the vessels to incarnate. The work, therefore, from the aspect of the vessels, is only completed through these souls. Now that the vessels of *Netzach, Hod* and *Yesod* are complete, this means that all the vessels of the head, middle and tail of the spiritual entity can draw on the full measure of the lights in the head, middle and tail, for all who are worthy of them. These are *Nefesh, Ruach* and *Neshamah* in their entirety. So only with the perfection of the lowest souls could the highest lights be revealed, and not prior to this.

63. This was a problem that also pre-occupied the rabbis of the Talmud. They raised it in their characteristically metaphorical way.

"Rav Papa said to Abaya, [of the fourth and fifth generation] 'How is it that for the former generations miracles were performed but for us miracles don't seem to happen? It cannot be because they were better at studying, because in the time of Rav Yehudah [of the second generation], all they learnt was the one tractate, *Nezikin*, whereas we study all six tractates of the *Mishnah*! And when Rav Yehudah was learning the law in the section *Uzkin*, "If a woman presses vegetables in a pot...," he used to say, "I see all the difficulties of Rav and Shmuel [of the first generation] here." [i.e. this passage presents as many difficulties as all the rest of the Talmud!] Yet we [of the fourth and fifth generation] have thirteen versions of this section, *Uzkin*! Nevertheless, when Rav Yehudah merely took off one shoe [in preparation for fasting to pray for rain], the rain used to arrive instantly, whereas we torment ourselves and cry loudly and no notice is taken of us!'

"Abaya replied, 'The former generations used to be ready to sacrifice their lives for the sanctity of God's Name. We do not sacrifice our lives for the sanctity of God's Name.'"

So, even though the later teachers were more skilled in answering difficult questions of law than were the earlier generations, it was clear to them that the former generations were of a holier essence than they were. Rav Papa and Abaya may have been considerably more skilled in Torah and its wisdom than were the earlier generations, but the former generations were closer to the level of the *Ein Sof* in the essence of their souls. The reason for this is that the purer vessels incarnate first whereas the wisdom of Torah [being the light] is revealed more and more to the later generations. As we have stated, it is precisely through its lowest vessels that the spiritual entity becomes completed. Then the more complete lights are drawn to the entity, even though the essence of the lowest vessels is furthest from the *Ein Sof*.

64. One need not ask then that if this is the case, why do we always follow the earlier generations in issues concerning the revealed Torah?

The matter, however, is as follows. With regards **practical** aspects of the *mitzvot*, the earlier generations had a more complete practice than do the later generations. This is because practice and practical matters are drawn from the holiest **vessels** of the *sephirot*, whereas the innermost aspects of Torah [the wisdom of Torah] and the reasons for the *mitzvot* come from the **lights** within the *sephirot*. We have already seen that vessels follow an opposite rule to that of lights. With regard to vessels, the highest ones develop first. Therefore the earlier generations had a greater understanding of practical Torah than the later ones. The opposite is true as regards lights, the lowest ones entering first. Thus, the later generations have a more complete understanding of the wisdom of Torah than the former generations had.

65. Now you must know that everything has an inner aspect and an outer aspect. In the world as a whole, Israel, the seed of Abraham, Isaac and Jacob, is considered to be the innermost aspect. The seventy nations are considered to be the outer aspect of the world. Within Israel itself, there is an inner aspect which consists of those people who are seriously committed to their spiritual work of serving God and there is an outer aspect consisting of those who are not involved in spirituality. Likewise, amongst the nations of the world, there is an inner aspect which consists of the saints of the world and an outer aspect which consists of those who are destructive and coarse.

Even amongst those of Israel who serve God, there is an inner aspect and an outer aspect. The inner aspect is those people who are privileged to understand the soul of the innermost aspects of Torah and its secrets, and the outer part consists of people who only deal with the practical aspects of Torah.

All this can also be considered likewise in one individual person. The individual has within him or her, the innermost aspect which is the aspect of "Israel" within the person. This is the point of Divine light within his or her heart. He or she also has an outer aspect which corresponds to the seventy nations of the world and relates to the will to receive. These internal "nations of the world" have the capacity for transformation. They can cleave to the innermost divine part of the person's soul and they then become like the righteous converts who join with the community of Israel.

66. A person may reinforce and respect his or her innermost aspect, which is the aspect of Israel within the person, over his or her external aspect, which is the aspect of the nations of the world within the person. He or she then strives to put most of his or her energy and labor into increasing and enhancing his or her innermost aspect for the soul's sake. To those aspects of himself or herself, which correspond to the internal nations of the world within that person, he or she gives only the minimum required. That is to say that the person only gives the minimum to his or her wills to receive for oneself, according to what is written in *The Ethics of the Fathers*, "Make your Torah your main occupation and your work secondary to it." The person's deeds affect both the inner aspect and the external aspect of the world as a whole. He or she causes the spiritual level of Israel to go up and the nations of the world, which comprise the external aspect of humanity, then recognize and value Israel.

But if, God forbid, the opposite occurs, that an individual of Israel reinforces and values his or her outer aspects, which is the aspect of the nations of the world within him or her, over and above his or her inner aspect of Israel, then, according to the prophecy of Deuteronomy, Chapter 28, "The stranger that is within you," which refers to the external aspects of the person, "will prevail over you higher and higher," "and you,"—as you are in yourself, in your innermost aspect, in your aspect of Israel within you—"will go down further and further" (Deut. 28:43). Then the person causes by his or her deeds that the externality of the world, which is the nations of the world, ascends higher and higher and has power over Israel and humiliates it to the dust, and they that are the innermost aspect of the world go down further and further, God forbid.

67. Do not be surprised by the fact that an individual person, through his or her deeds, can cause an elevation or degradation of the whole world. There is an unalterable law that the macrocosm [the totality] and the microcosm [the individual] are as like to each other as two drops of water. The same procedures that occur with respect to the macrocosm occur with regard to the individual and vice versa. Furthermore, it is the individual components themselves which make up the macrocosm and thus the macrocosm is only revealed through the manifestation of its individual components according to their measure and their quality. So certainly, the act of a single person, according to his or her capacity, may lower or elevate humanity as a whole.

This is how we can understand what is stated in the *Zohar* that through the study of the *Zohar* and the practice of the true wisdom, we can bring about an end to our state of exile and a complete redemption.

We could ask what studying the *Zohar* could have to do with redeeming Israel from among the nations?

68. From what we have already seen, it is easy to understand that the Torah, like the world itself, has an inner and an outer aspect. Likewise, the one who occupies himself or herself with Torah has these two levels. So to the degree that a person, when practising Torah, strengthens and focuses on the innermost aspects of Torah and its secrets, he or she gives strength in this measure to the innermost aspect of the

world, which is Israel. Then Israel begins to fulfill its true function with respect to the nations who then value Israel's role amongst them. Then shall the words of the prophet be fulfilled, "And the people shall take them and bring them to their place. And the House of Israel will settle in the Land of the Lord" (Isa. 14:2). Similarly, "Thus says the Lord God, 'Behold I will lift up My hand to the nations and set up My standard to the peoples. And they shall bring your sons in their arms and your daughters shall be carried on their shoulders. And kings shall be your foster fathers and their queens your nursing mothers'" (Isa. 49:22). [In other words, Israel, that is to say, the will to receive in order to serve God and each other will triumph over the will to receive for oneself alone, which will then act as support and hand-maiden to the will to receive in order to give.]

But, God forbid, the opposite could happen. A person of Israel might devalue the most intimate part of Torah with its secrets which deal with the ways of our souls and their levels, devaluing also the intellectual considerations and reasons of the Torah, emphasizing instead the outermost aspect of Torah that deals with practical issues alone. If such a person ever concerns himself or herself with the inner-most aspect of the Torah, he or she only sets aside a small portion of his time to it, not giving to it the attention it deserves but treating it as if it were superfluous material. By behaving in this way, he or she lowers and degrades the innermost aspect of the world, the Children of Israel, reinforcing the externality of the world over them, who are the nations of the world.

Then they, the nations of the world, cast Israel down and despise the children of Israel and consider Israel to be a superfluous entity in the world of which there is no need, God forbid. Not only this, but these people further cause the outer aspects of the nations of the world, who are coarse people who damage and destroy the world, to prevail over the inner aspects of the nations of the world, who are the righteous amongst the nations. They then cause terrible destruction, slaughter and holocausts, such as our generation has been a witness to, God preserve us from here onwards.

Therefore we can see that the redemption of Israel and all the worth of Israel is dependent on the learning of the *Zohar* and the innermost aspect of the Torah. The opposite is true also. All the afflictions and degradations that have come upon the Children of Israel are on account of their neglecting the most intimate part of Torah, and not having valued it but having related to it as something superfluous, God forbid.

69. This is what is said in the *Tikkunei haZohar*:

"Come and wake up, for the sake of the Holy *Shechinah*. Your heart is empty and you lack the understanding to know and comprehend her, even though she is in your midst.

"The inner meaning of the Scripture, 'A voice says, "Call out!"' (Isa. 40:3) is that a voice is knocking in the heart of each and every person to encounter and to pray for the raising up of the holy *Shechinah* which encompasses the souls of all Israel. The *Zohar* brings a proof that "calling out" means "prayer" by quoting from the book of Job, 'Call out now! Is there any that will answer you? And to which of the holy ones will you turn' (Job, 5:1)?

"The *Shechinah* herself says, 'But what shall I call out? I have no strength to raise myself from the dust because all flesh is as grass. Everyone is behaving like animals, eating grass and clover.'

"When they perform *mitzvot*, they do so in the way that animals would, without any inner understanding. Even all the kindness that they do, they really do primarily for their own benefit. They do not have the intention of carrying out the *mitzvot* in order to give pleasure to their Creator, but even the *mitzvot* they do perform are only done out of their own self-interest. Even the best amongst them who give of their time to the study of Torah, only do this to serve their wills to receive for themselves alone and without true intention of giving pleasure to God.

"It is said about such a generation that 'a spirit goes and does not return to the world.' That is the spirit of the Messiah who is needed to redeem Israel from all their sufferings and bring them to the final redemption, when the Scripture, 'The world will be full of the knowledge of God, just as the water covers the sea' (Isa. 11:9), will be fulfilled. It is this spirit that departs from the world and does not give light to the world.

"Woe to those people who cause the spirit of the Messiah to depart and leave the world, unable to return to it. They make the Torah a dry desert without any moisture of inner understanding and knowledge. They confine themselves to the practical aspects of Torah and they do not make any effort to try and understand the wisdom of the Kabbalah. They will not contemplate the innermost principles of the Torah and the deeper reasons for the *mitzvot*.

"Woe to them! They cause by their actions poverty, war, violence, pillage, killings and destructions in the world."

70. These words, as we have explained, concern those people who study Torah but disparage their own innerness and the intimate part of the Torah, leaving both aside. They treat them as if they are something unnecessary in the world and do not set aside the required time for them. In relation to their innermost aspects, they are like blind men groping along a wall. They strengthen the outermost aspects of themselves, that is their will to receive for themselves alone. They act similarly with regard to the Torah, emphasizing the outermost aspect of Torah over the innermost aspect of Torah. Thus they cause by their deeds that all the outer aspects of the world are strengthened over the innermost aspects of the world, each aspect according to its

essence. In this case, the outer aspects of Israel prevail and neutralize the innermost aspects of the community, who are the great Masters of the Torah. Likewise, the outermost aspects of the nations of the world, which are the warlords amongst them, prevail and hold sway over the innermost aspects which are the saints and pious ones of the nations of the world. Then the external aspect of the whole world, which are the nations of the world, prevail over and negate the children of Israel who are the innermost aspect of the world. In a generation such as this, all the warlords of the nations of the world raise up their heads and want primarily to destroy and kill the people of Israel. As it is written in the Talmud, "Sufferings only come to the world on account of Israel." This is exactly what we saw written in the above passage in the *Zohar*. This is what causes poverty, violence, robbery, killing and destruction in the whole world.

To our great sorrow, we ourselves have born witness to everything that has been said in the above passage. The finest of us were destroyed in the Holocaust. As the Talmud tells us, "The Righteous are the first to suffer." All that remains of the community of Israel that was destroyed in Europe is a remnant in the Holy Land and it is incumbent upon us, the remnant, to heal this grave error. Every one of us from now on should take upon himself or herself with all our soul and strength, the work of enhancing the innermost aspect of Torah to give it its true place as being much more important than the Torah's outward aspect. In this way, each of us will strengthen our own inner-most aspect, which is the aspect of Israel within us. This is the need of our soul as opposed to our external aspects which are our wills to receive for ourselves alone. This power will then touch all the community of Israel until the other nations, which are aspects within us, will recognize the value of the sages of Israel and they will then want to listen to them and obey them. Likewise, the innermost aspects of the nations of the world—the righteous ones amongst them—will prevail and subdue the outer aspect of the nations of the world—the violent and destructive elements. Then the innermost aspect of the world, Israel, will fulfill its true function with respect to the other nations who will recognize, appreciate it and value it. Then will the prophecies of Isaiah be fulfilled, "and the people shall take them and bring them to their place and Israel will settle in the land of the Lord" (Isa. 14:2).

This is why the *Zohar* states that **through studying this book of the *Zohar*, the redemption of the world will come about in love.**

Amen, may this be His will.

Chapter 4

Introduction to the Study of the Ten Sephirot

Rabbi Yehudah Lev Ashlag

At the beginning of this discourse, I discover a great need within myself to shatter an iron curtain which separates us from the wisdom of the Kabbalah since the time of the destruction of the Temple right up to our own generation. This barrier has burdened us to a very serious degree and awakens the fear that the Kabbalah might even be forgotten in Israel, God forbid.

When I begin to advise someone concerning the study of this subject, their first question always is, "But why do I need to know how many angels there are in heaven and what their names are? Surely I can keep the whole of the Torah in all its fullest details without this type of knowledge?"

Their second question is, "Didn't the sages already decide that before studying Kabbalah, a person must first 'fill his belly' with Talmud and Jewish Law? And who could possibly fool himself into thinking that he has already completed the entire revealed Torah and all that he lacks is the concealed Torah [the Kabbalah]?"

Thirdly, the person is afraid that he or she may go off the path as a consequence of this study. It has happened that there have been cases in the past where people strayed from the way of Torah as a consequence of studying Kabbalah. Therefore the person says, "Why should I risk it? Why should I be so foolish as to place myself in danger for no good reason?"

Fourthly, even those who love this learning only permit it to very saintly people who serve God, and not everyone who wants to take it up may do so.

But the fifth objection that the person may raise is the main one. There is a halachic principle that states that where there is a case of doubt we look at the general common practice. The person tells me, "When I look at the people who practise Torah in this generation, I see that they have all unanimously abandoned the study of this hidden wisdom. They even counsel those who ask them that, without any doubt, it is better to spend one's time studying a page of Talmud than to occupy oneself with Kabbalah."

2. However, if we consider only one very famous question, I am sure that all these questions and doubts will vanish over the horizon and disappear as if they had never been. The burning question which is asked of all the inhabitants of this world is, What is the point of our lives? Why do we live these number of years which cost us so dearly? We go through so much pain and suffering in order to complete them till their end. Who can really say that he enjoys his life? Or, even more pointedly, Is there anyone who benefits from my life? The truth is that the philosophers have left off pondering this question and it is certainly the case that in our generation no one even wants to consider it.

Nevertheless, the essence of this question still stands in all its force and bitterness. Sometimes it comes upon us unawares and bores into our brains, casting us down to the very dust until we hit upon the well-known strategy of allowing ourselves to be swept up thoughtlessly into the stream of life, just as we did yesterday.

3. Scripture gives the solution to this obdurate riddle in the phrase, "Taste and see that God is Good" (Ps. 34:9). Those people who fulfil Torah and *mitzvot* in the correct way are those who taste the true taste of life. They see and bear witness to the fact that God is Good. The sages have taught us that God created the worlds in order to benefit His creatures. It is in the nature of the Good to do good. But it is certainly the case that someone who has not yet tasted the life of fulfillment in Torah and *mitzvot* can neither understand nor experience that God is Good in the way that the sages taught; that God's whole intention in creating Man was only to give benefit to all. Therefore the best recommendation for such a person is to begin to practise Torah and *mitzvot* in the correct way. This is what the Torah itself says, "See, I have set before you this day, Life and Good or Death and Evil" (Deut. 30:15). Before the Torah was given, there was no choice. Only death and evil were present. This fits in with the remark of the sages that "wicked people within their lifetimes are called 'dead' because their death is better than their lives." The pain and suffering that they undergo just in order to survive, cost them dearly in comparison with the little amount of pleasure they receive in such a life.

However we have now been privileged to receive Torah and *mitzvot*, through whose fulfillment we can merit true and happy lives which give joy to others and to ourselves according to the true sense of the Scripture, "Taste and see that God is Good." Therefore, the Scripture says, "See, I have set before you this day Life and Good," which you did not have at all in the world before the giving of the Torah. The Scripture goes on to conclude, "…and thus choose Life, in order that you and your offspring will live" (Deut. 30:19).

The language here seems to be redundant. Obviously if you choose life, you will live! What the Scripture here is actually referring to is living a life of consciousness through the fulfillment of Torah and *mitzvot*. This is true life as contrasted to living without Torah and *mitzvot*. Such a life is more difficult than death. Thus the sages have said, "Wicked people within their lifetimes are called 'dead'." When Scripture says, "…in order that you and your offspring should live," it implies that a life without Torah not only gives no pleasure to oneself but cannot benefit others either. A person cannot even have pleasure from his or her own children since their lives are also harder than death. What sort of inheritance is that to pass on to them?

However, one who lives in the consciousness of Torah and *mitzvot* not only enjoys his or her own life, but he or she is happy to give birth to children to whom they bequeath this good life. This is the meaning of "…in order that you and your seed should live." A person then has additional joy in the life of his or her children, as he or she was a prime cause of them.

4. Through what we have said, you can now understand the words of the sages when they explained the meaning of the Scripture, "…and thus choose Life." Rashi's commentary on this verse is as follows: "I teach you that you should choose the portion of Life. This is like the case of a man saying to his son, 'Choose the best portion of my inheritance!' But then the man himself stands the son over the best part of the inheritance saying, 'This is the part that you should choose!' Concerning this the Psalmist says, 'God is the portion of my inheritance and cup. You support my lot' (Ps. 16:5). In other words, You have placed my hands on the best part of the inheritance saying, 'Take this part for yourself.'"

All this seems very odd. On the one hand, Scripture says, "Choose Life," which surely means that a person should choose for himself or for herself. But now the sages are saying that God Himself stands the person over the best part, in which case there seems to be no free choice here! Not only that but they go on to say that God Himself places the person's hand on the good portion. This is all very surprising, because if this is the case, where is the person's free choice?

We need to understand the sages' teaching because it is, in fact, completely true. God Himself **does** place the hand of the person on the best portion in life by giving him or her a life of contentment and delight right within a material life that is filled with pain and suffering, empty of all content. Of course a person will try to escape and run away from this life that is harder than death the moment he or she sees for themselves, even if only like one peeping through a lattice, some place of tranquillity to escape to. There is no greater direction of a person's choice on the part of God than this!

So the matter of Man's free choice involves only the question of to what extent a person is prepared to strengthen himself or herself. It is certain that a great deal of work and effort is involved until a person can purify his or her will to receive for themselves and thus come to fulfill Torah and *mitzvot* in the right way; that is, not for the sake of obtaining benefit for himself or for herself but for the purpose of giving pleasure to the Creator. This is called Torah *for its own sake.* Only in this way can the person merit the life of happiness and pleasantness which accompanies the fulfillment of Torah.

Before a person has come to this stage of purification, free choice is still operative. He or she can decide to what degree they will commit themselves to the work of purification. Using all manner of means and strategies, let the person do everything in his or her power to complete this work of purification, so that he or she will not stumble and fall under their burden in the middle of the journey, God forbid.

5. From what we have explained above, you can now understand the words of the rabbis which are quoted in the *Mishnah*, "This is the way of Torah: You should eat bread with salt. You should drink water in strict measure. You should sleep upon the earth and live a life of suffering and you should labor in Torah. If you act in this way, you will be happy and it will be well for you. You will be happy in this

world and it will be well for you in the world to come."

You might ask concerning this passage, why is the Torah different from the other wisdoms of the world which can be acquired without ascetic practices or the prerequisite of living a life of suffering? Effort alone is certainly sufficient to acquire these wisdoms, whereas it seems that even if we were to labor hard in Torah this would not be sufficient to acquire it without these ascetic acts of eating only bread and salt and suchlike.

The latter part of the above quotation is even more astonishing when the rabbis go on to say, "If you do so, you will be happy in this world and it will be well for you in the world to come." It is reasonable to suppose that it may be good for me in the world to come, but how can I say, "I am happy in this world," whilst I am afflicting myself over food, drink and sleep and I am living a life of great suffering? How can the Rabbis say about such a life, "Happy are you in this world"? Can such a life be called "happy" in the context of what is usually understood as happiness?

6. However, according to what we have already explained, the correct way to be involved in Torah and *mitzvot* in the strictest sense is with the intention of giving pleasure to one's Creator without gaining pleasure through satisfying one's own needs. It is only possible to come to this through great work and huge effort in purifying the body. The first tactic is to accustom oneself not to receive anything at all for one's own pleasure, even when dealing with matters that are permitted and necessary for one's bodily needs such as eating, drinking, sleeping and other essential requirements. In such a way, a person dissociates himself or herself from any accompanying pleasure even when dealing with only what is necessary and just partakes of them to the minimum degree for the purpose of keeping body and soul together. This is literally living a life of suffering.

Once a person has already accustomed himself or herself to this and he or she no longer has any more will to receive pleasure for oneself alone within the body, then it becomes possible for him or for her from this time on to practise Torah and fulfil the *mitzvot* only with the intention of giving pleasure to the Creator and not at all in order to give pleasure to oneself. When the person is worthy of this, then he or she merits to taste a happy life filled with all goodness and pleasure without any defect of suffering at all. This happy life becomes manifest through the practice of Torah and *mitzvot* for its own sake. As Rabbi Meir says:

"Whoever labors in Torah for its own sake merits many things, and not only that but the whole world is indebted to him. He is called Friend, Beloved, a Lover of God, a Lover of Mankind. Humility enclothes him, as does reverence. He is fit to be righteous, pious, honest and faithful. It keeps him far from sin and draws him near to purity. Through him, the world can benefit from counsel, sound knowledge, understanding and strength. As it is said, 'Counsel is Mine and sound knowledge; understanding is Mine, strength is Mine' (Prov. 8:14). It gives him sovereignty and governance and discerning judgment. The secrets of the Torah are revealed to him and he becomes like a flowing fountain that never stops, like a river that increases its flow. He is modest, long-suffering, forgiving of insult and he is magnified by Torah and exalted above all things."

It is of such a person that Scripture speaks when it says, "Taste and see that God is Good" (Ps. 34:9).

One who tastes the taste of the true practice of Torah and *mitzvot* for its own sake merits and sees for himself or for herself that the intention of Creation is only to benefit God's creatures. It is in the nature of the Good to do good. Such people are happy and joyful throughout all the years that God grants them and they find the world a happy place to be in.

7. Now you can understand the two sides of the coin concerning involve-ment with Torah and *mitzvot*. One side is the way of Torah which means the great preparation a person needs in order to purify the will to receive for oneself alone, before he or she can merit to truly fulfill Torah and *mitzvot* according to their essence. During this preparatory period, he or she has no alternative but to practise Torah and *mitzvot* not purely for its own sake, but mixing his or her own self-interest into the spiritual practice. The person has yet to sufficiently purify and cleanse the body from the will to receive those pleasures which belong to the vanities of this world. During this period the person has to live a life of suffering and to labor in Torah, as described by the above passage in the *Mishnah*.

Only when the person has finished and perfected the way of Torah and purified the body, making it fit to fulfill Torah and *mitzvot* for its own sake, in order to give pleasure to the Creator, does he or she come to the other side of the coin which is a life of delight and great tranquillity. This life of delight and great tranquillity is the expression of creation's purpose, which is God's desire to give good to His crea-tures; in other words, the happiest possible life in this world and in the world to come.

8. Now we have clearly explained the major distinction that lies between the wisdom of the Torah and that of the other wisdoms of the world. Their attainment does not benefit our life in this world at all as they cannot recompense us for the sufferings and pains that we endure throughout our lives. The other intellectual wisdoms do not require the transformation of our will to receive for ourselves alone. Regard-ing them, it is enough simply to work for them in order to acquire them just as we do for any other acquisitions of this world which are acquired through labor and effort. However this is not true of the practice of Torah and *mitzvot*. The whole purpose of Torah and

mitzvot is to qualify a person so that he or she will be fitting to receive all the Good inherent in the intention of Creation which is to do good to God's creatures. Torah thus requires the purification of the will to receive for oneself alone in order that a person should be fit to receive this divine Good.

9. This also fits very well with the above text, "If you do so, you will be happy in this world…" The language here is very precise, teaching us that the happy life of this world is only available to someone who has completed the way of Torah. The ascetic practices concerning eating, drinking, sleeping and the life of suffering mentioned here, are only relevant during the time of the pathway of Torah. Thus the sages said with great precision, "This is the way of Torah…" After a person has completed this way of Torah, which is not for its own sake, through a life of suffering and asceticism, the text then concludes, "you will be happy in this world," for you will merit the happiness and goodness that is intended by Creation. All the world will be worthwhile for you; both this world and even more so the world to come.

10. On the phrase, "And God said, 'Let there be light and there was light'" (Gen. 1:3), the *Zohar* comments, "Let there be light in this world and there was light in the world to come."

Explanation: The act of creation brought into being all creatures according to their true nature and in their full stature, in all their perfection and in all their glory. Thus the light that was created on the first day appeared in all its perfection, including even the life in this world, in complete delight and pleasantness, in consonance with the full measure expressed in the words, "Let there be light."

However, in order to prepare a place of free choice in which there exists the potential for spiritual work, this light was then hidden and concealed for the righteous to receive in the world to come, as the sages have explained. Thus they said in their clear language, "Let there be light in this world." But all that was left was, "And there was light in the next world." That is to say that those who practise Torah and *mitzvot* for its own sake merit the light but only in the future once they have purified their wills to receive through the way of Torah. Then they are worthy of this great light even in this world just as the sages have said, "You can see your world during your lifetime."

11. Despite all this we see that the sages of the Talmud have considerably eased the path of Torah for us to a greater degree than did the sages of the *Mishnah*. They said, "A person should always practise Torah and *mitzvot* even if it is not for its own sake, because the practice of Torah not for its own sake leads to the practice of Torah for its own sake." The light in the Torah itself has the capacity to bring a person to the good way.

The sages of the Talmud thus put the light of the Torah in place of the ascetic practices described above in the *Mishnah*. The light of the Torah is sufficiently powerful to work this transformation within us. It can bring a person to practise Torah and *mitzvot* for its own sake. They do not mention any ascetic practices here, only stating that the practice of Torah and *mitzvot* on their own is sufficient. The light which is within the practice of Torah and *mitzvot* can bring a person to the good way so that he or she can practise Torah and *mitzvot* in order to give pleasure to the Creator without mixing into it one's own self-interest. This way is called Torah for its own sake.

12. One might question the sages' words, however, as in practice we find that there are certain students whose practice of the Torah does not help them. They do not come to merit that the light within the Torah leads them to the transformation of Torah for its own sake. The reason is that although the person believes in God and in the Torah

and in cause and effect, and he or she practises Torah because God commanded him or her to do so, nevertheless they mix their own self-interest together with the service of God. If, after all the effort the person puts into the practice of Torah and *mitzvot*, it were to become known to him or to her that they would not get any pleasure or personal advantage from their work, then he or she would regret every bit of effort that was put in since the person had deluded himself or herself right from the very beginning into thinking that they would also get personal benefit from their labor. This state of mind is called not for its own sake, as is stated in the Talmud, "Do not be like slaves who serve their master only for the sake of their reward."

Nevertheless, the sages permitted us to begin working with Torah and *mitzvot* even when it is not for its own sake on the grounds that working in Torah not for its own sake, will lead to Torah for its own sake. However it is certain that if the person who practises Torah in this way has not merited to believe in God and in His Torah but is filled with doubt, then the sages were not referring to him or to her when they said that the light within the Torah will bring a person back to the good way. For the light which is in Torah only shines forth for those who believe that it does so. Not only that, but the measure of the strength of the light of Torah directly accords with the degree of a person's belief. But for those who lack this faith, the reverse happens: "For those who use it wrongly, it becomes the drug of death," for they receive darkness from Torah and their eyes are dimmed.

13. The sages created an apt parable to explain the Biblical statement, "Why do you want the day of God? Why is it the day of God for you? For you it is darkness and not light" (Amos 5:18)! This is analogous to a rooster and a bat, both of whom are waiting for the dawn. The rooster says to the bat, "I am waiting for the light as it is my light. What do you want the light for?" The analogy here is exact. From it,

we can clearly understand those who study but do not progress from the stage of practising Torah not for its own sake to the stage of practising Torah for its own sake. It is because of their lack of faith that they do not receive any light from the Torah. They walk in darkness and will die without wisdom. But those who have the merit of complete faith can be sure that the practice of Torah and *mitzvot*, even when undertaken not for its own sake will shine its light upon them and will reform them and they will even merit to practise Torah for its own sake without going through prior afflictions and a life of suffering. Practising Torah for its own sake will bring them a life of happiness and good, both in this world and in the world to come. About such a person it is written, "Then you shall delight in the Lord and I will cause you to ride upon the high places of the earth and feed you the inheritance of Jacob your father, for the mouth of the Lord has spoken it" (Isaiah 58:14).

14. In a similar fashion, I once explained the proverb of the sages, "He whose Torah is his craft." According to the way a person practises Torah, so can the measure of his or her faith be known. The Hebrew word *amanah* (craft) has the same letters as the Hebrew word *emunah*, (faith). A man has a certain measure of faith in his friend and lends him some money. He may believe in him to the extent of loaning his friend $1 but, if his friend would ask for $2, he would refuse to lend it to him. Maybe he has faith in his friend to the extent of $100 but no more than that. Or it is possible that he may have faith in his friend to the extent that he is willing to loan him up to half his property, but not all of it. It is possible, too, that he might have so much faith in his friend that he would loan him everything he owns without any shadow of fear. This last example of faith is considered to be complete faith. The previous modes are counted as partial faith, some more, some less.

So one person, for example, may budget for themselves, according to the measure of his or her faith in God, one hour of the day to practise Torah and spiritual work. Another may assign two hours of the day to this work according to the measure of his or her faith in God. A third does not let a single moment of his or her free time pass without practising Torah and spiritual work. Only in this third example do we see someone whose faith is complete. He or she believes in God to the extent of their whole property. This is not true of the people in the previous examples. Their faith is not complete. We need not labor this point as it is understood.

15. Thus a man or a woman should not expect that simply practising Torah and *mitzvot* not for its own sake will automatically bring him or her to practise Torah for its own sake unless they know within their own heart that they have merited the required faith in God and Torah. Then the light that is inherent in Torah will bring the person to reform and he or she will merit the day of God that is all light. For the sanctity of faith purifies the eyes of Man so that he or she may enjoy the light of God until the illumination that is inherent in Torah brings the person to the good way.

On the other hand, people who lack faith are similar to bats who cannot bear the sight of daylight. The daylight for them is a darkness worse than the black of night as they only receive nourishment during the dark of the night. So it is with people who lack faith. Their eyes are blinded to the light of God. Therefore, for them, this light turns into darkness and the elixir of life becomes the drug of death. It is about such people that the Scripture spoke, "Woe to you, who desire the day of the Lord! Why would you have this day of the Lord? It is darkness and not light!"

So, first and foremost on the spiritual journey, a person has to work to acquire full faith.

16. Now we can settle a difficulty that arises in the Talmud. The Talmud tells us, "The Torah becomes the elixir of life for those who practise it for its own sake, but it becomes a drug of death for those who practise it when it is not for its own sake." The commentators here raised the following objection: "But didn't the sages say that a person should always practise Torah and *mitzvot* even if it is not for its own sake, for through being engaged in Torah and *mitzvot* even when it is not for its own sake, the person will come to practise Torah and *mitzvot* for its own sake?"

    Clearly from what we have learnt we can resolve the contradiction by simply saying that these two passages refer to different cases. The one case concerns someone who is practising Torah for the sake of learning the Torah. He or she believes, at the very least, in cause and effect, but the person includes his or her own pleasure and self-interest together with their intention of giving pleasure to the Creator. However in this case, the light of Torah will bring the person to the good way and he or she will come to practise Torah for its own sake.

    The other case refers to someone who practises Torah not for the sake of the study of Torah itself. He or she does not believe in cause and effect to the extent that they are prepared to put themselves out. Rather, they study Torah for their own purposes alone. Here, the Torah becomes a drug of death for them because the light in it becomes darkness.

17. Therefore before a person begins to study Torah, he or she must first strengthen his or her faith in God and in His Divine Providence with respect to cause and effect. As the rabbis have said, "The Master is faithful to pay you the wages for your work." Thus the person should intend that his or her labor should be for the sake of the *mitzvah* of Torah itself and in this way, he or she will merit to benefit from its light. The person's faith will then also get stronger and will grow by

virtue of this light, as it is written, "It shall be health to your navel and marrow to your bones" (Prov. 3:8).

Then the person can be certain in his or her heart that through the practice of Torah, even when it was done not for its own sake, he or she will come to practice Torah for its own sake. Even a person who knows for himself or for herself that they have not yet attained faith can also hope that through practising Torah and *mitzvot* with this particular intention, they can come to have faith in God. There is no commandment more important than this. The Talmud tells us, "Habakkuk came and put faith at the very center of the religion as it is written, 'A righteous person lives through his faith'" (Hab. 2:4).

What is more, there is not actually any alternative. As another passage of the Talmud tells us:

Raba said, "Job sought to excuse all the world from judgement. He said, 'Lord of the Universe, You have created the ox with cloven hooves [kosher] and you have created the ass with whole hooves [not kosher]; You created paradise and You created hell. You have created righteous people and you have created wicked people, and who can stay your hand?'"

The commentator Rashi explains here, "You have created the righteous through the means of the good inclination. You have created the wicked through the means of the evil inclination. Therefore none can be delivered from Your hand for who can prevent himself? Sinners are compelled to sin by their own nature!"

Raba continued, "But Job's companions answered Job, 'You are incorrect. You nullify fear of sin and limit prayer before God' (Job 15:4). It is true that God created the evil inclination, yet He also created the Torah as its medicine.'"

Rashi comments here that the Torah acts as a medicine to nullify sinful thoughts, as is said in another passage of the Talmud, "If this knave attacks you, drag him to the *Beit HaMidrash* (house of learning). If he is made of stone, he will dissolve." In other words, if a person is attacked by the evil inclination as when the thought of sin first occurs to him or to her, then the remedy is to turn one's thoughts to Torah because this will act against the evil inclination. From this it follows that sinners are not, in fact, coerced into sin because they can save themselves from sinning through the means of Torah.

18. It is clear that the sinner can therefore not excuse himself or herself from the consequences of their sin.

A person may say that he or she is studying Torah but still be troubled by sinful thoughts. This means that they are troubled by doubts and their evil inclination is still not softened. In such a case, the person must know that just as the Creator, Blessed be He, created in him or in her the evil inclination in all its force, God also created the medicine and antidote which can be relied upon to weaken the power of the evil inclination and can eliminate it completely.

If someone is engaged in Torah and does not succeed in removing the evil urge from themselves, then one of the following alternatives must be the case: Either he or she was negligent as regards the requirement of putting sufficient effort into the practice of Torah, as it is written, "Do not believe someone who says, 'I didn't labor but nonetheless I found.'" Or it is possible that the person put in the appropriate *quantity* of effort but was negligent regarding the *quality* of their work. That is to say that whilst involved in the practice of Torah, they did not focus their heart and mind on the need to attract to themselves the light that is in Torah which brings faith to the heart of Man. They practised in an unmindful manner, removing their attention from the most important aspect required, which is that the light which is in Torah should bring them to faith. Even though they may have had this intention at the beginning, they became distracted from it during their learning.

In either case, one may not exempt oneself from responsibility on the grounds that one's evil inclination compelled one. As the sages have stated, "I created the evil inclination. I created the Torah as its medicine." There are no exceptions to this rule. If there were, then Job's argument would stand, God forbid!

19. By what we have said above I have removed a large allegation against the following words of Rabbi Chayim Vital which appear in his *Introduction to the Sha'ar HaHakdamot* of the Ari and which perplex many people.

"A man should not say, 'I will go and practise Kabbalah before I practise the Torah of the *Mishnah* and Talmud,' for the Rabbis have already said, 'No one should study Kabbalah if they have not already filled their belly with *Mishnah* and Talmud. This would be like being a soul without a body, lacking any contact with this physical world. A person is not fully incarnate until he becomes involved at the physical level with the *mitzvot* of the Torah.' But the opposite is also true. If someone studies *Mishnah* and Talmud without also spending time in studying the innermost aspects of Torah and its secrets, he is like a body sitting in darkness, lacking a human soul which is the light of God that shines within. The body becomes dry because it is not taking from Torah, the source of life. Therefore a student who wishes to practise Torah for its own sake needs to start by occupying himself with Bible, *Mishnah* and Talmud, absorbing from that as much as his intellect can gather. Afterwards, he should turn to the practice of Kabbalah and come to know his Creator through it in the way that King David commanded his son Solomon, 'Know the Lord your Father and serve Him' (Chron. 1 28:9). But if the student finds that the study of Talmud is burdensome and hard for him, it is best that he leave it and turn to the practice and study of the true wisdom, which is the Kabbalah. This is what is meant by the passage in the Talmud,

'If a student of Torah does not see a sign of blessing in his studies after five years, then he never will.' However, everyone who does put their focus on the study of Kabbalah should spend a small portion of the day studying *halachah* and practising answering practical questions." This ends our quote of his holy language, word for word.

20. The words of Rabbi Chayim Vital here are seemingly very surprising. He says that a student who has not yet succeeded in learning revealed Torah such as the Talmud, should go and study Kabbalah. But this is in contradiction to what he said earlier, that the wisdom of Kabbalah without the revealed Torah is like a soul without a body, because it has no relation to the physical world of activity.

   The proof that Rabbi Chayim Vital brings from the Talmud about a student who has not seen a transformation in himself after five years of study is even more surprising. Surely the sages did not intend that a person should give up studying Talmud altogether! What they intended was to caution him to re-examine his ways and possibly consider studying under another teacher or changing the tractate of Talmud that he is studying. They certainly did not mean that he should give up these studies completely.

21. There is another difficulty in Rabbi Chayim Vital's understanding of the passage that he quotes from the Talmud. This passage seems to suggest that a person needs a degree of preparation and special talent in order to attain the wisdom of Torah. But surely the sages have said, "The Holy One, Blessed be He said to Israel, 'By your life! All this wisdom and all this Torah is easy! Anyone who fears to be separate from Me and practises the words of Torah will find all the wisdom and all the Torah in his heart!'" So, in fact, we do not require any prior excellence. Just by virtue of being afraid to be separated from God and by carrying out the *mitzvot*, we can come to merit all the wisdom of the Torah.

2. However, if we pay close attention to the words of Rabbi Chayim Vital, they become as clear as a blue sky. For he wrote that if one is not succeeding in his studies of revealed Torah [i.e. Talmud], he should instead turn his hand to the study of Kabbalah. By the term, "not succeeding", Rabbi Chayim Vital does not intend intellectual understanding or expertise, but rather, he means that which we discussed above in the explanation of the phrase, "I created the evil inclination, I created the Torah as its medicine." That is to say that although the person is studying and laboring in the revealed Torah (Talmud), nevertheless, he finds that his evil urge is still active within him in all its force and has not softened at all. He finds that he still has sinful thoughts, just as Rashi described above (paragraph 17) in his explanation of "I created the evil inclination. I created the Torah as its medicine." So Rabbi Chayim Vital advises a person in such a situation to leave his study of revealed Torah and turn to the study of Kabbalah, because it is easier through the practice and effort of the study of Kabbalah to draw to oneself the illumination which is inherent in Torah, than it is through labor in revealed Torah.

The reason for this is very simple. The wisdom of the revealed Torah (the Talmud) is clothed in external physical garments. It deals with issues such as stealing, robbery, damages and the like. For this reason it is very difficult for anyone to keep his or her heart pure and focused on God in order to draw to himself or herself the light of Torah whilst they are learning this material. This is even more so for one who finds the study itself difficult. How is he or she meant to remember God during his or her study, when the subject matter pertains to the physical world? How can he or she possibly keep his or her intention directed towards God when dealing with material matters?

Therefore Rabbi Chayim Vital counsels the student to occupy himself or herself with the wisdom of the Kabbalah, because this wisdom is entirely clothed in the names of God. Thus, naturally, the student will be able to direct his or her mind and heart towards God during study, without effort. Even though the subject matter is extremely difficult, nevertheless since this wisdom and God are one, it becomes a simple matter.

23. Now we can see that the quotation that Rabbi Chayim Vital brings from the Talmud is entirely appropriate. "If a pupil has not seen any transformation in himself after five years of learning, he will not see it in the future." The reason as to why the student did not see a good sign in his or her learning is only because of the student's lack of intention and is not due to lack of talent. The inner wisdom of Torah does not require talent, but as we have said in the above quotation from the sages, "The Holy One Blessed be He said to Israel, 'By your life! All the wisdom and all the Torah is easy! Anyone who fears being separate from Me and practises the words of Torah, will find all the wisdom and all the Torah in his heart.'"

However one has to give the process time during which one can accustom oneself to the light within the Torah and *mitzvot*. The question is, how much time? One might think that the process could take all the seventy years of one's life! Therefore the Talmud here comes to warn us not to wait longer than five years, with Rabbi Yossi of the Talmud saying that just three years is certainly sufficient to merit the wisdom of the Torah. If the person did not see any sign of transformation in themselves within that period of time, then he or she should not delude himself or herself with vain hopes. Rather, he or she should know that they are unlikely ever to achieve a transformation through this approach. Therefore, without wasting any more time, the student should try another tactic through which he or she may come to merit the practice of Torah for its own sake and to merit the wisdom of Torah. The Talmud itself does not explain what this other way might be, but it does warn the person not to simply sit and wait in their present situation. So Rabbi Chayim Vital tells us that the best and surest tactic is for the person to become involved in the wisdom of Kabbalah, and to leave off studying Talmud completely as he has already tried that and it did not work for him. The student should put all his or her energies into the study of Kabbalah and he or she will certainly succeed in that, for the reason that we have explained above.

4. It is important to point out that Rabbi Chayim Vital is not suggesting that a person should renounce the study of the revealed Torah in as much as it pertains to practical *halachah*. As it is said, "an ignorant person cannot be a pious person," "an inadvertent error may cause a person to make a deliberate error," and "even an inadvertent error may nevertheless incur a loss of much benefit" (Eccles. 9:18).

Everyone is therefore required to review practical *halachah*, so that he or she will not make any mistakes in practice. So, we can see that Rabbi Chayim Vital, in his remarks above, is not talking about the study of practical *halachah*. He is referring, rather, to the systematic study of Talmud for its inner wisdom. A person must be sure that he or she can deal with practical issues in *halachah*, as Rabbi Chayim Vital himself makes clear. The aspect of studying that he is suggesting that we can give up under these circumstances is the realm of theory that does not come into practice. Under these circumstances, it is permissible for a person to learn *halachah* from compendia of laws and not from the sources. One has to be very careful with this, however, as you cannot compare someone who has a profound knowledge of the source material of *halachah* to someone who knows it only from summaries.

It was in order to be sure not to mislead here, that Rabbi Chayim Vital makes the point right at the beginning of his words that the soul requires the contact with the body which occurs in the practical work of the *mitzvot*.

25. Now you can see how all the questions that we listed at the very beginning of this *Introduction* are completely empty of worth. They are snares laid by the evil urge in an attempt to hunt and capture pure souls in order to harass them and entrap them in a world where there is no delight.

You will remember that the first question that people ask is, "Why can't I simply observe the whole Torah without any knowledge of Kabbalah?" To such people I say, "On the contrary! If you are able to fulfill the study of Torah and to practise the *mitzvot* in full, for its own sake only in order to give pleasure to the Creator, then you really do not have to learn Kabbalah. For it is said about you that "the soul of the man will teach him." Then, the secrets of Torah will be revealed to you like a spring overflowing with water, without your needing help from books.

"But if you are still involved in Torah in a way that is not for its own sake and your hope is to be able to practise it for its own sake, then I have to ask you how many years have you been studying like this? If you have been studying for less than five years according to the first opinion or less than three years according to Rabbi Yossi, then you should still wait and hope to see this transformation in yourself. However if you have been involved in learning Talmud not for its own sake for more than three years according to Rabbi Yossi or for more than five years according to the first opinion in the Talmud, then the Talmud itself warns you that you will never see the transformation you are looking for if you continue on your present path. Why waste your life in pursuing a false hope when you have a sure and handy tactic, that is to study the wisdom of the Kabbalah which, as I have shown above, is one with God Himself?"

26. Now we will come to grips with the second objection raised at the beginning of this work which was this: People say that before beginning to study Kabbalah, a person must first have "filled his belly" with the study of Talmud and *halachah*.

This is certainly the case in everyone's opinion, if you have already merited to learn Torah for its own sake or if you are still within the first three or five years of this study. However if you have been studying for more than this time period and you have not progressed with your inner work, then the Talmud cautions you that you may never see the transformation you are looking for and you should definitely change to studying Kabbalah.

27. You need to know that there are two parts to Kabbalah. The first part is called the *sitrei Torah* (secrets of Torah). This part is forbidden to be revealed except by way of hints by a Master Kabbalist to one who has acquired an advanced level of understanding. This category includes the *Ma'aseh Merkavah* (the Wisdom of the Chariot) and the *Ma'aseh B'reshit* (the Wisdom of Creation). The sages of the *Zohar* designate this part of Kabbalah as relating to the first three *sephirot*, which are *Keter*, *Chochmah* and *Binah*. It is also referred to as the head of the spiritual entity.

The second level in Kabbalah is known as the *ta'amei Torah* (reasons of Torah). Not only is it permitted to reveal this level, it is an extremely meritorious act to do so. It is known in the *Zohar* as the seven lower *sephirot*, or the body of the spiritual entity. In every holy entity there are ten *sephirot*, which are called, *Keter*, *Chochmah*, *Binah*, *Chesed*, *Gevurah*, *Tipheret*, *Netzach*, *Hod*, *Yesod* and *Malchut*. The first three *sephirot* are considered as the head of the entity and the seven lower *sephirot* are considered as the body of the entity.

Likewise, even the soul of the human has within it aspects of the ten *sephirot* according to their names as, indeed, has every single entity, whether in the higher worlds or in the lower worlds, as will be explained further on. The reason why the seven lower *sephirot* which comprise the body of the spiritual entity are called the *ta'amei Torah* (the reasons of the Torah) is in accordance with the inner meaning of the scriptural expression, "The palate tastes (*ta'am*) food," as is written in this passage from Job, "But ask now the beasts and they shall teach you, and the birds of the sky and they shall tell you, or speak to the earth and it will teach you and the fishes of the sea shall declare to you. Who amongst all these does not know that the hand of the Lord has done this? In this hand is the soul of every living thing and the spirit of all humankind. Does not the ear discern words just as the palate tastes food? Wisdom belongs to the aged and length of days brings understanding. With Him is wisdom and might. He has counsel and understanding" (Job 12:12–14).

The lights that are revealed below the level of the first three *sephirot*—that is they are revealed below the level of the head of the spiritual entity—are designated *ta'amim* (reasons or tastes). The lowest *sephirah* of the head, the *Malchut* of the head, is designated as equivalent to the palate. Therefore these lights are called the *ta'amei Torah*. This is to say that they are revealed at the level of the palate of the head of the spiritual entity which is the source of all the *ta'amim* and corresponds to the *Malchut* of the head. From this level and lower, there is no restriction on revealing them. On the contrary, the reward for revealing them is great beyond all measure.

Now everything that exists, whether in the macrocosm or in the smallest microcosm, is made up of these first three *sephirot* together with the last seven *sephirot*. So, if we take as an example, the *Malchut* which belongs to the end of the world of *Assiyah*, the first three *sephirot* even of this low level belong to the *sitrei Torah*, the concealed aspect of Torah which it is forbidden to reveal. Equally, the seven lower *sephirot* of the *Keter* of the world of *Atzilut*, which is the very highest of the highest, belong to the sphere of the *ta'amei torah*, which is permissible to reveal and these matters are published in books of Kabbalah.

28. Now the source of these matters may be found in the Talmud, where it is written:

"It is quoted in the book of Isaiah (Isa. 23:18), 'And her merchandise and her hire shall be sacred to the Lord. It shall neither be stored nor treasured, for her gain shall be for them that dwell before the Lord to eat sufficiently and for stately clothing.'"

The Talmud further asks, "What does the reward of stately clothing refer to?"

It answers, "This refers to one who conceals those same matters which God concealed."

"What matters are they?"

"They are the *sitrei torah* (secrets of Torah)."

"Others say that this passage refers to one who reveals matters which God concealed."

"And what matters are they?"

"They are the *ta'amei Torah* (reasons of Torah)."

The commentator Rashbam clarifies: The term *sitrei torah* refers to the *Ma'aseh Merkavah*, the *Ma'aseh B'reshit*, and to the inner meaning of God's name, as it is written, "This is My Name for concealment" (Exod. 3:15).

The term, "one who conceals" implies one who only reveals the secret matters of *Ma'aseh B'reshit* and *Ma'aseh Merkavah* to a person who has a specific concern with them, as is taught in the Talmud: "One does not expound on the subject of forbidden relations in the presence of two, nor the *Ma'aseh B'reshit* in the presence of two nor the *Ma'aseh Merkavah* in the presence of one unless he is a sage and understands intuitively of his own knowledge."

The term, "one who reveals matters which God concealed" refers to one who teaches matters which were originally concealed, then subsequently God revealed them and gave permission to reveal them, and whoever does reveal them merits to receive all the good stated in the above quotation from Isaiah.

29. Here you can see explicitly the large distinction between the *sitrei torah* (secrets of Torah) and the *ta'amei torah* (reasons of Torah). One who knows the *sitrei torah*, receives a great reward for concealing them and not revealing them. Exactly the opposite is true for the *ta'amei torah*. One who understands them and reveals them receives a great reward for teaching them to others.

   There is some argument in the Talmud here [see *Notes* for full discussion] but all the sages agree that the secrets of Torah must be concealed and the reasons of Torah must be revealed.

30. Now we have a clear answer to the fourth and fifth questions that we asked at the very beginning of this *Introduction*. The fourth question relates to the teaching of the sages of the Talmud—which is also to be found in books of Kabbalah—to the effect that this wisdom should only be taught to people who have reached a certain level of spirituality.

   We can now see that this injunction refers to that portion of Kabbalah that is known as the *sitrei torah*, which is the aspect of the first three *sephirot* and the head of the spiritual entity. This is indeed only taught to individuals who have learned to conceal their spiritual attainment and only under particular known conditions. In all the books of Kabbalah which are either in manuscript or printed, you will not find even a trace of this wisdom. These are the matters that God concealed, as we learnt in the Talmud. You cannot conceive that any of our holiest and most saintly sages would reveal them. You will not find a mention of these matters in the *Sefer Yetsirah*, in the *Zohar*, in the *Braita of Rabbi Yishmael* or in the writings of any of the early Kabbalists up to and including Nachmanides, or in the work of the Ba'al HaTurim. Nor will you find a mention of this wisdom in the *Shulchan Aruch*, in the writings of the Vilna Gaon or of Rabbi Schneur Zalman of Liadi, or in the writings of any of the other righteous sages, may their memory be for a blessing. From these righteous sages has come to us all the revealed Torah by which we live, to know the way we can serve God, may He be blessed. Furthermore, all these men wrote and published books on the wisdom of Kabbalah. After all there can be no greater revelation of something than to write a book on it! The author has no idea who will come across his book. It is possible that even completely wicked people could look at his book. If so, there can be no greater revelation of the mysteries of Torah than this. We can certainly not conceive of these holy and pure sages deviating in the slightest degree from what is written explicitly in the Talmud, concerning not revealing that which should be concealed. Therefore everything that has ever been written and published on the subject of Kabbalah is only at the level of the *ta'amei torah*, that God first concealed and then revealed according to the inner meaning of "the palate will taste food." Not only is there no prohibition on revealing these matters, but, on the contrary, it is a very beneficial act to do so. The reward of someone who knows this material and teaches it is very great, for it is on the revelation of these lights to the general population that the coming of the Messiah depends.

31. It is very important that we should explain now why the coming of the Messiah is dependent on making this teaching available to everybody, as is taught in the *Zohar* and also in all the books of

Kabbalah. The explanation of this matter is brought in the *Tikkunei haZohar (tikkun* 30):

"We learn from Scripture (Gen. 1:2), 'And the spirit of God hovered over the waters.'

"We may ask, 'What is the spirit of God?'

"Since the time when the holy *Shechinah* descended into exile, this spirit of God rests with those who occupy themselves with Torah, because the holy *Shechinah* is to be found amongst them...

"But, 'All flesh is grass' (Isa. 40:6).

"Everyone has become like animals eating grass, and all their grace is as the flower of the field. This means that even all the good that people do, they are doing for their own benefit... and even those who do practise Torah are doing so only for their own benefit. At that time 'He remembered that they were but flesh, a spirit that passes away and never returns' (Ps. 78:39). This is the spirit of the Messiah.

"Woe to those who cause the spirit of the Messiah to disappear and never return! They make the Torah into a parched land and do not want to study the wisdom of Kabbalah. These people cause the flow of wisdom to cease, wisdom being the first letter *Yud* of the holy four-letter name of God...The spirit that departs is the spirit of the Messiah. It is the Holy Spirit, the spirit of Wisdom and Understanding, the spirit of Sound Advice and Strength, the spirit of Knowledge and fear of being separate from the Lord.

"Furthermore 'And God said, "Let there be light," and there was light' (Gen. 1:3).

"This refers to love; the love of loving-kindness.

"As it is said, 'With eternal love I have loved you, therefore I have drawn loving-kindness to you' (Jer. 31:2).

"And it is also written, 'Do not stir up nor awaken My love, till it please'" (Song of Sol. 2:7).

"Love and fear of sin are the central elements, used for good or for bad. If it is for bad, then love is exploited for personal gain. If it is for good, then God says, "I charge you, O daughters of Jerusalem, by the hinds and the gazelles in the field: Do not stir up nor awaken My love, till it please' (Song of Sol. 2:7) …

"This refers to the case whenever love is given completely selflessly, without any expectation of receiving anything in return. The love of God and the fear of sin, when they are exploited for personal gain, pertain to the maidservant who is referred to in the following passage:

"'For three things the earth is angered, and for four it cannot bear: for a slave when he becomes king, and a fool when he is filled with food, for an unloved woman when she is married and a maidservant who disinherits her mistress'" (Prov. 30:21).

32. Now we will begin our explanation of this passage from the *Tikkunei haZohar* at its end. It tells us that the fear and the love that a person has when he or she practises Torah and *mitzvot* with the intention of getting something out of it personally, has the aspect of being the maidservant, about which it is written, "The earth is angered… when a maidservant disinherits her mistress." It is difficult for us to understand this. We have learnt the principle that a person should always engage himself or herself in Torah and *mitzvot* even when they are practising Torah not for its own sake. So why should the earth be angered? We further need to understand the relationship between practising Torah not for its own sake and the position of a maidservant. We also have to understand the phrase, "the maidservant who disinherits her mistress." What kind of inheritance is referred to here?

33. You may understand this matter by considering all that we have explained so far in this *Introduction*, that the sages only permitted the practice of Torah not for its own sake, on the condition that through such practice one would come to the state of practising Torah for

its own sake via the light within it that transforms one. Therefore involvement in Torah which is not for its own sake is considered as a maidservant who helps and does the menial jobs for her mistress, the holy *Shechinah*. After all, the end result is to come to the practice of Torah for its own sake, thus meriting to give life-force to the *Shechinah*. Then this maidservant, which has the aspect of practising Torah not for its own sake, is yet considered to be a holy maidservant in that she helps and prepares the way for holiness. She is called "the maidservant of the holy world of *Assiyah*."

However, if a person's faith is not complete and he or she practises Torah and *mitzvot* only because they feel that God is commanding them to do so [i.e. in the hope of receiving a reward], then, as we have previously seen (paragraphs 11–13), such practice of Torah and *mitzvot* will in no way help to reveal the light within Torah. The person's eyes are defective and they transform the light within Torah into darkness, as in the example of the bat that we looked at above. This type of work in Torah is no longer in the category of the holy maidservant because through such practice of Torah a person cannot come to the practice of Torah for its own sake. Therefore such work comes into the domain of the maidservant of the shells (the domain of evil), who inherits this work in Torah and exploits it for her own benefit. This causes the earth to be angry. That is to say the holy *Shechinah*, which is called "earth", is angry because the Torah and spiritual work that should have come to her as her possession have been exploited by the maidservant of the shells who brings them down into the possession of the framework of evil. Thus the maidservant disinherits her Mistress, God forbid.

34. The *Tikkunei haZohar* explains the inner meaning of the oath from the *Song of Songs*, "I charge you, O daughters of Jerusalem, by the gazelles and the deer of the field, that you do not stir up nor awaken My love till it pleases." Why is such punctiliousness required? It

is because Israel has the potential to attract the highest light of loving-kindness which is called "the love of loving-kindness" which is that which is so desired. This light is attracted particularly through practising Torah and *mitzvot* selflessly, not in order to receive a reward.

The reason that this light is so desirable is because through the means of this light of loving-kindness, the light of the highest wisdom is attracted to Israel and is revealed and enclothed by the light of loving-kindness which Israel has drawn to itself. The light of this wisdom is referred to in Isaiah, "And the spirit of the Lord will rest upon him, the spirit of Wisdom, and of Understanding, the spirit of Counsel and Might, the spirit of Knowledge and of the Fear of the Lord and his delight shall be in the fear of separation from the Lord" (Isa. 11:2). This refers to the Messiah, as is made clear later on in the same chapter, verse 12. "And he shall set up a banner for the nations, and shall assemble the outcasts of Israel and gather together the dispersed of Judah from the four corners of the earth." For when Israel brings down the light of wisdom through the means of the light of loving-kindness, then the Messiah is revealed and he gathers up the scattered ones of Israel.

Therefore everything depends on one's involvement in Torah and spiritual work for its own sake which can attract this great light of loving-kindness, which in turn attracts the light of wisdom to itself and enclothes it. This is the deeper meaning of the oath, "Do not stir up nor awaken My love till it pleases." For the complete redemption of humanity and the gathering up of the exiles cannot come about without this work and the presence of these lights, because the channels for the lights of holiness are organized in this way.

35. We can now go deeper into the passage we quoted above: "And the spirit of God hovered over the waters." What is the spirit of God? This expression refers to the time when the holy *Shechinah* is in

exile. This spirit rests on those who are studying Torah, because the *Shechinah* is found amongst them. The time of exile referred to here is the period in which Israel is still practising Torah and *mitzvot* but not for its own sake. However, if they are doing so in order to get from the stage of Torah which is not for its own sake to the stage of practising Torah for its own sake, then the *Shechinah* nevertheless dwells amongst them, albeit in a state of exile because they have not yet reached the stage of the practice of Torah for its own sake. This accords with the concept of the holy maidservant, as we learnt above. This is the meaning of the phrase "the holy *Shechinah* is found amongst them." The *Shechinah* is there, but hidden. In the end, Israel will be worthy to attain the open revelation of the *Shechinah*. The spirit of the Messiah hovers over all those who practise in this way. It awakens them to strive for the level of Torah for its own sake, by virtue of the illumination within the Torah which transforms them to the good way, helping and preparing them for the inspiration of the spirit of the *Shechinah*, which is the holy Mistress.

However, if this practice of Torah which is not for its own sake is conducted without the required intention of arriving at Torah for its own sake for the reasons explained above, then the *Shechinah* grieves and says, "All flesh is as grass; all are like animals eating grass." This implies that even among those practising Torah, the spirit of Man which has the potential to ascend higher is not to be found, but those who are practising Torah suffice with an animal-like consciousness that descends lower.

The reason for this is explained here. "All the loving-kindness that these people do is as the flower of the field [it fades and dies]." They do it for their own benefit, self-advancement and pleasure. This applies even to those who study Torah. All the loving-kindness that they do is done out of self-interest alone. Their practice of Torah and *mitzvot* is for their own benefit and pleasure. Such practice of Torah is unable to bring them to the state of Torah for its own sake.

And this is what is said in the *Tikkunei haZohar*, "'At that time, He remembered that they were but flesh, a spirit that passes away and does not come again' (Ps. 78:39). Know that this is the spirit of the Messiah." This means that the spirit of the Messiah does not hover over them but leaves them and does not return. The maidservant of uncleanness exploits their Torah and disinherits her Mistress because those who are practising are not on the path that leads from Torah which is practised not for its own sake, to Torah which is practised for its own sake. And thus the *Zohar* concludes that it is such people, who are practising Torah not for its own sake without the required intention to come to Torah for its own sake, who make the Torah like a parched land. Furthermore, these people do not even try to study the wisdom of the Kabbalah.

Even though such people do not benefit from their study of the revealed Torah because there is no light in it for them and it has become like a parched land due to their small-mindedness, nevertheless they could turn the situation around if they were to study Kabbalah because the light that is in it is enclothed in the garments of God; that is to say, the Holy Names and the *sephirot*. Then, they would be able to access the path which leads from Torah which is practised not for its own sake to Torah which is practised for its own sake much more easily. The spirit of God would then hover over them, as in the inner meaning of the phrase, "the light that is in it would return them to the good way."

But sadly they don't even want to learn Kabbalah and thus the *Tikkunei HaZohar* says about them, "Woe to those who cause poverty, destruction, shame, persecution and war in the world. The spirit that departs is the spirit of the Messiah. It is the Holy Spirit, the spirit of Wisdom and Understanding, the spirit of Sound Advice and Strength and the spirit of Knowledge and fear of being separate from the Lord."

36. This passage from the *Tikkunei haZohar* clarifies the fact that there is an oath that the light of loving-kindness and love will not awaken in the world until the deeds of Israel in the work of Torah and *mitzvot* will only be performed with the intention of not receiving any reward through them, but with the sole intention of giving pleasure to the Creator, Blessed be He. This, then, is the inner meaning of the oath, "I charge you, O daughters of Jerusalem, by the gazelles and by the deer of the field, that you do not stir up or awaken My Love till it pleases."

Now we see that the duration of the exile and the sufferings that afflict us, depends upon us and is only waiting for us to be worthy of the practice of Torah and *mitzvot* for its own sake. If only we could merit this, then instantaneously this light of love and loving-kindness would awaken, which has the capacity of bringing with it the higher light of wisdom according to the inner meaning of the Scripture, "And then will rest upon him the spirit of Wisdom and Understanding, the spirit of Sound Advice and Strength, the spirit of Knowledge and the fear of being separate from the Lord," and then we will merit the complete redemption.

We have also clarified that the only way that the whole community of Israel can come into this pure state of consciousness is through learning the Kabbalah, which is the easiest way, appropriate even for people of modest intellectual capacities. This is not true, however, of the study of revealed Torah on its own, through which it is impossible, other than for a few exceptional people, to merit this transformation. Even for these few exceptional people, the path of revealed Torah requires great effort. This path is certainly not for the majority of people, as we have explained above.

With this, we end our explanation of why the fourth and fifth objections that were raised at the very beginning of this Introduction have no meaning or value to them.

37. We now turn to the third question which concerned the fear that people have, that through the study of Kabbalah they might become lax or heretical in their beliefs or practices. There is no reason at all to worry about this although this has happened on occasion in the past. These cases occurred for one of two reasons. Either they ignored the advice of the sages and matters were revealed to them which it is forbidden to reveal, or they took the words of the Kabbalah according to their literal meaning, using material imagery, and thus transgressed the commandment of not making a graven image.

For this reason, there really was a strong wall surrounding this wisdom, which lasted right until this generation. Many people began to study the Kabbalah but were forced to give up because of a lack of understanding which arose due to the material terminology used in Kabbalah. For this reason, I have labored to explain the great work of Rabbi Yitshak Luria entitled *Etz Chayim* (Tree of Life) in my commentary *Panim Me'irot* and *Panim Masbirot* in which I strip the concepts of their material forms and set them within the laws of spirituality that are beyond the dimensions of space and time. In this way, even a beginner can understand these matters according to their true sense with clarity of thought and great simplicity.

38. Now we must continue to expand our understanding of this obligation of practising Torah and *mitzvot* for its own sake about which I have begun to write.

We need to understand the expression, "Torah for its own sake." Why is the complete and satisfactory practice of Torah defined as Torah practised for its own sake, and why is the unsatisfactory practice of Torah called "not for its own sake"? According to our straightforward understanding, the intention of someone who practises Torah and *mitzvot* should be to give pleasure to the Creator, and he or she should not be acting from any motive of self-benefit. This being the case, this level of relating to Torah should have been designated and defined as Torah for *His* sake, meaning Torah for God's sake. So why is it called Torah for *its* own sake, meaning for the sake of the Torah itself? It is clear that there is a deeper teaching here than is at first apparent.

The language seems to indicate that involvement in Torah for God's sake, meaning in order to give pleasure to one's Creator, is still not sufficient. There is a further requirement that a person's study of Torah should be for the Torah's own sake. This needs an explanation.

39. The matter is as follows. It is known that the Torah is called "the Torah of Life" as it is written, "And it is Life to those who find it and Health to all their flesh" (Prov. 4:22), also, "It is not something empty for you but it is your Life" (Deut. 32:48). This being so, the implication of the expression, "Torah for its own sake" is that someone who is involved in Torah and *mitzvot* in the right way draws to himself or to herself life and longevity, the Torah acting according to its name. However a person who is involved in Torah and *mitzvot* without focusing their heart or intention in this way, brings upon himself or upon herself exactly the opposite of life and length of days, God forbid. This is a relationship to Torah which is entirely in opposition to the meaning of its name, the name of the Torah being the Torah of Life. Understand this well!

These matters are explained in the Talmud where it is written, "For the person who practises Torah not for its own sake, the Torah becomes a drug of death, whereas for the person who practises Torah for its own sake, the Torah becomes the elixir of life." These words need clarification in order to understand how, and in what way can the holy Torah become a drug of death! After all, isn't it bad enough that a person strives vainly and in a futile way, not receiving any benefit from his or her labor and trouble, but in addition to this, his or her Torah and spiritual work become a drug of death for them? This is very astonishing!

40. First we must understand the remark of the sages of the Talmud. They said, "If a person says, 'I labored and subsequently I found,' believe him! If a person says, 'I did not labor and yet I found,' don't believe him!"

There is a difficulty here with the language; "laboring" and "finding" appear to be mutually contradictory ideas. Labor is a matter of work and effort. One has to pay the price for every purchase worth having. For an important acquisition one labors a lot, whereas for something of much less worth, one puts in less work. But "finding" works in a totally different way. It tends to come upon a person when he or she least expects it, without preparation, effort, labor or cost. So how can one say, "I labored and subsequently I found?" If labor is involved, it would have been better to say, "I labored and then I acquired," or "I labored and then I merited," or some similar phrase, but not "I labored and then I found."

41. Now there is a discussion in the *Zohar* on the Scriptural quotation, "Those who really search for Me will find Me" (Prov. 8:17). The *Zohar* asks, "Where can we find God?" And it answers, "We can only find God in Torah." It further discusses the Scripture, "Behold You are a hidden God" (Isa. 45:15), implying that God hides Himself in the holy Torah.

We have to understand the sages' words here in the right way. It would seem more likely that God is hidden amongst the highways and byways of the material world and in all the vanities of this world that lie outside the Torah! How, then, can the *Zohar* claim the opposite and state that it is only in Torah that God hides Himself? Also, in the general sense that God conceals Himself in such a way that we need to search for Him, one can ask what is this concealment for? What we have understood from the quotation from Proverbs is that all who search for God will find Him. We need to investigate the matter of this search for God and the matter of the finding of God. What do they consist of and why are they necessary?

42. You need to know that the distance that we feel ourselves as being so far away from God that makes us so liable to sin, has only one single cause. It is the source of all the pains and sufferings we experience and is the source of all our arrogant acts and mistakes over which we stumble. It is obvious that if we were able to remove this one single cause, then we would instantly be free of all our suffering and we would immediately merit to cleave to God with all our heart, soul and might. I say to you that this root cause is none other than the minimal understanding that we possess of the way that God involves Himself in the life of His creatures, which is termed His Divine Providence. We do not understand Him as is fitting.

43. Let us imagine how the world would be were God to relate to us in a completely open way. Suppose, for example, a Jew ate something that was not kosher. It would cause him or her to choke immediately on the spot. Equally, anyone who performed a *mitzvah* would straight away experience the most wondrous ecstasy equivalent to the best possible delights of this physical world. Of course, under these circumstances, no Jew would contemplate even tasting something that was not kosher if he or she knew for certain that it would cause them to lose their life. One would no more think of doing such a thing than one would of jumping into a fire! In the same way, who would miss an opportunity of running to perform a *mitzvah* as fast as they could? It

would be just like a person, who, when offered a great material delight, cannot refrain or hesitate but runs to accept it with all the alacrity he or she can muster. Therefore, if the Divine Providence were to be openly manifest, everyone in the world would be a complete *tzaddik*.

44. So you can see, then, that in our world, all we lack is that Divine Providence should be revealed. If the Divine Providence were revealed then all human beings would be complete *tzaddikim*. All would cleave to God in total love. It would be considered the greatest honor for each one of us to be friends with God and to love Him with all our heart and soul, cleaving to Him continually, never missing a moment.

However, this is not the case. There is a basic principle in Jewish thought that we do not see the reward of *mitzvot* in this world. Similarly, we do not witness the punishment of sinners. God appears to have great patience with them. Sometimes it even seems to us that we see exactly the opposite, just as the Psalmist observed, "Behold these are the wicked. Always at ease, they increase in riches" (Ps. 73:12).

The consequence of this is that not everyone who wants to profess a true relationship with God is able to do so. We stumble over every step, to the extent that the sages, commenting on "I have found one man out of a thousand" (Eccles. 7:28), said that if a thousand people enter to learn, only one will emerge as fit for instruction. The right understanding of God's relationship to His creation is the source of all good, and its wrong understanding, the root cause of all evil. So we find that this understanding is the still point around which all people revolve, attracting to themselves either correction or kindness.

45. When we consider more deeply how we perceive God's Providence with respect to our feelings, we find that our feelings fit into four categories. Each category experiences God's Providence in a uniquely different way so there are four levels of perception of Divine Providence.

These four categories are actually two main divisions which are termed the *concealment of God's face* and the *revelation of God's face*. However these two categories subdivide into four because there are two aspects of perception of Divine Providence within the category of the concealment of God's face and two aspects of perception of Divine Providence within the category of the revelation of God's face. The two levels of concealment are *single concealment* and *concealment within concealment*. The two levels of revelation of God's face are *the clear perception of God's involvement with Man with regard to cause and effect* and *the clear perception of God's eternal involvement with His creation*. We will explain all this now, with the help of God.

46. Scripture says, "Then My anger will burn against him on that day and I will forsake them and I will conceal My face from them and they shall be for a prey and many bad evils and troubles will find them. Then he will say on that day, 'It is because God is not within me that all these troubles have come upon me.' And I will doubly conceal My face on that day for all the evils that he has perpetrated in that he has turned to other gods" (Deut. 31:17–18).

When we look at the actual words we see that at first the Scripture says, "Then My anger will burn...and I will conceal My face." This is the first level of concealment. After that Scripture continues, "And I will doubly conceal My face on that day." This is the level of concealment within concealment. We need to understand just what this level of double concealment is.

47. The first step in this understanding is to become clear as to what "the face of God" means, as in the above expression, "and I will conceal My face." We can understand this from a familiar example. When a person sees his friend's face, he recognizes him immediately. This is not the case if he only sees his back. Then he may not be sure exactly

who it is. He may feel doubt and think that it is someone else and not his friend at all.

It is the same here. We all know and feel that God in His essence is Good and it is in the nature of the Good to do good. Therefore when God bestows abundant good on the creatures He created in accordance with His ample and beneficent hand, this state is designated as revealing His face to His creatures. Then everyone knows and recognizes Him as He is acting in a way that is fitting to His name, as we have explained in paragraph 43 with respect to open providence.

48. However when God relates to His creatures in a way which is opposite to the way that we have mentioned, in other words when people are suffering and receiving pain in this, God's world, this state is designated as the *back* of God. The face of God, which is His attribute of perfect goodness, is completely concealed from them since this behavior is not compatible with His name. This is like someone who sees his friend from the back and then may have a doubt and think that it is someone else. This is according to the quotation, "Then My anger will burn and I will conceal My face from them." For we designate the time that God's anger burns and His creatures experience pain and suffering as *God hiding His face*, His face being His aspect of perfect goodness. Only His back is revealed. Under these circumstances a person has to strengthen his faith mightily in order not to fall into sinful thoughts, as it is difficult to recognize God from His back. This state is known as single concealment.

49. However if peoples' troubles and sorrows multiply, this can bring about a double concealment. This is referred to in the books of Kabbalah as *concealment within concealment*; in this state, even God's back is not perceived. It implies that people make no connection between their pain and suffering and the thought that God is correcting them

through it. They claim that this fate has come upon them as a result of chance or due to the nature of things. This is complete denial of the Divine Providence as having a role in cause and effect. This state is referred to as "I will doubly conceal My face." Such people have, in fact, turned to other gods. They are in a state of denial and turn to false causes.

50. This is not the case with the passage quoted immediately prior (paragraph 46) which refers to single concealment. The passage concludes, "He will say on that day, 'It is because God is not within me that all these troubles have come upon me!'" That is to say that, in this case, the people still believe in Divine Providence with regard to cause and effect. They say that their pain and suffering occurred because they did not cleave to God. Their perception accords with the Scripture, "It was because God was not within me that all these troubles have come upon me." This state is regarded as one in which people still perceive the Divine but only from God's back. Hence it is called single concealment, since it is only God's face that is concealed.

51. Now we have explained the two different ways that His creatures perceive God's Providence when it is in the aspect of being concealed, that is to say single concealment and concealment within concealment. In single concealment, God's face is concealed but His back is revealed to people. People in this state believe that God has caused them this suffering as a consequence of their own actions. Even though it may be hard for them, under these circumstances, to recognize God from His back and this may lead them into sin, nevertheless, such people are referred to as having the characteristic of not being completely wicked. The sins that they commit are considered as inadvertent errors as they only came to sin on account of the magnitude of their suffering and, generally speaking, they still believe in cause and effect.

2. This is contrasted with the state of concealment within concealment in which even God's back is hidden from people. Such people no longer believe in cause and effect. Their sins are considered as acts of arrogance. These people are designated as complete evil-doers. They believe that God has abandoned them and has no relationship to His creatures, and so they turn to other causes as the Scripture says, "he has turned to other gods" (ibid.)

3. It is important that you know that all the work we do in actively and consciously choosing the path of Torah and *mitzvot*, as a matter of free choice, takes place primarily during this time when Divine Providence is concealed. Concerning this period, [Rabbi] Ben Haha said, "The reward is according to the degree of suffering," seeing that His Providence is not openly manifest and one cannot perceive God as He really is. His face is concealed and He can only be perceived from His back.

This is similar to a man who sees his friend's back and therefore is liable to doubt if it really is his friend or someone else. In this manner, the choice is always in a person's own hands. A person always has the choice whether to do God's will or to transgress His will, for the pain and sufferings he or she undergoes bring him or her to doubt the reality of God's good Providence over His creatures.

This doubt leads the person to transgress as in the single level of concealment, in which case the transgressions are mistakes. In the state of double concealment, the transgressions are considered as deliberate sins. In either case, the person finds himself or herself in great pain and longing. Scripture says about this period in a person's life, "Whatever you are able to do, do it with all your strength" (Eccles. 9:10). For the person will not merit the revelation of God's face, which means the perfect attribute of God's goodness, unless he or she tries and does everything he or she possibly can. And the reward is according to the suffering.

54. However, once God sees that a person has put in the required amount of effort for himself or for herself and has done all he or she could to manifest their choice and has strengthened himself or herself in their faith in God, then God helps the person to attain the perception of the Divine Providence in its open manifestation, so that the face of God is revealed to him or her. Through this perception the person comes to be completely transformed and he or she cleaves to Him with all their heart, soul and might, inspired by their perception of the revelation of God's true role in a person's life.

55. This perception of the Divine Providence and the transformation that goes together with it come to a person in two stages. The first stage is the clear awareness of a definite cause and effect. Not only does the person clearly perceive the good consequences that result from a *mitzvah* which he or she receives in the world to come, but he or she also experiences wondrous pleasure at the moment of performing a *mitzvah* in this world. In the same way, not only does the person perceive that there is a bitter consequence of a loss of light attendant on each sin after one's death, but he or she also merits to experience the bitter taste of a sin whilst still in this life.

   It is obvious that one who has merited such direct perception of God's Providence, can be quite sure of himself or of herself that he or she will not sin any more, in just the same way as a person would not contemplate cutting off one of his or her own limbs and thus causing terrible suffering to themselves. It is equally certain that the person would not let the opportunity of a *mitzvah* go by if it presented itself to one, in just the same way that a person may be sure not to forego any pleasure of this world or great profit that might come his or her way.

56. By this you may understand what the sages implied when they asked, "What constitutes transformation?" and answered, "when God

Himself testifies that the person will never again return to his foolishness." This is a surprising definition, as who is going to go up to heaven to hear God's testimony? What is more, to whom is God expected to give this testimony? Is it not enough that God Himself knows that the man or woman has transformed with all their heart and will not sin anymore?

Yet from what we have already clarified, the matter is quite simple. In truth, a person can never be completely certain that he or she will not sin again unless they have already merited the perception of God's Providence, which is, that He acts with cause and effect. This is the revelation of God's face. This direct revelation of God's face, coming as it does as a grace from God, is termed *testimony*, as it is God's grace itself that enables a person to attain this perception of cause and effect which ensures that he or she will not sin again. Thus we can say that it is God Himself who testifies for the person.

So when the sages asked what constitutes transformation, they meant, "When can a person be sure that he or she has reached a perfect transformation?" The answer comes as a clear sign, when God Himself testifies that the person will no longer return to his or her foolish ways. In other words, the person merits the direct revelation of God's face when God's grace itself testifies for him or for her that he or she will not return to their foolish ways.

57. The transformation discussed here is known as *transformation from fear of sin*. Whilst it is the case that the person has returned to God with all their heart and soul, to such a degree that God testifies about the person that he or she will never return to their foolish ways, nevertheless the certainty that the person will not sin any more arises from his or her perception and feeling of the terrible suffering consequent on sins. Therefore the person can be sure of himself or of herself that he or she will not sin any more in the same way; that they can be certain of themselves that they would not bring upon

themselves terrible suffering.

In the last analysis, however, this transformation and certainty only comes about through the person's fear of the suffering that is consequent on sins. His or her transformation comes about only through fear of consequence and therefore this stage of consciousness is called *the transformation from fear of sin.*

58. Now we may understand the words of the sages that when a person comes to the level of transformation from fear of sin, he or she merits that the acts of arrogance that he or she committed earlier in their life become transformed into the category of sins which were committed because they fell and became confused.

How can this be?

We explained above (paragraph 52) that a person's sins of arrogance were committed due to the perception of Divine Providence as in the state of double concealment which is concealment within concealment. This is characterized by a person's not believing in God's role in cause and effect. This state should be contrasted with that of single concealment wherein a person believes in the role of Divine Providence with respect to cause and effect, but due to the greatness of the suffering the person sometimes has thoughts of sin. For even though he or she believes that their suffering came to them as a consequence of their behavior, nevertheless, they are like the person who sees a friend's back and is liable to doubt whether it is the friend or someone else. These sins are therefore only inadvertent errors since the person does, in general, believe in the role of Divine Providence with regard to cause and effect.

59. Therefore once a person is worthy of the transformation in his or her consciousness at the level of fear of sin, which implies that he or she has a clear perception of Divine Providence with regard to cause and

effect, then he or she may be quite certain that they will no longer sin. At this stage, the aspect of double concealment that the person once experienced is completely healed. Now the person sees, black on white, that God *is* involved with the world through cause and effect. It is now clear to the person that the many sufferings that he or she experienced all their life were brought about by Divine Providence as a consequence of the sins that he or she had committed. Now the person understands the matter retroactively. He or she realizes that they had made a bitter mistake. Thus the person uproots these arrogant acts from their very root. Not completely however, but they become like inadvertent errors, that is to say, similar to those that the person commits in the stage of single concealment when he or she stumbles into sin simply due to the confusion caused by the greatness of their suffering which tends to push one out of his or her normal state of consciousness. These sins are considered as inadvertent errors.

60. However, at this level of transformation, the state of single concealment is not healed at all. This state is only healed from this level onwards, once the person has attained the revelation of God's face. But the aspect of single concealment of God's face and all the inadvertent errors still remain as they were, unhealed and unchanged.

The reason for this is that both then and now the person believes that their difficulties and suffering came about as a result of punishment according to what has already been quoted, "They will say on that day, 'It is because God is not in me that all these troubles have come upon me!'"

61. Therefore such a person is still not called a complete *tzaddik*. Anyone who merits the revelation of God's face, which means the measure of His complete goodness as is fitting according to His Name, is called

a *tzaddik*. The person justifies (Heb. *matzdik*) God's Providence as it truly is, which is that God treats His creatures with absolute goodness and in absolute perfection, such that God is Good both to the evil doer and to the good person.

So since the person has become worthy of the revelation of God's face, it is fitting that he or she should be called by the name of *tzaddik* from this time onwards. However since, as yet, he or she has only completely healed the stage of double concealment but has not yet healed that aspect of his or her life that was in single concealment, the healing of which only occurs after this stage, he or she is not yet considered to be a full *tzaddik* but, rather, is called an incomplete *tzaddik*. He or she must still heal this aspect of their past, that is, the stage of single concealment.

62. Another term for the person now is a *benoni* (intermediate person). He or she has already become worthy of the stage of transformation resulting from fear of sin. Now he or she is ready through the perfected practice of Torah and *mitzvot* to come to the next level which is transformation from love of God. Then the person will merit to become a complete *tzaddik*. Thus, at this present time, which is an intermediate stage between the fear of sin and the love of God, he or she is called a *benoni*; a person who has the characteristic of being intermediate. Before this time, such a person was not capable of even preparing for transformation through love.

63. Now we have thoroughly clarified the first stage of perception of the revelation of the face of God. This is the actual perception and experience of Divine Providence as cause and effect, to the degree that God testifies about the person that he or she will never again return to sin. This is called transformation from fear of sin and through it, the person's arrogant acts are healed to the extent that they become like

inadvertent errors. Such a person is called an incomplete *tzaddik* or a *benoni*, as we have explained.

64. Now we will go on to clarify the second level of attainment of the revelation of the face of God which is the perception of this complete, true and eternal Providence, namely that God watches over His creatures with His attribute that He is Good and He does good to both evil doers and good doers. When the person perceives this, he or she is called a complete *tzaddik*. He or she has attained transformation from love of God through which he or she merits that his or her arrogant acts are transformed into virtues.

We have now examined all four ways in which people commonly perceive the Divine Providence (see table 4). The first three levels—double concealment, single concealment and direct perception of cause and effect—are actually only preparatory phases through which a person merits to come to this fourth phase which is the perception of God's true and eternal Providence which we will now explain, with the help of God.

65. We need, first, to understand why the third stage in which the person has an actual living perception of cause and effect is not enough and why the person must still go deeper into God's relationship with Man. Although God has testified that a person, when he or she comes to this level of development, will never sin any more, he or she is nonetheless still referred to as a *benoni* or an incomplete *tzaddik*. These names themselves imply that the person's work has not yet come to completion. There still exists a lack and a blemish in his or her Torah and spiritual work.

66. But before we go into this, we must first discuss a question that the sages raised concerning the *mitzvah* of loving God. "How could it be", they asked, "that the holy Torah commands us to do something

Table 4

How we experience God's Providence.

Concealment of God's Face

a) **concealment within concealment**
Man does not connect his pain and suffering with God's involvement with him at all.
Stage of arrogant acts or deliberate sins.

b) **single concealment**
Man perceives God's back. He ascribes his pain and suffering to punishment as he projects his anger onto God.
Stage of inadvertent errors.

Revelation of God's face

a) **transformation from fear of sin**
Man has a clear perception of God's involvement with him as cause and effect. God testifies that he will not return to his foolish ways. This is manifest by the "opening of his eyes" in Torah. He is known as an incomplete *tzaddik* or *benoni*, an intermediate person.
Stage of arrogant acts transformed into inadvertent errors.
Inadvertent errors not yet healed.

b) **transformation from love of God**
Man sees and knows that God is Good and does good as befits His Name.
He is good to the evil doer equally as to the good person.
Man justifies God's actions in the world and knows that all are destined to come to love God.
Complete *Tzaddik*. All sins transformed into virtues.

that is absolutely not within our power to do? A person can force or compel himself or herself to perform all other *mitzvot*, but as regarding love, no force or compulsion in the world can ever induce love." They answered, that when a person observes all the other 612 *mitzvot*, the final *mitzvah* of loving God is drawn to the person as a grace. It can then be considered as if the person does have the power to do this *mitzvah*. After all, he or she can compel themselves to do the other 612 *mitzvot*, fulfilling them properly and then he or she merits the *mitzvah* of loving God.

67. However these words need a lot of explanation. Even if the above analysis is correct, love should still not be considered to be a commandment as it does not involve any action on our part. It is, rather, something that comes naturally after we have fulfilled the previous 612 *mitzvot*. Therefore, it would have been quite sufficient to have been given 612 *mitzvot* as commandments. So the question remains as to why we have also been given the 613th one, namely the *mitzvah* of loving God?

68. In order to understand this more deeply, we must first come to a true understanding of the essence of the love of God, as it is in itself. You should know that all the tendencies and characteristics that the human being has inherently within him or within her with which he or she functions in relationships with friends, are the very same natural characteristics that one needs in order to serve God. Actually, right from the start, these characteristics were only implanted in Man for this ultimate purpose. This is the inner meaning of the text, "That none of us shall be banished" (2 Sam. 14:14). Every tendency or characteristic is needed in order to complete the pathways of bounty and to completely fulfil the desire of God. As it is written, "All are called by My Name, for I have created him for My Glory. I have formed

him. Yes, I have made him" (Isa. 43:7). And, "The Lord has made everything for His own purpose" (Prov. 16:4). However in the meantime, a whole world is prepared for each and every person in order that all their natural tendencies and attributes may be developed and perfected through practising them on one's fellow human beings in such a way that these attributes become fit for their ultimate purpose. For this reason the sages said, "A man should say, 'The world was created just for me!'" All the creatures of the world are necessary for each individual as it is they that develop and train a person's natural tendencies and attributes until they have become fit to constitute a tool for the service of God.

69. This being the case, we can come to understand what the essence of one's love for God is, by looking at the qualities of love with which a person behaves towards his or her fellow human beings. It is certainly the case that a person's love for God is influenced by these ways of expressing love. A person was only given these attributes in the first place in order to bring them into the service of God.

   Now when we study the qualities of the love with which a person loves his or her fellow men, we find four levels of love, each one higher than the other. In actual fact, one can consider them as two basic levels which, when further refined, become four.

70. The first level is that of conditional love. This means that due to the great measure of goodness, pleasure and help a person receives from his or her friend, his or her soul cleaves to that friend with wondrous love. This level of love has two aspects to it. The first aspect is that before the two came to know and love each other, they actually caused harm to each other. But now they do not want to recall this because "love covers all transgressions" (Prov. 10:12).

   The second aspect of conditional love is that from the first moment, the two friends only acted kindly towards each other and there was never any trace of harm or ill-feeling between them at all.

2*. The second (basic) level is that of unconditional love. Here the person recognizes that the qualities of his or her friend are so wonderful that they are vastly greater than anything he or she could have expected or imagined. As a result of this, the person's soul cleaves to the friend with a great love that has no limits.

There are also two aspects here. In the first one, the person understands how the friend relates to him or to her but the person does not yet know of all of the friend's dealings and conduct with others. So this aspect of unconditional love is still uncertain because the friend sometimes has dealings with others which seem, at least on the surface, to be causing damage and evil out of negligence. If the lover would see these dealings, then the value of the friend would be lessened in his or her eyes and the love between them would be spoiled. However as he or she has not yet seen these dealings, their love remains great and whole in wondrous measure.

73. The second level of unconditional love, which is the fourth of the four levels of love, is one in which he or she recognizes the worth of the friend as above, but additionally, he or she now knows of all the friend's dealings with every single person, with not one of them omitted. He or she has checked and discovered that not only is there not the slightest flaw in the friend's relationship but the friend's goodness towards all has no limits and exceeds anything the person could possibly have surmised or imagined. This level of love is eternal and absolute love (table 5).

74. All these four levels of love, which characterize the love between human beings, also characterize the love between a person and God. Not only this, but they become stages through which the love of God

* There is no paragraph 71 in the original text.

develops, each stage being the precursor of the next. It is thus impossible to arrive at any of them without first meriting the first stage of conditional love. When the person has fully completed this level, this first level itself causes the second level to appear. Once the person has merited to fully grasp the second level right to its end, it causes the third level to appear, and this in turn, brings into being the fourth level which is eternal love.

75. This awakens the question, "How can a person become worthy of the first level of the love of God?" This is the first level of conditional love, which means the love that comes through an appreciation of the great goodness that the person has obtained from the Beloved. But the fact remains that the reward for *mitzvot* is not found in this world [so how could the person ever see this great goodness?]. The question is all the greater when we bear in mind that everyone has to go through the first two levels of perception of Divine Providence as concealment of God's face, meaning that God's face which is the attribute of God's Goodness—that God is Good and does good—is concealed from the person during this time. As a result of this, the person experiences his or her life as filled with pain and suffering.

As we have already explained, the main thrust of work with Torah and *mitzvot* through conscious choice occurs during this time of the concealment of God's face. Since the person must go through this stage of concealment of God's face, it is difficult to understand how he or she could ever arrive at the second level of conditional love, in which he or she feels that from the very beginning of their relationship, the Beloved only offered him or her great and wondrous good without even the tiniest bit of evil. All the more so, how can the person ever arrive at the third and fourth levels of love?

Table 5

Four Levels of Love

Two Levels of Conditional Love

Love is dependent on the perception of goodness received

a) First aspect: before he came to know his friend, they actually caused harm to each other. Now they do not wish to recall this as love covers all transgressions.

b) Second aspect: from the first moment, they only did good to each other and there was never any trace of damage or ill-feeling at all between them.
Stage of arrogant acts transformed into merits.

Two levels of Unconditional Love

The person loves his friend with a wondrous, infinite love.
He perceives his friend's worth as being beyond all he could imagine.

c) First aspect: He knows his friend's worth with regard to his own dealings with him.

d) Second aspect: He knows his friend's worth also through his dealings and conduct with others and they are better than he possibly could imagine.

He has tilted the balance for himself and the whole world for good.
Eternal and absolute love.

76. Here we have plunged into deep waters from which we must bring up at least one valuable pearl. To help us in this endeavor, we need to understand the following teaching of the Rabbis:

"When the Rabbis were taking their leave of the school of Rabbi Ami, they said to him, 'May you see your world in your lifetime, and may you merit that your latter end will be in the world to come ... May your mouth declare wisdom and your tongue whisper songs ... May your face shine like the brightness of the firmament. May your lips utter knowledge ... and your steps run to hear the Ancient of Days [God].'"

But why didn't they say to him, May you *receive* your world within your lifetime? ["world" meaning his reward for all the *mitzvot* he had done.] Why did they only say, "May you *see* your world"? If they were going to give him a blessing, why didn't they give him the best blessing they could; that he should attain and receive his world within his lifetime?

Furthermore, what is the meaning of the blessing that they did give him? What would a person benefit by *seeing* his or her reward in the world to come whilst still in this life? After all, if he or she were only to be blessed to merit that their latter end would be in the world to come, that in itself is no small blessing! Why did the sages add this particular blessing of seeing one's reward whilst in this life and why did they put it first?

77. First of all, we need to understand what this *seeing* of the world to come within one's lifetime actually consists of. It is obvious that with our physical eyes we cannot see anything that is spiritual. Also it is not God's way to change the laws of nature. Right from their inception, the laws of nature were only ordered so by God because they are the most favorable for achieving their objective; that a person should merit, through them, to come to cleave to God, as it is written, "All

God's activities are directed towards this purpose" (Prov. 16:4). So we must understand what it would mean for a person to *see* his or her world within their lifetime.

78. I say to you that *seeing* comes about **through a person's eyes being opened in the holy Torah.** As it is written, "Open my eyes, that I may see wonders in Your Torah" (Ps. 119:18). It is concerning this that an oath is administered to the soul before it incarnates in a body. "Even if the whole world were to say to you that you are a *tzaddik*, see yourself in your own eyes as a *rasha* [an evil doer or one who is still liable to sin]." Specifically, "in your own eyes." As long as your eyes have not yet been opened in the Torah, regard yourself as one who could still sin. Do not mislead yourself by the fact that you are generally known in the world as a *tzaddik*.

Now you can also see why the Rabbis placed the blessing of *seeing* one's world in one's lifetime first in the string of blessings as, prior to this opening of one's eyes in Torah, a person is not yet even an incomplete *tzaddik*.

79. But if a person truly knows for himself or for herself that he or she observes the whole Torah, and the whole world agrees with him or her on this, why is this not considered sufficient? Why is he or she still sworn to regard himself or herself as one who could still sin? Is it because he or she still lacks this wonderful level of opening of one's eyes in Torah, of seeing one's world within one's lifetime, that the person must still regard himself or herself as having the possibility of coming to sin? This is all very astonishing.

80. We have already clarified the four ways through which human beings perceive God's Providence, which are the two levels of concealment of God's face and the two levels of revelation of God's face. We have explained that there is a profound intention behind the concealment

of God's face, namely of giving people an opportunity to make the effort of serving God through Torah and *mitzvot* from their own free choice. Then God experiences great satisfaction from their work in Torah and *mitzvot*, even more than He receives from the angels above, who have no choice in what they do, but are compelled in their service. There are other important reasons for this concealment of God's face, but this is not the place to go into them.

81. Despite the great value attached to this stage of concealment of God's face, it is not considered to be a complete stage but is a transitory stage. It is the stage from which one can become worthy of all the desired wholeness. All the reward that is laid up for us, only comes about as a result of our striving in Torah and *mitzvot* during this time of concealment of God's face. At the time when a person exercises conscious choice in the practice of Torah and *mitzvot*, he or she experiences considerable suffering as part of his or her experience of intensifying one's faith and doing God's will. And all the reward for *mitzvot* is given in proportion to the suffering that the person experiences in working with them, according to the words of Rabbi Ben Haha, "The reward is according to the suffering".

82. Therefore everyone has to go through this transitional phase of concealment of God's face. When the person completes this stage, he or she then merits the attainment of revealed Providence, which is the revelation of God's face. Before he or she merits the revelation of God's face, even though the person may perceive God's back, it is not possible to completely avoid coming into sin. Not only is the person not able to fulfill all 613 *mitzvot* because the *mitzvah* of loving God cannot be induced through force or coercion, he or she cannot even fulfill all the other 612 *mitzvot*, because the person cannot yet experience fear of sin on a permanent basis. This is illustrated by the fact

that the numerical value of the word "Torah" in the system of *gematria* is 611. So at this stage of consciousness the person cannot even fulfill the 612 *mitzvot* properly. But in the end a person will merit the revelation of God's face as it is written, "He will not always chide, neither shall He keep His anger forever" (Ps. 103:19).

83. The first level of revelation of God's face is the actual perception of Divine Providence as operating through cause and effect in complete clarity. This only comes to a person through Divine grace whereby he or she merits the opening of one's eyes in the holy Torah in wondrous perception. The person becomes like an overflowing spring of water, as Rabbi Meir said (paragraph 6). For every *mitzvah* of the holy Torah that the person has fulfilled by their work during the period of free choice, he or she now merits to *see* the reward which is waiting for them in the world to come. Likewise, they *see* the great loss involved in every sin.

84. Even though the person cannot actually experience this reward in this lifetime, because the reward of the *mitzvot* does not belong in this world, nevertheless their clear perception of the reward of *mitzvot* causes them to experience great joy at the time of performing each *mitzvah*. This is according to the principle: "if anyone is certain of collecting money that is owed them, it is as if they have already collected it." Take, for example, a businessman who has made a very profitable transaction. He has made a great deal of money. Even though the money will not be paid to him for a long time, yet he is sure, without any shadow of a doubt, that his profit will come to him in due course, then he is just as happy as if he already had the money in his hand.

85. It goes without saying that such open Providence testifies for the person that from now on, he or she will cleave to Torah and *mitzvot* with all their heart, soul and might. Similarly, he or she will distance

themselves and run away from sins as one who flees from a fire. Although the person is not yet a complete *tzaddik* as he or she has not yet merited the transformation through love of God, nevertheless, their great devotion to Torah and to good deeds helps them very gradually to come to merit the transformation of loving God which is the final level of the revelation of God's face. Then the person is able to fulfill all 613 *mitzvot* completely and becomes a complete *tzaddik*.

86. Now we can resolve the question that we had concerning the oath that the soul is required to swear before coming into this world (paragraph 78): "Even if the whole world were to say to you that you are a *tzaddik*, see yourself in your own eyes as a *rasha* [an evil doer or one who is still liable to sin]."" We asked why should a person need to regard himself or herself as one who still has the possibility of sinning, when all the rest of the world regards him or her as a *tzaddik*. Can the whole world be wrong?

We can ask, too, what is the significance of the testimony of the whole world here? Surely a person knows himself or herself better than the whole world does! This being the case, the oath ought to read, "Even if you know *for yourself* that you are a *tzaddik*, consider yourself as one who may still sin."

But in another passage from the Talmud, "Raba said, 'A person should know in his heart whether he is a complete *tzaddik* or not!'" This is to say that there really is such a reality and an obligation of becoming a complete *tzaddik* and furthermore, a person is required to examine himself or herself and to know one's own truth for oneself. If this is the case, why do they make the soul swear an oath that it will always regard itself as having the characteristic of an evil person and never come to know the truth about itself, when the sages have explicitly obliged the opposite?

87. However these matters are extremely precise. As long as a man or woman has not yet merited the opening of his or her eyes in Torah in wondrous perception to the extent that he or she obtains a clear perception of the Divine Providence as operating through cause and effect, it is certain that he or she will not be able to deceive themselves and think of themselves as a *tzaddik*. The person clearly feels that he or she lacks the two most all-inclusive *mitzvot* of the Torah, namely love for God and fear of sin. Without the opening of one's eyes in Torah, the person cannot come to the level of fearing sin completely to the extent that God testifies that he or she will never again return to their foolish ways. As we wrote above, this comes about due to the person's fear of sin being so great and through his or her perception of the consequence and loss attendant upon the sin. A person cannot conceive of this before he or she has attained a perfectly clear and certain perception of Divine Providence as it operates through cause and effect. This is the first level of revelation of God's face which comes to the person through having one's eyes opened in Torah. This is not to speak of loving God which is completely beyond the person's ability since the love for God is dependent on the understanding within the heart. No amount of effort or coercion helps here at all.

88. Thus the language of the oath is, "even if the whole world says you are a *tzaddik*, you should still see yourself as liable to sin," for these two commandments of love for God and fear of sin are given only to the man or woman for themselves. No one else in the world besides the person can in any way discern or know whether these *mitzvot* are present or not. So if people see someone properly practising 611 *mitzvot* they then automatically assume that they must also have the *mitzvot* of the love of God and fear of sin. Since it is natural for a person to believe what the world says about them, he or she might easily fall

into a bitter mistake. For this reason, the soul is made to swear an oath before it comes into incarnation and hopefully that might help the person. However a person certainly has the obligation to examine himself or herself within their heart to know if he or she is a complete *tzaddik* or not.

89. Now we can answer the question that we raised above concerning the love for God. We asked, "How can a person even come to the first level of love when the reward for *mitzvot* is not given in this world?" We can now understand that one does not actually have to *receive* the reward for one's *mitzvot* in one's lifetime. Thus the sages were very precise in their language when they offered the blessing, "May you *see* your world in this lifetime and later receive it in the world to come." This teaches that the reward for *mitzvot* is not in this world but in the world to come.

    However, in order to see, know and feel the reward for *mitzvot* that will manifest in the world to come, a person must in truth know this with complete clarity whilst still incarnate in this life. This comes through the wondrous perception in Torah. Through this the person merits, at the very least, the aspect of conditional love, which is the first stage that leads a person out of concealment of God's face into the revelation of God's face. So this opening of one's eyes in Torah is a precondition for a person's being able to properly observe *mitzvot* such that God can testify about him or her that they will never return to their old ways (see table 6).

90. From now on, the person endeavors to keep Torah and *mitzvot* from the perspective of conditional love, on the basis of the future reward in the world to come, according to the principle that someone who is sure to collect money is regarded as having collected it already.

Table 6

How the four ways we perceive God's providence and how the four stages of love relate to each other in a person's development.

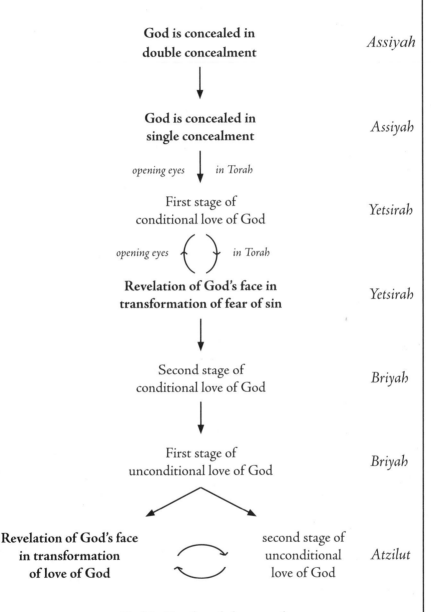

God is concealed in double concealment — *Assiyah*

God is concealed in single concealment — *Assiyah*

opening eyes — *in Torah*

First stage of conditional love of God — *Yetsirah*

opening eyes — *in Torah*

Revelation of God's face in transformation of fear of sin — *Yetsirah*

Second stage of conditional love of God — *Briyah*

First stage of unconditional love of God — *Briyah*

Revelation of God's face in transformation of love of God — second stage of unconditional love of God — *Atzilut*

*God is Good and does good
to the evil doer and the good alike.*

Then the person continues and comes to the second level of revelation which is the true perception of God's relationship to the world. This arises from His Truth and His Eternity, which is to say that He is Good and does good to both evil-doers and to good people. Then the person merits the stage of unconditional love, and the arrogant acts that he or she did in the past are transformed into good deeds. From here onwards, such a person is called a complete *tzaddik*, because he or she is able to fulfill the Torah and *mitzvot* through fear of sin and through love for God. The person is called "complete" because he or she observes all 613 *mitzvot* in their full sense.

91. Now we have answered the question that we asked above; namely, why someone who has already reached the third level of perception of God's Providence, that is, that of cause and effect, about whom God has already testified that he or she will not sin any more, is still only called an incomplete *tzaddik*. We can now understand this clearly as they still lack one *mitzvah*, which is the *mitzvah* of love. So the person is certainly not complete, as he or she needs to attain the entire complement of 613 *mitzvot* which is the first step on the threshold of perfection.

92. In all that has been said, we have now clarified the question we raised above. How did the Torah command us to love God when it is not at all within our power to occupy ourselves with this *mitzvah* or even to come close to it by the slightest touch? We have seen concerning this issue that the sages have cautioned us, saying, "Do not believe one who says, 'I labored, but I didn't find.'" They also said, "A person should always practise Torah and *mitzvot* even if it is not for its own sake, for through the practice of Torah and *mitzvot* which is not for its own sake, he will come to practise Torah and *mitzvot* for its own sake," on which the Bible, testifies, "Those who seek Me will find Me" (Prov. 8:7).

93. This is the language of the sages:

"Rabbi Yitshak said, 'If a person should say to you, "I labored, but I didn't find," don't believe him.'

"'I didn't labor, but I nonetheless found,' don't believe him.

"'I labored and I found,' believe him."

This is referring to matters of Torah. In matters of business, this rule may not apply.

We questioned (in paragraph 40) the connection between the term "laboring" and the term "finding" where the language appears to be self-contradictory, "laboring" being associated with an acquisition and "finding" implying something coming to you without effort and by chance. Therefore the text should have read, "I labored and I acquired."

However you should know that the language of "finding" that the Talmud uses here, comes from the above Biblical phrase, "Those who seek Me will find Me," (Prov. 8:17) and hinges on the finding of God's face. As the *Zohar* says, we only find God in the Torah. That is to say, through laboring in Torah, we become worthy of finding the revelation of God's face.

Therefore the sages were perfectly precise in their language when they said, "I labored and I found, believe it!" For the labor is in Torah and the finding refers to the revelation of God's face in the true perception of Divine Providence. They purposely did not say, "I labored and I merited, believe it" or "I labored and I acquired," as then it would have been possible to mistake their meaning and think that the merit or acquisition of direct perception depends on the acquisition of Torah alone. But the word "finding" teaches us that they intended an aspect additional to that of the acquisition of Torah alone, and this is the grace of the revelation of God's face as being the true nature of Divine Providence.

94. This also resolves our surprise over the statement, "I did not labor and yet I found. Do not believe him!" which seems odd, as who would even have imagined in the first place that one could merit to Torah without first laboring in it? However now we see that these words hinge on the Biblical phrase, "Those who seek Me will find Me," their meaning being that anybody, regardless of capacity or talent, who truly seeks God, will immediately find Him. This is implied by the expression, "those who seek Me."

A person might then think that there is no need for such a great effort and that even a person of inferior motivation, who is not prepared to put in any effort, will also "find" God. Therefore our sages caution us not to believe in such an explanation. Effort is an essential part of the spiritual path and one should not believe someone who says that they put in no effort at all but nonetheless found.

95. From this we can understand why the Torah is called by the name "Life." As is written, "See, I have set before you today both Life and Good and Death and Evil…Therefore choose Life" (Deut. 30:15,19)! Likewise, it is also written, "My teachings are Life to those that find them" (Prov. 4:22). The Torah derives this name from the Scripture, "In the Light of the King's face is Life" (Prov. 16:15), since God is the source of all life and all good, therefore life is transmitted from Him to all those branches that cleave to their source. This may be said concerning all those who have labored and found the light of God's face in the Torah. They have merited that their eyes are opened in Torah in wondrous perception until they came to the revelation of God's face, which means the perception of the true nature of Providence that befits God's Name as "the Good." It is in the nature of the Good to do good.

96. Those who merit this state of consciousness cannot refrain from performing any *mitzvah* in its proper way in just the same way that a

person finds he or she cannot forego a great pleasure which has come to him or to her. Similarly, people in such a state of consciousness flee from sin like one who runs away from a fire. About them it is written, "But you who cleave to the Lord your God are all alive this day" (Deut. 4:4). God's love reaches and benefits them as a completely natural love, flowing through the natural channels prepared for the person as part of the nature of the created world, for now the branch is found to be in affinity with its root, as is fitting. Life flows through the person in great bounty from its Source without any pause. For this reason, the Torah is called by the name, "Life."

97. The sages have thus cautioned us in many places regarding the necessary requirement that our practice of Torah should be carried out for its own sake. Then through the Torah we will gain life, because the Torah is a law of life. It was for this purpose that it was given to us, as it is written, "and you shall choose life."

Therefore when a person engages in Torah, he or she should do so with their whole mind and heart in order to find within it the light of the face of the Living King. This is the perception of Divine Providence in its revealed state which is called "the light of His face." Everyone has the capacity to attain this as it is written, "All those who seek Me will find Me." A person lacks nothing except effort as we learnt, "I labored but I did not find—don't believe it."

The Talmud tells us, "When a person occupies himself with Torah for its own sake, then the Torah becomes an elixir of life for him." That is to say, only when a person puts his or her whole mind and heart to Torah, will he or she merit life and this is what is meant by Torah for its own sake.

98. Now you can see that the problem that the sages raised concerning the *mitzvah* of loving God—namely that as love cannot come by force

or compulsion it is not in our hands—happens not to be a problem after all. As it turns out, love is completely in our own hands. After all, everyone can make the effort in Torah until he or she achieves the attainment of the revealed aspect of God's Providence, as it is written, "'I labored and I found'—believe!" And when a person merits the revelation of God's Providence as it really is, then love is drawn to the person of itself through natural channels, as we have already explained. Whoever does not believe that one can attain this level through one's own effort, for whatever reason, does not believe in the teaching of our sages, but imagines that effort alone is not sufficient for everyone. This is contrary to what we have just learned, "'I labored but I did not find'—don't believe!" This view also contradicts the Biblical passage that says, "Everyone who seeks Me will find Me." This is true of everyone regardless of capacity; however, effort is definitely required.

99. From what we have clarified, we may now understand the sages' statement, "One who practises Torah not for its own sake, his Torah becomes a drug of death for him." Also, we are now able to understand the discussion in the *Zohar* of the Scripture, "Surely You are a God who conceals Himself" (Isa. 45:15). The *Zohar* states that God conceals Himself in Torah! (See paragraph 41). We pointed out that it would make more sense to say, on the contrary, that it is in the trivial and empty things of this world, that are outside the Torah, that God conceals Himself, and it is in the Torah that He *reveals* Himself. We also asked what benefit we gain from the fact that God conceals Himself, in order that we should find Him.

100. We can see from what we have already explained that the concealment whereby God hides Himself in order that people may search for Him, refers to the hiding of His face that He conducts with His creatures

according to the two modes of single concealment and concealment within concealment. The *Zohar* informs us that it should not even cross our minds that God wants us to remain with this perception of ours which sees His Divine Providence in the aspect of concealment of His face from His creatures. Rather, it is like a man who purposely hides so that his friend will look for him and find him. So it is with God. When He conducts Himself with His creatures in this aspect of concealment, it is only because He wants people to desire the revelation of His face, and then they will find Him. In fact, there is no other entry or route for the creatures to come to merit the light of the face of the Living King, unless His dealings with them begin with concealment of His face. All concealment is merely a preparation for the revelation of His face.

101. Now this is what is meant by God concealing Himself in Torah. A person feels suffering and pain during the time of concealment of God's face. However, one cannot compare the situation of a person who has many sins and few good deeds and knows little of Torah, to that of a person who has acquired much Torah and performed many good deeds. The first person is much more capable of justifying God's actions in that he or she realizes that in some measure they caused their own suffering. However the one who has acquired much Torah finds it extremely hard to justify God seeing that in his or her own opinion he or she is not deserving of such afflictions. Not only this but they see other people who are much inferior to themselves, suffering less! Just as it is written, "Behold these are the wicked. Always at ease, they increase in riches" (Ps. 73:12). A person then feels that all the efforts to cleanse himself or herself have been in vain.

Thus we see, paradoxically, that as long as a person has not yet merited to perceive Divine Providence according to the aspect of the revelation of God's face, it seems that the Torah that he or she has learned, and the many *mitzvot* that he or she have done, make the concealment of God's face much worse. Thus it is written that God conceals Himself in Torah. But in truth, this greater weight that a person feels because of the Torah is only a wake-up call. It is the holy Torah itself that is calling to the person through these experiences, telling him or her to awaken as fast as possible and to hurry and put the required effort into their spiritual work in order to merit immediately the revelation of God's face, which is what God Himself wants. Understand this thoroughly!

102. For this reason, it is written that the Torah of one who learns not for its own sake becomes a drug of death for that person. Not only does the person never leave the state of concealment of God's face in order to come to the revelation of God's face, as after all, he or she didn't put their attention into the effort to merit Torah. But the more Torah they acquire, the more God becomes concealed for them, until they fall into double concealment, which is a form of spiritual death. In this state they are completely cut off from their root and the Torah has become a drug of death for them.

103. With this in mind, we can clarify the two adjectives associated with Torah; namely *revealed* Torah [the Bible, the *Mishnah* and the Talmud] and *concealed* Torah [Kabbalah]. We must, particularly, understand the nature of the concealed Torah and why we need it. Why, for example, is not all of Torah revealed? Here, there is a very deep intention. The notion of concealed or secret Torah hints at the fact that God conceals Himself in Torah, as is explained above. For this reason, this part of Torah [the Kabbalah] is called "concealed." The revealed aspect of Torah [Bible, *Mishnah* and Talmud] is so called because God becomes revealed through the Torah.

For this reason, the Kabbalists said—and this is also found in the prayer-book of the Gaon of Vilna—that a person's attainment of Torah *begins* in concealment, that is to say, with the study of Kabbalah, and *ends* with understanding the simple meaning of Torah, which is the Bible. Through putting all one's effort *first* into the study of concealed Torah, which is Kabbalah, a person comes to understand the revealed Torah, which is the Bible. Thus a person should begin his or her study of Torah with the concealed Torah and when he or she is worthy they end in understanding the meaning of the revealed Torah.

104. We asked above (in paragraph 75), "How can we arrive at the first level of love for God which is a conditional love when the reward for *mitzvot* is not given in this world?" Nevertheless, the *perception* of the reward for *mitzvot* is in this world. It comes to us through the opening of our eyes in the Torah. This clear perception of the reward is perceived by the person exactly as if he or she received the reward of the *mitzvah* on the spot (paragraph 84).

Thus, the person feels the wondrous goodness that is part of the thought of Creation, which is to give pleasure to His creatures according to His good and ample hand. From this abundant goodness that he or she perceives, a wondrous love reveals itself between themselves and God. It showers on the person unceasingly, using the same pathways and channels as those used by natural love.

105. A person receives all this once he or she has a clear perception of God's face, that is, of His Goodness. But all the reality of the suffering that they underwent because of God's concealment before they merited the revelation of God's face still exists. Even though the person does not wish to recall it because of his or her love for God, it nonetheless constitutes a serious defect. If this is true with respect to relationships between people, then how much more so will it be true of a person's relationship to God?

How will a person be able to truly feel God's Providence in the sense that He is Good and does good to both good people and evil doers? How can a person reach true love of God? How can he or she reach a stage wherein the person both feels and knows that God only acted well towards him or towards her ever since they were born and never caused him or her any harm at all which, as we have stated, is the second stage of the love of God? (See tables 5 and 6.)

106. In order to understand this, we need to go more deeply into the words of the sages who said, "Whoever comes to God through love, his arrogant acts become virtues." This means that God does more than just forgive the person's arrogant acts. God transforms every single arrogant act or sin into a *mitzvah*.

107. Thus, once a person has merited the illumination of God's face to such a degree that every sin which he or she ever did—even those that were done deliberately—has become transformed into a *mitzvah*, then that person becomes happy and rejoices over all the feelings of suffering, the bitter pain and the many troubles that he or she went through during their life whilst in the two levels of concealment of God's face. It was the fact of the concealment of God's face that was the cause of the transgressions that have now been transformed into *mitzvot* by the most wondrous light of the face of God. All the pain and suffering that took the person out of his or her right mind and led the person to sin inadvertently, as in the first state of concealment, or to sin deliberately, as in the state of double concealment, are transformed and now become an opportunity to fulfill a *mitzvah* and receive a great, wonderful and eternal reward for it. Thus all suffering is transformed into great joy and all evil into wondrous good.

108. This is brought out in the folk-story of the Jew who was a faithful servant in the house of a certain master who loved him as much as

life itself. It once happened that the master went on a journey and left his business in the hands of a deputy. This deputy was an antisemite. What did he do? He took the Jew and gave him five lashes in front of everyone in the village in order to humiliate him. When the master returned, the servant went to him and told him what had happened. The man was very angry. He called to his deputy and commanded him to give the Jew one thousand rubles in cash for each stroke of the lash that he had received. The Jew took the money and went home where his wife found him crying. She said to him in great dread, "What happened when you met the master?" He told her and she responded, "But then, why are you crying?" He said to her, "I'm crying because he only gave me five lashes. If he had given me ten lashes, I would have ten thousand rubles!"

9. So now we have been shown that once a person merits that their sins are forgiven in such a way that their arrogant acts become as virtues, then the person's relationship with God comes to the second stage of love in which the Beloved never caused his or her lover any harm, not even a shadow of the least degree. He only bestowed much and wondrous good upon the person, right from the very beginning of their relationship. So transformation from love and the transmutation of arrogant acts into virtues come together, just as the sages have said.

0. Up to now, we have only explained how a person comes to the first two levels of *conditional* love, but we have yet to investigate how a person can come to relate to the Creator according to the two levels of *unconditional* love. In order to reach clarity on this issue, we must first study the following Talmudic passage:

"The Tanna said, 'A man should always consider himself as if he is half liable and half meritorious. If he does one *mitzvah*, he should be happy that he tilted the balance to the side of merit. If he does one sin, woe to him that he tilted the balance to the side of liability. As Scripture says, "One sinner can destroy much good" (Eccles. 9:18).'

"Rabbi Eliezer, the son of Rabbi Shimon said, 'The world is judged according to the majority of its deeds and the individual is judged according to the majority of his deeds. If he does one *mitzvah*, then happy is he who tilted himself *and the whole world* to the side of merit. If he did one sin, woe to him who tilted the balance of himself *and of all the world* to the side of liability. As it is said, "One sinner can destroy much good" (ibid). Because of the one sin that the person did, much good is lost to him *and to all the world*.'"

III. Rabbi Eliezer's words seem to be riddled with difficulties from beginning to end. He says that someone who does one *mitzvah*, immediately tilts his or her balance to the side of merit, because a person is judged according to the majority of his or her deeds. But surely this would only apply to an individual of whom it could be said that half of his deeds were good and half of his deeds were bad? But Rabbi Eliezer the son of Rabbi Shimon is not in fact talking about such a situation. The most important part of his words is, in fact, missing from our text, but the commentator Rashi explains his meaning. Rabbi Eliezer is referring to the statement of the Tanna, that a person should always consider himself or herself as being half liable and half meritorious, but he adds that the person should also look at the whole world as if the world itself is half liable and half meritorious. If this is what he meant, why didn't he use the same language as the Tanna did (paragraph 110)?

112. But the most difficult matter we need to consider here is how can a person consider himself or herself as if he or she is only half liable? This is a mystery! If one knows for oneself that one has many sins,

should he or she lie to himself or to herself and say that they are only half and half? The Torah itself says, "Keep your distance from a lie" (Ex. 23:7)! Furthermore, if we take literally the statement that the one who commits a sin can lose much good, then this would imply that because of that one sin, the person tilts the balance for himself or for herself together with the world to the side of liability. But we are not here to discuss some hypothetical situation that a man or woman might imagine. We are talking of reality as it is, for ourselves and for the world.

13. Rabbi Eliezer's words are even more puzzling when we consider the fact that in every generation there are many people who do at least one *mitzvah*, yet the world is still not tilted to the side of merit. It seems that the situation does not change at all but the world just carries on in the same old way. So we see that we need to understand this text at a much deeper level. According to a superficial reading, we can't make any sense of it.

The text is not talking about a man or a woman who knows for himself or for herself that their sins are many. It is not trying to persuade the person to believe something false about themselves, namely that he or she is half sinful and half meritorious, and thus to entice the person and persuade them that all they lack is one *mitzvah*. That is not the way of the sages at all. Rather, the Talmud is talking here about a person who feels or considers himself or herself to be a complete *tzaddik*. The person feels that he or she has achieved complete perfection. This is because they have already become worthy of the first level of love through the opening of their eyes in the Torah, through which, as we have learned above, God has already testified that he or she will never return to their old ways. It is to such a person that the Tanna is speaking, clarifying his or her path and proving to him or her that they are still not a [complete] *tzaddik* but are, as yet, a *benoni*. That is to say that the person is half liable and half meritorious. He or she is still not a [complete] *tzaddik* as they still lack one *mitzvah* from the 613 *mitzvot* in the Torah, namely the *mitzvah* of the love of God.

The testimony of God that the person will no longer sin is only based on the clarity of his or her perception of the great loss that would be experienced were they to commit a sin. This is called the fear of sin. For this reason, the state of consciousness of the person at this time is called transformation through fear of sin, as we have explained at length above (paragraph 57).

114. We have also discussed above that this stage of transformation through fear of sin only heals a person from the time of his or her transformation onwards, but not retroactively. All the pain and suffering that was undergone before meriting the revelation of God's face, have stayed exactly as they were without any healing at all. Also the sins that the person committed then are not completely transformed but they remain in their status of sins which were committed inadvertently.

115. It is for this reason that the Tanna is telling such a person who is still lacking the one *mitzvah*, that he or she should see himself as if they are half liable and half meritorious. That is to say, they should consider the moment when they merited transformation as the halfway point of their life. In this way, the liable half corresponds to that half of the person's life that he or she lived before reaching transformation. This half is certainly liable, as transformation from fear of sin does not heal it. Yet he or she may also be considered as half meritorious inasmuch as the second half of their life, which transpires from the time of transformation and onwards, is certainly meritorious since the person is sure never to sin again. Therefore, for the first half of one's life one is liable and for the second half, one is meritorious.

16. The Tanna says to such a person that he or she should think for themselves that if they were to practise the one *mitzvah*, which is the only one that they lack out of the 613 *mitzvot*—namely that of loving God—then, "happy is he that he tilted his balance to the side of merit." For whoever is worthy of the *mitzvah* of loving God which is transformation from the love for God, merits that their arrogant acts are transformed into virtues. Then, all the sorrow and sadness that they suffered in their lives before this transformation are transmuted into wonderful, limitless pleasure, to such a degree that they are sorry that they did not suffer a great deal more, as in the above story about the Jewish servant and his master!

This is called, "tilting the balance to the side of merit." A person's feelings, together with his other mistakes and acts of arrogance, have become transformed into virtues. This is indeed tilting the balance to the side of merit as the pan of the scales that was filled with liability has transformed and become filled instead with virtuous acts. In the language of the sages this transformation is called "tilting the balance."

17. The Tanna warns such a person that as long as he or she is still a *benoni* and has not yet merited to that one remaining *mitzvah* that he or she lacks out of all the 613 *mitzvot*, they should not rely upon themselves that they will not sin until the day of their death. They should not even rely on the testimony of God that they will not return to their old ways, as they still might come to sin. Therefore they should think for themselves that if they should do one sin, woe to them that they have tilted their balance to the pan of liability. Such a person would immediately lose the wonderful insight in Torah and the revelation of God's face that they had experienced. Their consciousness would fall once more into the concealment of God's face and then they would really have tilted themselves to the negative side. They would have lost all the positive and the good which would

have come in the second half of their life. Concerning this, the Tanna brings to such a person the scriptural proof, "One sinner can lose much good."

118. Now we are in a position to understand the addition that Rabbi Eliezer made to the Tanna's words. We can also see why he doesn't use the language of "half liable" and "half virtuous" as the Tanna does. The Tanna was talking within the framework of the second and third levels of the love for God (see tables 5 and 6) whereas Rabbi Eliezer the son of Rabbi Shimon is talking from the perspective of the fourth level of love which is eternal love and involves the insight that God is Good and does only good to evil doers and good people alike which is the revelation of God's face as it truly is.

119. We have already learnt that it is only possible to come to this fourth level of love when a person is well-versed, recognizes and knows all the dealings of his or her Beloved; how He behaves towards all people without leaving even one out. Therefore, even the great virtue that a man or woman attains in tilting the balance for themselves to the side of merit is still not enough for him or for her to attain the perfected love of God, which is the fourth level of the love of God. This is because at this point he or she still does not perceive the attribute of God as being Good and doing good to evil people as well as to the good. He or she only perceives God's Providence with regard to himself or herself but he or she still does not yet know how God's Providence operates in this most sublime and wondrous way with regard to all the other creatures of the world.

As we have explained above: As long as the person does not know all the dealings of the Beloved with others without exception, then his or her love cannot be eternal. He or she still has to tilt the balance of the whole world to the pan of merit. Only then will eternal love be revealed to the person.

o. This is what Rabbi Eliezer is saying when he states that the world is judged according to the majority of its deeds, and the individual is judged according to the majority of his or her deeds. Since Rabbi Eliezer is talking about the whole world, he cannot say, as does the Tanna, that the person should see the whole world as if it is half liable and half meritorious. An individual person only reaches this level regarding himself or herself when he or she becomes worthy of the revelation of God's face and of transformation from fear of sin. How could a person possibly say such a thing with regard to the whole world when most of the world has not yet come to the transformation from fear of sin? Therefore Rabbi Eliezer has to say that the world is judged according to the majority of its deeds and a person according to the majority of his or her deeds.

It is possible to think that one could only attain the level of a complete *tzaddik* if he or she had never sinned or transgressed in their life, and that those who have stumbled into sins and transgressions are no longer worthy to become complete *tzaddikim*. But, as Rabbi Eliezer teaches us, this is not so. Just as the world is judged according to the majority of its deeds, so is the individual. That is to say that when someone arrives at the quality of consciousness of being a *benoni*, which is to say that he or she has reached transformation through fear of sin, then that person merits 612 commandments which, as we have seen, divide one's life into half, the liable half of the past and the meritorious half of the future. At this point, if the person adds just one more *mitzvah*, which is the *mitzvah* of the love for God, then that person is judged according to the majority of his or her deeds which are now meritorious and he or she tilts the balance completely to the pan of merit. That is to say that the pan of the scales that was filled with sins is completely transformed into virtues, as we learnt above. So even if the person had a whole pan filled with sins and transgressions, they are all transformed into virtues (as above, paragraph 116) and then he or she is certainly comparable to someone who has never sinned in their life and they are now considered to be a complete *tzaddik.*

So Rabbi Eliezer teaches that "both the world and the individual are judged according to the majority of their deeds." Any sins committed before transformation through love of God do not come into the calculation at all. They are transformed into merits. So even completely wicked people, after they have become worthy of transformation through love for God, are considered to be complete *tzaddikim.*

121. Therefore Rabbi Eliezer says that if a person who, having reached the stage of transformation from fear of sin where only one *mitzvah* is lacking, then acts from that one *mitzvah* which is the love for God, then "Happy is he that he tilts the balance of himself and the whole world to the side of merit." Not only do they become worthy of transformation through the love with which they act, tilting themselves decisively to the side of virtue in accordance with the words of the Tanna, but we find that they also merit tilting the balance of the whole world to the side of virtue.

This means that such a person merits to ascend in wondrous perception in the holy Torah until it is revealed to him or to her that it is the destiny of every single human being to reach transformation through love for God. Then to all human beings will be revealed and shown the same wondrous Providence that such a person perceives for themselves. All the rest of the world, too, will have the balance tilted to the side of merit and then, "sins will cease from the Earth and wickedness will exist no longer" (Ps. 104:35).

Thus, even though most of the rest of the world still has not even come to the stage of transformation from fear of sin, nevertheless, since this one person clearly and decisively perceives the tipping of the balance that will come to everyone in the future, he or she is moved by the joy of it. It is exactly analogous to the situation we discussed earlier concerning the blessing of the Rabbis in the Talmud, "May you see your world in your lifetime!" when, referring to the transformation from fear of sin, a person becomes as excited and delighted as if he or she has already attained all the delight and wonder that is destined for him, according to the principle that if someone is certain to collect money, it is as if he or she has already collected it.

This is the case here too. For the individual who clearly perceives the transformation of the whole world, it is as if they have already merited to attain the level of transformation from love for God. He or she has tilted the balance for each and every person such that each person's pan of sins has transformed into a pan of merits. As a result, the individual knows God's dealings with each and every person in the world in the most complete way. That is why Rabbi Eliezer the son of Rabbi Shimon said, "Happy is he who has tilted the balance of himself *and that of the whole world* to the side of merit."

From now on, the person knows all the ways of God's Divine Providence with each and every creature, from the true aspect of the revelation of His face which is that God is Good and does good to both evil and to good people. Now that the person knows this, he or she also merits the fourth aspect of love, which is the eternal love about which we have spoken above (in paragraph 73).

Still, Rabbi Eliezer, like the Tanna, warns such a person that even though he or she has the merit to tilt the balance of the whole world from sin to virtue, nevertheless, they still should not become overconfident till the day they die. If, God forbid, they should stumble over one sin, all their wonderful insights and experiences would be lost immediately, according to the Scripture, "and one sinner can destroy much good," as the Tanna pointed out.

Now we have explained the difference between the words of the Tanna and the words of Rabbi Eliezer the son of Rabbi Shimon in this Talmudic passage. The Tanna is talking from the point of view of the second and third levels of love, therefore he does not mention the tilting of the balance of the whole world. However Rabbi Eliezer, the son of Rabbi Shimon is talking from the perspective of the fourth level of love, which can only be envisaged through the perception of the tilting of the balance of the entire world to the side of merit, as we have explained.

However, we still have to understand exactly how a person comes to this wondrous level of consciousness in which he or she tilts the balance of the whole of humanity to the side of virtue.

122. We need now to look at the following words of the sages in the Talmud:

"When the community is in a time of trouble, a man should not say, 'I will go to my house and I will eat and drink and all will be well with me.' For if he does so, then Scripture says of him, 'And the Lord God proclaimed that day for crying, for mourning, for baring one's head and for wearing sackcloth. And behold joy and gladness, slaying of oxen and killing of sheep, eating meat and drinking wine; let us eat and drink for tomorrow we die' (Isa. 22:12–14).

"The following verse states, 'And the Lord of Hosts revealed Himself in my hearing; surely this sin will not be atoned for by you till you die.' This is the quality of the *benoni*.

"But what does Scripture say of the quality of the wicked? 'Come you, I will fetch wine and we will get drunk and tomorrow shall be as this day' (Isa. 56:12).

"What follows after this verse? 'The *tzaddik* perishes, and no one takes it to heart. It is because of the evil that the *tzaddik* died' (Isa. 57:1).

"But rather a man should share in the distress of the community, then he will merit to participate in the consolation of the community."

3. At a superficial glance, the passages of Scripture brought here seem to have no connection with what the Talmud is trying to prove. The Talmud wants to bring scriptural proof that a person is obliged to feel distress together with the community. If this is its purpose, then why does it distinguish between the quality of a *benoni* and the quality of an evil-doer? Why does the Talmud use the specific language of the *quality* of the *benoni* and the *quality* of the evil-doer? Why does it not simply refer to intermediate people and wicked people? The word "quality" seems to be superfluous here. What is more, how does the Talmud know that Scripture here is discussing the sin of one who does not share in the community's pain?

A further difficulty is that there does not appear to be any punishment for the quality of the evil-doer but rather, "the *tzaddik* perishes and no one takes it to heart." If the wicked sin, what has the *tzaddik* done that he or she should be punished? What would the wicked care if the *tzaddik* dies?

4. You should know that the qualities of the wicked person, the *benoni* and the *tzaddik*, mentioned in this passage, do not refer to separate people, but all three qualities are to be found within each and every person. We can discern these three qualities in every human being. During the person's period of concealment of God's face, before the person merits to transformation from fear of sin, he or she is considered as having the quality of the wicked. After that, if one is worthy to attain transformation from fear of sin, that person is considered as having the quality of a *benoni*. When the person merits the transformation of love for God in its fourth level, which is eternal love, then

they are considered to be a complete *tzaddik*. For this reason, to show that it is referring to different states of a single person, the Talmud does not discuss "the wicked" or "the benoni," but rather the quality of the wicked or the quality of the *benoni*.

125. We must also remember that it is impossible to attain this fourth level of love without previously attaining the perception of the revelation of God's face as being the future destiny for all humanity. Through this perception, the person has the ability to tilt the balance of the whole world to the side of merit, as Rabbi Eliezer has said.

We have already explained that the revelation of God's face transforms all the pain and suffering that were endured during the time of concealment into such wondrous pleasures that a person is actually sorry that they did not suffer more!

Since this is so, we have a question: A man or a woman, when they tilt the balance for themselves to the pan of merit, certainly remembers all the pain and suffering that they suffered when they were in the state of concealment. The reality therefore exists that all that pain and suffering can then be transformed into wondrous delight, as we have said. But when the person tilts the balance of the whole world to the pan of merit, how can he or she know the measure of suffering and pain that all the creatures of the world suffer? Each person needs to understand their fellow creatures in order to see how they can be tilted to the side of merit in just the same way as we have described for a person who tilts the balance for himself or for herself.

In order that the pan of merit for the whole world should not be lacking at the time when the person can tilt the balance of the world to the side of merit, there is no other tactic than to always take care to truly feel the distress of the community, just as a person feels distress over their own troubles. In this way, such a person will feel the pan of liability of the world within them in the same way as they feel their own liability. Then, if the person is worthy to tilt the balance for himself or herself to the side of merit, he or she will also be able to tilt the balance of the whole world to the side of merit and thus become a complete *tzaddik*.

6. Now we can understand the words of the Talmud (paragraph 122) clearly. If a person did not distress himself or herself with the sorrow of the community, then even if they arrive at the level of transformation of fear of sin, which is the quality of the *benoni*, then Scripture says of them, "Behold joy and gladness, slaying of oxen and killing of sheep." This refers to the blessing of perceiving the world in one's lifetime and as the person sees the reward of their *mitzvot* prepared for him or for her in the world to come, then the person is certainly filled with joy and gladness and says to himself or herself, "Slay oxen and kill sheep, eat meat and drink wine, eat and drink for tomorrow we die." This is to say that they are filled with great happiness on account of the reward promised them in the world to come. So they say with great joy, "for tomorrow we die, and I will collect my reward in my life in the world to come."

But what is written afterwards? "Then the Lord of Hosts revealed Himself in my hearing, 'surely this sin will not be atoned for by you until you die!'" This is to say that Scripture reproves the person on account of the inadvertent sins that he or she still has. We have learnt that for one who reaches transformation through fear of sin, the sins that were done out of arrogance are transformed, but only into inadvertent sins. Thus, since he or she did not feel distress on account of the sorrow of the community, they cannot merit to attain the transformation of love for God, wherein their sins would have been transformed into virtues. As it is, the person still has his or her inadvertent sins which cannot this be atoned for during his or her lifetime. Then how will such a person enjoy their life in the world to come?

Thus Scripture says, "Surely this sin will not be atoned for until you die!" referring to the inadvertent sins before the person dies, as their atonement has been prevented.

127. The Talmud informs us that this is the quality of the *benoni*, which is to say that this Scripture is dealing with the period of a person's transformation from fear of sin and onwards, during which time he or she is called a *benoni*. But concerning the quality of the *rasha* (the wicked), what does the Scripture say? What are the consequences that follow from that period when the person was immersed in concealment of God's face that is called the period of the wicked? Now it is clear that transformation from fear of sin does not deal with the person's past before he or she has reached transformation, and so the Talmud brings another Scripture, "Come you, I will fetch wine and we will get drunk and tomorrow shall be like today." Those days and years which were spent in the concealment of God's face, which have not yet been corrected and which are called "the quality of the evil person" do not want the person to die because they have no part in the world to come after death, since those days and years belong to the *quality of the rasha* within him.

So at the very moment that the quality of the *benoni* within the person is happy and rejoicing "because tomorrow we die" and we will then merit the life of the world to come, simultaneously the quality of the *rasha* which is in the person does not agree but says that "tomorrow shall be like today." That is to say, that aspect of him or her wants to be happy and live in this world forever, as it still has no part in the world to come, because the person has still not healed this aspect within himself or herself as this aspect is only healed by transformation from love for God.

128. The Talmudic passage concludes that "the *tzaddik* perishes." In other words, the aspect of the complete *tzaddik* which the person should

merit is lost to him or to her. "... and no man takes it to heart. It is because of the evil the *tzaddik* died." Because the person at the intermediate level (*benoni*) did not feel the pain of the community, he or she cannot merit the transformation through love for God because of this omission. Transformation through loving God would transform one's arrogant acts into virtues and one's evil actions into great joys. Instead, all the mistakes that the person made and the evils that were suffered before the person reached transformation through fear of sin still exist within him or within her in the aspect of the quality of the *rasha* which feels badly on account of God's Providence. And it is because of these bad feelings which he or she still experiences that the person is not able to merit the state of the complete *tzaddik*.

Now this is what Scripture means when it says, "... and no man takes it to heart." This means that the man or woman does not notice that because of the evil, namely those bad feelings that they still have from the past with respect to God's Providence that "the *tzaddik* is lost." The aspect of the person that is the *tzaddik* within them is lost, and the person will die and leave this world as only a *benoni*.

All this comes about as whoever does not feel sorrow over the suffering of the community does not merit to see its consolation because they were not able to tip the balance for the community to the side of merit and witness their consolation. Thus such a person can never attain the aspect of the *tzaddik*.

29. There is no one in the world, born of a woman, who does not have in potential the three qualities mentioned above, namely the quality of the *rasha*, the quality of the *benoni* and the quality of the *tzaddik*. They are called "qualities" because they stem from the quality of the person's perception of God's Providence. As the Rabbis of the Talmud have said, "As a man perceives, so others perceive him."

Those who perceive the quality of God's Providence as in the aspect of concealment of God's face are considered as having the quality of the *rasha*, whether incompletely wicked as in single concealment, or completely wicked, as in double concealment. This is because, according to their perception and their feeling, God conducts the world with a providence that is not good. They indict themselves when they receive affliction and pain from God's Providence and feel badly the whole day long. They are further most condemning in that they think that everyone else in the world suffers in the same way from God's poor supervision. Thus those who perceive Divine Providence only from the point of view of concealment are called wicked (Heb. *rasha*) or people who condemn (Heb. *Harshia*). Understand this. This name reflects the depth of their feelings. This matter depends only upon the understanding of the heart. Speech or thought here is irrelevant, as a person may justify God's providence in speech or thought whilst they feel differently in their body or their senses which do not know how to lie and cannot be coerced. Therefore, those people who perceive God's Providence according to the condemning quality of the *rasha* have tilted the balance for themselves and for the whole world to the pan of liability, as we learn from the words of Rabbi Eliezer. They imagine that all of humanity suffers as they do from God's bad management and not in a way that is fitting to God's Name, which is that He is Good and does good to evil doers and good people alike.

130. Those who are worthy of attaining and feeling God's Providence as the revelation of God's face at its first level, which is termed transformation through fear of sin, are considered as having the quality of the *benoni*. This is because their feelings are divided into two parts, as in the two pans of a set of scales. On the one hand, they have already merited the revelation of God's face in the sense of "you will see your world in your lifetime." At least from now on, they perceive God's good Providence as is fitting to His blessed and good name. Therefore they have a pan of merit. However all the bitter pain and suffering

of the past is still strongly etched into their emotions stemming from all the days and years of the concealment of God's Providence; that period of their past before they gained this transformation. These feelings still stand in all their pain and constitute the pan of liability. These two pans are arrayed, one opposite the other, such that before the person's transformation, the pan of liability outweighs the positive one, and from the moment of the person's transformation onwards, the pan of merit prevails. Thus, at the moment of transformation, the two pans are finely balanced between negativity and merit and therefore a person at this stage is thus called an intermediate person or a *benoni*.

31. Those who merit the revelation of God's face at the second level, which is called transformation through love for God, wherein their acts of arrogance become as merits, have thus tipped the scale of liability to the scale of merit. This means that all the pain and suffering which was engraved in their bones when they lived under the providence of concealment of God's face, has now decisively tipped the balance and become a pan of merit. All their suffering and sorrow has been transformed into wondrous and eternal joy. Such a person is now called a *tzaddik* because he justifies (Heb. *matzdik*) God's relationship with the world.

32. One needs to know that the quality of the *benoni* can function even whilst a person is still under the influence of the concealment of God's face. By making a great effort of belief in cause and effect, a light of great trust in God is revealed and a person may merit the revelation of God's face on a temporary basis as in the aspect of a *benoni*. But there is a defect in that the person cannot as yet sustain this level in a permanent way. For it to become a permanent state of consciousness, the person has to attain the level of consciousness of transformation through fear of sin (paragraph 63).

133. Concerning what we said earlier, that free choice only operates during the period of concealment of God's face, we need to know that this does not imply that once a person has become worthy of perceiving Divine Providence through the revelation of God's face, he or she no longer has to work and labor in Torah and *mitzvot*. On the contrary, the main work with Torah and *mitzvot* in the correct way begins only after a person has attained the transformation though love for God. Only then is it truly possible for him or for her to practise Torah and *mitzvot* with love of God and fear of sin as we have been commanded. As it is written in the Talmud, "The world was created only for the sake of the complete *tzaddik*."

We can understand this better by analogy with the following story:

There was once a King who wanted to choose the most faithful subjects of his kingdom and bring them into his service in his innermost palace. So what did he do? He issued a public proclamation throughout his kingdom, that everyone who so desired, whether great or small, should come to him and work in his innermost palace. But he appointed many guards from amongst his servants whom he stationed at the entrance to the palace and along all the roads leading to it, commanding them to cunningly deceive all those approaching the palace and to lead them away from the road which led to the palace.

Naturally, all the citizens of the country began to run to the king's temple, but they were led astray by the cunning of the diligent guards. Still, many of them managed to overcome the guards, and succeeded in approaching the door of the palace. But those who guarded the doorway were the most diligent of all. If anyone actually arrived at the doorway, they deflected him with their great cunning until he went back the way he came. But these people would return more forcefully, stronger than ever and come back again and again and so it would go on for days, even years, until they would give up and not try any more. Only the most valiant of all, whose patience stood them in good stead, overcame those guards and opened the door. They immediately merited to see the face of the King who assigned each one to the duty most suited for him.

From then onwards, they no longer had any more dealings with those guards who had deflected them and embittered their lives for so many days and years, as they were going to and fro, for now they were worthy to work and serve facing the majestic light of the face of the King in his innermost palace.

The same is true of the work of the complete *tzaddik*. The free will that functions at the time of concealment of God's face certainly no longer operates once he or she has opened the door to perception of the revealed providence. However he or she begins the main service of God at the moment of the revelation of God's face, when the *tzaddik* begins to tread the many steps on the ladder whose base rests on the ground and whose head reaches up into heaven, as it is written, "And the *tzaddikim* will go from strength to strength" (Ps. 94:8). Each *tzaddik* is helped by his fellow. Their service trains them to do God's desire so that through them the Purpose of Creation, which is to give pleasure to His creatures according to His good and generous hand, may be fulfilled.

134. One should know the supreme spiritual law that revelation can only occur in a place where there was once concealment. This is also true with regard to matters of this world, in which absence precedes coming into being. For example, wheat only grows in the place where the seed was first sown and then the husk has rotted. Similarly, in spiritual matters, there is a direct relationship between concealment and revelation, like that of the wick of a candle to the light which it holds. For every concealment, once it has been healed, reveals a light that is

specific to that particular concealment; and the light that is revealed is connected to it just as the flame is caught by the wick. Remember this in all your ways.

135. Now we can understand what the sages meant when they said that the whole Torah consists of the names of God. At first glance this is a most surprising statement. We find many coarse matters in the Torah. There are the names of evil people; Pharaoh, Bilaam and others; things that are forbidden; things that are unclean; cruel curses which are to be found in the section of reproofs and such like. How can we understand all these as being names of God?

136. In order to understand this, we need to know that God's ways are not our ways. Our way is to go from the imperfect and come to the perfect. In God's way, however, all revelations emanate from the perfect and come to the imperfect, for creation originates and comes forth from God in a completely perfect state. This perfect state separates from the face of God and evolves through many levels until it comes to its final and most contracted level which is the level most suited to our material world, and then it can be revealed to us here in this world.

137. Thus you may know that the holy Torah, of whose virtue there is no end, did not originate before God in the form in which it appears in this world. It is known that "the Torah and God are One", but we cannot see this in the Torah of this world at all. Not only that, but for one who practises Torah not for its own sake, the Torah can even become a drug of death.

In the beginning, when the Torah was formed before God, it came forth in the highest degree of perfection and it embodied the aspect of the unity of the Torah and God in actuality. This is called the Torah of the world of *Atzilut*, of which it is written, "He and His life-force and His vessels are One." Then the Torah went forth from God and underwent many contractions, stage after stage, until it was given on Mount Sinai to Moses in the form that we recognize in this world; enclothed in the coarse garments of this physical world.

8. However you should know that even though there is a huge difference between the garments of the Torah in this physical world and its garments in the world of *Atzilut*, the Torah itself—which is to say, the light which is inside those garments—does not change in any way at all. The light of the Torah of *Atzilut* is just the same as that of the Torah of this world, as is written, "I, God, do not change" (Mal. 3:6).

Furthermore, the coarse garments in which the Torah is enclothed in our world of *Assiyah* do not in any way diminish its light. On the contrary, these coarse garments are incomparably more important for the task of completing the transformation, than the more spiritual ones which the Torah wears in the higher worlds, as concealment is the first cause of revelation. When concealment has been healed and transformed into revelation, it becomes like the wick of a candle with respect to the light that it holds. The greater the concealment has been, the greater the light it will reveal and hold at its healing. Therefore the coarse clothing the Torah wears in this world does not in any way cause the light of the Torah to diminish at all.

9. The Talmud tells us:

"When Moses ascended on high, the ministering angels spoke before the Holy One, blessed be He. 'Lord of the Universe, what business has one born of a woman amongst us?'

"He answered, 'He has come to receive the Torah!'

"They asked Him, '... You desire to give this to flesh and blood?'

"The Holy One, Blessed be He, said to Moses, 'Answer them!'

"So Moses said to them, '...'Do you feel jealousy?'...Do you have an evil side to your nature?'"

This passage illustrates that, as we have explained, the greatest concealment reveals the greatest light. Moses demonstrated to the angels that it is impossible for the greatest lights to be revealed through the pure garments which the Torah wears in the world of the angels. This is only possible through the garments of this world.

140. So there is no difference at all between the Torah of *Atzilut*, where the Torah and God are One, and the Torah of this world. The only difference lies in the garments. It is the garments of this world that conceal God and hide Him.

You should know that by virtue of His being clothed in the *Torah* [Heb. instruction], God is known as *Moreh* [Heb. teacher]. This is to inform us that at the time of single and even of double concealment, God is present and enclothed within the Torah, for God is the *Moreh*.

The coarse garments of the Torah of our world act like wings that cover and conceal the Teacher, may He be blessed, who is enclothed and concealed by them. However, when a person merits the revelation of the Divine face through the transformation of love of God in its fourth level, it is said of him, "Your Teacher will no longer be covered over by wings and your eyes will see your Teacher" (Isa. 30:20). From then onwards, the garments of the Torah no longer conceal the Teacher and it is revealed to the person for eternity that the Torah and God are One.

141. From this, you can understand the sages' comment on the Scripture, "Forsake Me, but keep My Torah." This, they explained, means, "If only you would forsake Me but keep My Torah, for the light which is in it will transform you." This seems, superficially, to be rather surprising. However, the sages are referring to people who fast and afflict themselves trying to induce a revelation of God's face. "They desire the

nearness of God. They say, 'Why have we fasted and You do not see it? We have afflicted our souls and You take no notice'" (Isa. 58:3). And then they are told in the name of God, "Please forsake Me, for all your striving is worthless and useless because I am only to be found in the Torah. Therefore observe the Torah and seek Me in it, for the light within it will bring you back to the good way, as it is written, 'Those who seek Me will find Me' (Prov. 8:17)."

2. Now it is possible to explain the essence of the wisdom of the Kabbalah, at least to a small degree, in a way that is sufficient for a reliable understanding of the quality of this wisdom. In this manner, a person will not be misled by false images such as many people imagine.

You should know that the holy Torah has four different aspects which embrace the whole of reality. The first three are called *world*, *year* and *soul* and the fourth aspect is the many ways in which the first three can combine themselves in different circumstances.

3. The outermost aspect of reality comprises the sky and the land-masses, the earth and the waters and so on, which the holy Torah calls *world*. The inner aspect of this reality comprises Man, the animals, the birds and the beasts, according to their species, which are mentioned in the Torah. These are called *soul*. All the causal factors mentioned in the Torah in the sense of cause and effect—as, for example, the chain of generations starting from Adam until Joshua and Calev, who entered the promised land, are called *year*, the father representing the cause and the son representing the effect. This causal aspect of reality is called *year*. All the various ways in which both the outer and the inner aspects of reality function and combine, that are discussed in the Torah, are called *the existence of reality*.

144. You should know that in Kabbalah, the four worlds are called *Atzilut*, *Briyah*, *Yetsirah* and *Assiyah*. These worlds emanate one from another just as a seal embeds its impression in wax. Everything which is found in the seal is then found in the impression of the wax to which the seal was applied, without any feature being added or subtracted. It is the same for the unfolding of the worlds. All the four aspects of the world of *Atzilut*, that is *world, year, soul* and their various combinations, which are called *the existence of reality*, are transferred like a seal with its impression, to the world of *Briyah*, and from there to the world of *Yetsirah* and right down to *Assiyah*.

Thus, all the three aspects of reality that we experience in this world, which are called, *world, year* and *soul* together with all their combinations, are derived and come into this world from the world of *Yetsirah*. They come into *Yetsirah* from the world above it, in such a way that the source of everything in this physical world is in the world of *Atzilut*. Even brand new inventions, which never existed previously in the world, have their being first in the world of *Atzilut* and from there they descend and are revealed to us in this world. And this is what the sages taught, "There is not a single blade of grass that does not have an angel and a guide above who beats it and tells it to grow," and "A man cannot even bang his finger in this world unless it has first been proclaimed above that he will do so."

145. So you should know that the Torah is enclothed within these three aspects of reality; *world, year* and *soul* plus all their myriad combinations in this material world. It is from here that the matter of the forbidden and the unclean, which are spoken of in the revealed Torah, is derived. God is enclothed in this Torah, according to the principle that God and the Torah are One, albeit in great concealment and hiddenness. The material garments are the wings that cover and conceal Him, may He be blessed. However the enclothing of the Torah

in the purer aspects of *world*, *year* and *soul* and their combinations as they manifest in the three higher worlds of *Atzilut*, *Briyah* and *Yetsirah* appear in this world as the wisdom of the Kabbalah.

6. The wisdom of Kabbalah and that of the revealed Torah are actually one. However when a person is in the state of consciousness of concealment of God's face, then he or she finds that God is similarly concealed by the Torah. Under these circumstances, when a person studies the revealed Torah, he or she cannot receive the light of Torah which pertains to *Yetsirah* and, one need not add, certainly not that which pertains to a higher level. Only when a person attains the consciousness of revelation of God's face, do the garments of the revealed Torah start to become more transparent and the revealed Torah becomes one with the Torah of *Yetsirah* which is the wisdom of Kabbalah. As for one who attains the level of the Torah of *Atzilut*, the letters of the Torah are in no way changed. It is just that these very same garments of the revealed Torah in this world have become transparent to the person and no longer conceal God. As it is written, "And your Teacher will no longer be covered by wings and your eyes will see your Teacher." Thus, that which is written in the *Zohar*, "He, His life force and his vessels are One," is fulfilled.

7. In order to understand this better, I will give you a practical example. As long as a person is in the state of concealment of God's face, the letters and garments of the Torah conceal God. As a consequence of being in this state, the person inevitably stumbles into sin. Then the person comes up against the prospect of the consequences of their acts and they have to deal with the coarse garments of the Torah; the unclean, the forbidden, the defective and suchlike. However, when the person becomes worthy of the revelation of God's Providence and the transformation from love for God, then all their arrogant acts

are changed into virtues. All the sins and mistakes through which the person stumbled during the time when he or she lived under the concealment of God's face are now stripped from their coarse and extremely bitter garments and are now dressed in garments of light, *mitzvot* and merits, for it is these very same coarse garments themselves which are transformed into virtues. They now have the aspect of garments that stem from the worlds of *Atzilut* or *Briyah*, where they do not hide or conceal the Teacher, may He be blessed. On the contrary, "… and your eyes will see your Teacher," becomes a reality.

It must again be emphasized that there is no difference between the Torah of *Atzilut* and the Torah of this world; between the wisdom of Kabbalah and the revealed Torah. The only distinction lies in the perspective of the person who is studying it. Both deal with exactly the same principles and the same language. Nevertheless one will experience the Torah from the point of view of the wisdom of Kabbalah, the Torah of *Atzilut*, and the other will experience the Torah as revealed Torah, the Torah of *Assiyah*. Understand this well.

148. In the light of this, we can understand how wise were the remarks of the Vilna Gaon who wrote that when we start studying Torah, we [usually] first engage with its most hidden aspect. That is to say that we study the revealed Torah of *Assiyah* in which God is completely hidden. Next, we study the level called *remez* (hint) in which God is a little more revealed. This is the Torah of *Yetsirah*. Eventually a person comes to the Torah in its simple meaning. This is the Torah of *Atzilut*, which is here called the simple meaning of the Torah (Heb. *pshat*). This is so because at this level, all the garments that conceal God are removed (Heb. *hitpashet*).

149. We can now come to some understanding of the four holy worlds which are known in the wisdom of Kabbalah by the names: *Atzilut*,

Briyah, Yetsirah and *Assiyah* of holiness and the four worlds of *Atzilut, Briyah, Yetsirah* and *Assiyah* of uncleanness which are arranged as two frameworks each opposed to the other. We can understand these four worlds through the four levels through which we understand God's Providence and through the four levels of love. We will begin by discussing the four holy worlds of *Atzilut, Briyah, Yetsirah* and *Assiyah* and we will start from the bottom with the world of *Assiyah.* (See table 6.)

o. We have already explained above that the first two aspects of our experience of God's Providence are the two aspects of concealment. You should know that they both belong to the world of *Assiyah.* As it is said in the *Etz Chayim* of the Ari, "Most of the world of *Assiyah* is evil and the little bit of good that is in it is so mixed up with the bad that it is impossible to recognize it." From the consciousness of single concealment of God's face, the suffering and pain experienced by people at this level of awareness of God's Providence leads to the experience of the world as being mostly bad. From the aspect of double concealment, even what good there is, is mixed with the bad and is not recognized as good at all.

Revelation of God's face begins in the world of *Yetsirah.* Concerning this level, the *Etz Chayim* tells us that the world of *Yetsirah* is perceived as being half good and half bad. Here, the person reaches the first stage of God's revelation, which is the first level of conditional love. This is termed transformation from fear of sin. Such a person is called a *benoni* (intermediate person) since he is still half liable and half meritorious as explained above (paragraphs 60–63).

The second level of love is also conditional, except that at this level, there is no remembrance of any damage or evil that occurred. This is also true of the first level of unconditional love. Both of these two levels are associated with the world of *Briyah,* which the *Etz Chayim* tells us is mostly good and a little evil, and the small amount of evil within it is not recognizable as such. This is because, were the *benoni* to merit one *mitzvah* [that of the love of God], he or she would tilt their balance wholly to the side of virtue. Thus the world of *Briyah* is mostly good. The little bit of bad that is present at the level of *Briyah* but is not recognizable there, stems from the third aspect of love which is unconditional. It comes from the fact that even though the person has tilted the balance for himself or herself to the side of merit, he or she has still not tilted the balance for the whole world to the positive side. This is the source of the little amount of bad, as this love for God is still not eternal. However this little bit is not recognizable as he or she has not yet felt badly on behalf of others.

The fourth level of love is that which is unconditional and eternal. It is associated with the world of *Atzilut*. As the *Etz Chayim* states, this world has no evil in it at all, as it is written, "No evil dwells with You" (Ps. 5:5). Once the person has tilted the whole world to the side of the positive, his or her love for God is eternal and certain. There can never again be any possibility of covering or concealment of God. This is a place of complete revelation of God's face according to what is written, "Your Teacher is no longer concealed by wings and your eyes will see your Teacher." Now a person is familiar with God's dealings with all His creatures and sees them all in the aspect of the true Divine Providence which is openly revealed in accordance with His Name, implying that God is Good and does good both to evil doers and to good people, alike.

151. In this way, we can understand, too, the matter of the four worlds, *Atzilut, Briyah, Yetsirah* and *Assiyah* of uncleanness, which are arranged opposite the four worlds, *Atzilut, Briyah, Yetsirah* and *Assiyah* of holiness, as it is written, "God created them, one against the other" (Eccles. 7:14). The world of *Assiyah*, which belongs to the framework of the unclean, consists of the two levels of concealment of God's

face. This framework dominates at these two levels in order to bring a person to tilt both himself or herself and the world into negativity, God forbid.

The world of *Yetsirah* of the framework of evil exploits the pan of liability which was not healed in the holy world of *Yetsirah* and thus can have power over the *benoni* who receives his or her light from the level of this world of *Yetsirah*, according to the inner meaning of "God created them, one against the other."

The world of *Briyah*, which belongs to the framework of evil, has the same power of extinguishing conditional love, as it can take away that on which the conditional love depends. Thus, the second level of love is still incomplete.

The world of *Atzilut* of the framework of evil exploits the little bit of evil which exists but is unrecognizable within the world of *Briyah*. Even though the love for God at this level is a true love from the perception that God is Good and does good to evil doers and good people, which is associated with the holy world of *Atzilut*, still, since a person at this level has not yet merited to tilt the whole world to the side of holiness, there is still strength in this shell to undermine this love from the point of view of questioning the Divine Providence with regard to other people.

52. Thus, the *Etz Chayim* tells us that the world of *Atzilut* of the shells corresponds to the holy world of *Briyah* and not to the holy world of *Atzilut*. The holy world of *Atzilut* is associated with the fourth level of love, at which level the framework of evil has no influence whatsoever as the person has already tilted the balance of the whole world to the side of merit. The person already knows God's dealings with all His creatures according to the Divine Providence appropriate to His Name, which is that God is Good and does good to evil doers and good people. However, at the level of the holy world of *Briyah*, which

is associated with the third level of love, the person has not yet tilted the balance of the whole world to the side of merit. Therefore there is still a foothold for the shells to get a grip. This is the world of *Atzilut* of the shells, which is associated with this third level of love, which is the first level of unconditional love.

153. We have now thoroughly explained the four worlds of holiness of *Atzilut, Briyah, Yetsirah* and *Assiyah* and the shells or framework of evil which are arranged against each and every world. These shells represent the lack which exists in each of the worlds of holiness and they are called the four worlds of *Atzilut, Briyah, Yetsirah* and *Assiyah* of the shells.

154. These words of explanation are adequate for anyone to get a feel of the essence of the wisdom of Kabbalah, at least in a small degree. You should know that most of the authors of books on Kabbalah intended them to be read only by people who had already merited the revelation of God's face and all the highest perceptions that we described above.

You might then ask that if such a person had already reached the final level of unconditional love, they would know all that is written about Kabbalah by virtue of their own experience. Why should he or she then study books of Kabbalah that other people have written?

This question can easily be answered. Imagine a person studying the Torah of this world but who knows nothing of the ways of this world, in the sense of *world, year* and *soul*. He or she has no idea how people conceive of themselves or how they relate to others, nor is he or she familiar with any of the animals, the birds and beasts of this world. Could you even begin to think that such a person would be able to understand anything of the Torah properly? They would have no idea what it was talking about and would confuse evil with good and good with evil. They would not be able to make sense of a single aspect of Torah. So, too, in our case. Even if a person has reached a level where his or her perception is of the Torah of *Atzilut*, all he or she knows of this Torah is only that which is relevant to their own soul. Such a person still lacks a knowledge of the three dimensions of *world*, *year* and *soul* as they manifest themselves in the world of *Atzilut* and how they relate and combine with one another. In order to understand matters of Torah and how they relate to each particular world, the person needs this information in precise detail. This is provided by the *Zohar* and authentic books of Kabbalah. Everyone with a deep inner understanding should study this material day and night.

55. This being so, we can ask why the Kabbalists said that it was important for *everybody* to study Kabbalah?

In this lies an important matter, which should be stated publicly. Studying Kabbalah is of inestimable value in a person's spiritual progress. Even though a person may not understand what he or she is studying, through his or her great desire and strong will to understand, they awaken the lights which surround their soul.

The meaning of this is that everyone is destined to arrive at this wondrous level of consciousness which God intended to bestow on all His creatures according to His Purpose of Creation. If a person does not reach this level in this incarnation, he or she will certainly reach it in a subsequent one until he or she should become worthy of fulfilling the specific purpose that God has planned for that person. As long as a person has not yet reached his or her perfection, the lights which are destined for him or for her in the future remain as surrounding lights. This means that these lights are ready and prepared for the person but are waiting for the person to merit suitable vessels for the lights and then the lights will be enclothed in the transformed vessels.

Therefore, even at a time when the person lacks such vessels, but is occupying himself or herself in the study of this wisdom, whenever he or she mentions the names of the lights and the vessels with which their particular soul has a connection, they immediately shine upon him or her to a certain degree. However they shine without being enclothed in the innermost part of the soul, as the person still lacks the transformed vessels to receive the lights. However the illumination that the person receives time after time, whenever he or she studies Kabbalah, brings down upon that person favor from the higher worlds, and the higher worlds bestow upon him or her an abundance of holiness and purity, which bring a person very close indeed so that he or she may come to perfection.

156. However, there is one strict condition to the study of this wisdom, which is not to make any materializations concerning either imaginary or physical terms. If a person is not careful with this, he or she will infringe the commandment, "You should not make any idol or graven image for yourself." The person would then be damaged rather than helped by this material. It was for this reason that the sages warned that this material should only be studied by someone over the age of forty or directly from a master, as a precautionary measure so that they would not fall into the above-mentioned trap. I have prepared, with God's help, my explanations of the *Etz Chayim* with just this purpose in mind to ensure that the reader does not come into error regarding his or her understanding of terms which are borrowed from the physical world but refer to purely spiritual realities.

However after the first four volumes of this explanation were printed and distributed, I saw that I had still not fulfilled my obligation in explaining this material as well as I had thought. All the tremendous effort that I had put into explaining and expanding on this material so that it would be readily understandable, was almost completely wasted. This was because those who studied the material did not feel the great necessity of being absolutely clear about the meaning of every single word used and the need to go over each word many times. It is important to remember the precise meaning of each word in every place it occurs throughout the book. Through forgetting the precise meaning of even one word, the matters under discussion become confused, as due to the sensitivity of the material, a misunderstanding of one word is enough to undermine one's whole understanding.

In order to rectify this, I began to write an explanation of essential terms, according to the alphabet. I included all the words brought in books of Kabbalah that require an explanation. In this book, I gathered together the Ari's explanations with those of other early Kabbalists listing everything they had to say about the word in question. I also included a summary of all these explanations and I gave my own definition of the term. This material is quite sufficient for anyone interested in understanding the meaning of a word, whenever he or she should come across it in any true book of Kabbalah written by either the early or the later Kabbalists. I continued with all the frequently used words in Kabbalah. I have already published, with God's help, the words beginning with the letter *Aleph* and some of the words that begin with the letter *Bet*. This material already runs to almost a thousand pages. However, due to lack of funds, I had to cease this work in its early stages. It has been almost a year during which I have been unable to continue with this most important work. Only God knows what will be its fate, for it is very costly and at present I have no one to help me.

Therefore I have taken another course, on the basis of the Talmudic maxim, "A limited goal is very achievable. A vast goal is difficult to achieve" and have written the book, *The Study of the Ten Sephirot of the Ari* to which this is the Introduction. In this book, I have taken from all the writings of the Ari and especially from his book, the *Etz*

Chayim, all the principle articles which are relevant to the explanation of the ten *sephirot*. I have placed the words of the Ari at the top of each page. I have written one comprehensive commentary on his words, which is called *Or P'nimi* (Inner Light) and a further, more general commentary, called *Histaclut P'nimit* (Inner View) which together explain every word and concept to be found in the words of the Ari as set out at the top of the page, as simply and as clearly as I can. I have divided the book into sixteen chapters, in which each chapter studies a particular aspect of the ten *sephirot*. The *Or P'nimi* primarily explains the words of the Ari found in that chapter and the *Histaclut P'nimit* explains the general issues that are discussed. I have set out a table of questions and answers concerning the words and the concepts discussed in each chapter. After the reader has completed each chapter, he should try to answer all the questions by himself. Then he should compare his answers with those provided. Even if he remembers the answers very clearly, he should go over the questions very many times until he is utterly familiar with the concepts. Then he will remember the meaning of every word when he needs it or, at the very least, he will remember where to look up its definition, and God will help him to succeed.

Chapter 5

Keywords, Definitions and Concepts

Mark and Yedidah Cohen

Rabbi Ashlag does not explain all the concepts he uses in the *Introductions*. There are two reasons for this. The first is that some of the concepts, for example, "Torah and *mitzvot*" or "free will" do not belong particularly to the world of Kabbalah but, rather, are central ideas in Jewish thought. For this reason, Rabbi Ashlag assumes that his reader will be familiar with these basic concepts, although they will not know the particular nuance that Kabbalah puts on them, and which Rabbi Ashlag explains in the *Introductions*. The second, is that many of the concepts which are mentioned in the *Introductions* and which are central to the study of Kabbalah, for example, "light" and "vessel", are exactly defined in the works that these essays introduce.

We have therefore provided definitions of these terms, set out in approximately the order in which they arise in the text, followed by a section of short discussions of fundamental concepts. An alpahabetical list of all the terms heads the chapter.

Alphabetical list of terms.

Light

In Kabbalah, light is the direct emanation of Divinity. It exists eternally. Its nature is giving. It is referred to as "is from is" [Heb. *Yesh me Yesh*]. That is to say, it is not something new or created but it always *is*. "I am God. I do not change" (Mal. 3:6).

Vessel

The vessel is *the will to receive*. This is something new, something created, [Heb. *Yesh meAyin*]. It did not exist in an active form in God prior to the creation. While the light has the quality of abundance, of giving, the vessel has the quality of receiving. The desire to receive the light is the vessel for the light.

Thus the vessel is a lack, a desire, or a will to receive. From its beginnings within God to its final form where it has its own consciousness, it must undergo a certain development.

The Formation of the Vessel (The four aspects, the ten Sephirot, the four letter Name of God)

In order to reach its final form, the vessel must first come into being and go through four stages of evolution. This is necessary as the vessel starts out united with the light, and has to become empty of the light in order to act in a true capacity as a vessel. These four stages are needed in order to enable the vessel to a) know what it wants to receive—therefore it needs to have experienced the light and b) to lack that which it wants to receive—it needs to be empty of the light. Only then it has become a vessel suitable for the light. This is true of all vessels from those in the highest spiritual worlds down to the smallest particle in this world. These four stages are called the four aspects. They also subdivide into the ten *sephirot* and they correspond, too, to the four letter Name of God. They begin with the vessel subsumed within the light and they end with a complete vessel with its own consciousness and existence, empty of light.

Giving
The very nature of the light is to give; to bestow, to benefit.

Receiving
The very nature of the vessel is receiving. If the vessel is empty then it desires to receive. This is the *will to receive.*

Affinity of Form; Difference or Antipathy of Form
When two spiritual entities act in an identical way, or have identical desires, they are said to have affinity of form and thus to be at one with each other. Two spiritual entities which act in different or opposite ways have antipathy of form.

Thus affinity of form leads to cleaving and to unity, while antipathy of form leads to separation and spiritual distance. Rabbi Ashlag gives this example: There are two friends who love each other and have identical ideas and aspirations. Even though they may be physically separated by distance, their affinity of form ensures that spiritually, they are at one with each other. However, two people may be physically close yet their aims and aspirations may be different from each other to such a degree that they come to hate each other. This is antipathy of form. However close they may be physically, they are as far apart as the East is from the West.

Will to Receive for Oneself Alone
Now we can understand that if the very nature of the light is giving and the very nature of the vessel is receiving, this is the basis of the antipathy of form and separation between ourselves (the vessels) and God (the light). And indeed, if we act as pure receivers, using the will to receive for ourselves alone, only receiving according to the dictates of our own desires or egos, we could not be further away spiritually from God. This is referred to as the will to receive for oneself and often also referred to in the *Introductions* as "the body." It represents

the domination of evil (the shells) over the souls as they are here in this world.

The will to give (for the sake of giving)

Here the person, wanting to become closer to God, limits his or her use of their will to receive, even though that is their nature, and uses as much as he or she possibly can of their will to give alone. It is a form of the vessel that has affinity of form with God. However it is an incomplete form of the vessel as it does not receive and therefore fails to fulfil the Purpose of Creation which is for God to give His creatures pleasure.

The Will to Receive in Order to Give Pleasure to the Creator

This is the form of the will to receive that is in affinity of form with God, in oneness with the Source [Heb. *d'vekut*].

Rabbi Ashlag explains the concept by the following example:

A wayfarer comes to a man's house. He is hungry and there is food laid out. The host, seeing his guest's hunger, invites him to eat. But the wayfarer does not want to receive for himself alone, so he refuses. This refusal leads the host to entreat him saying, "Please eat. We have not had a guest for so long. It would give me so much pleasure if you would eat." When the wayfarer sees that his host would receive so much happiness were he to eat, and would be very sad if he did not do so, then under these circumstances he agrees to eat because by eating he gives pleasure to his host. By receiving (food) from his host he is giving (pleasure) to his host. Receiving that is done with the purpose of giving is considered to be pure giving.

The explanation of this parable is that we are the wayfarer and the host is God. The food is the light. The vessel is the wayfarer's hunger. By not eating directly only in order to satisfy his hunger, but only eating for the purpose of pleasing his host, the wayfarer is receiving the light only in order to give pleasure to the Creator. In other words, here the receiving is transformed into giving—receiving the light only because it causes pleasure to the Creator.

In Kabbalah, giving to each other is likened to giving to God. By using the will to receive in order to give, we become in affinity of form with the Source. We become one with the Creator [Heb. *d'vekut*]. This is a new and complete form of vessel that did not exist prior to the creation of the worlds. This vessel now fulfills the ultimate purpose of creation in that it enables God to give pleasure to His creatures without leading to separation between the vessel and the light.

The Purpose of Creation (also called "The thought of Creation")
The Purpose of Creation or original thought of Creation is that God wants to give pleasure to His creatures. This obligates the new creation of the will to receive God's gifts, which is the vessel or the will to receive, and which characterizes the created being.

The Healing of Creation [Heb. Tikkun]
This is the work we do on ourselves as vessels in order to transform the act of receiving into that of giving. In doing this, we become in affinity of form with the light. We may then receive the light, enabling God to fulfill the Purpose of Creation. At the same time, we give it selflessly to others. We have transformed our finite vessels of desire into infinite channels of God's goodness.

To enclothe
When we use the term "to enclothe," the meaning is that a lower aspect has attained affinity of form with a higher aspect. So a vessel which originates from a will to receive and is thus lower in the sense of being further away from God's essence, may enclothe light when it acquires an affinity of form with the outermost or coarser aspects of that light.

Head/Body or Head Part/Middle Part/End Part
These are the subdivisions of the spiritual entity. The head is the planning aspect or potential of the vessel. It is the aspect of the

spiritual entity in which the primary interaction with the light occurs. In the case of receiving only to give, the light is first reflected back as an act of giving, thus enabling the vessel to subsequently receive whilst still being in affinity of form with the Giver.

The body or the middle part of the vessel is the part of the vessel into which the light enters. It is that part of the vessel that acts like a vessel enclothing the light within it.

The end part of the vessel is that aspect of the vessel that restricts that part of the light from entering that it cannot receive for the purpose of giving. Since it remains in holiness and is committed to not receiving for itself alone, it puts a stop or boundary to the light.

Fear of God/Fear of Sin

Yirat HaShem is usually translated as fear of God, fear of sin, or simply fear of making a mistake. It can be more accurately understood as "I so much want to be one with my Beloved, that I am afraid of doing the wrong thing." It is more accurately translated as fear of sin, fear of separation, or simply fear of making a mistake. In Kabbalah, it is a very high level of holiness.

Love of God

We love God when things are going well and are not so enamoured when we are having a hard time. This is called conditional love—conditional on our circumstances. It is not a perfect love.

True love of God is unconditional, no matter what. In good or bad circumstances, in suffering or in happiness. In loving God unconditionally, we reach a stage of loving God the way He/She loves us.

For its own sake/Not for its own sake

When we serve God for God's sake, we serve from an ego-less point. We give to God and to others only to please the One and to serve His/Her creatures. We do not ask or want for ourselves. We can also learn the One's wisdom—Torah—for its own sake and so that the illumination that is in Torah will shed its light on our souls and enable us to grow closer to our Source.

Not for its own sake is the opposite. Our motives are mixed. Our ego is involved. Although we may be serving God, we are also serving our egos at the same time. Still, by remembering our overall intention of wanting to purify ourselves, it is nevertheless a valuable stage that leads to Torah for its own sake. It is only a negative stage if there is no overall intention to grow in purity but the person's inner motive is self-serving. Then it can lead to a state in which the Torah becomes the drug of death, God forbid.

Revealed Torah

Revealed Torah comprises the written Torah, which is the five books of Moses together with the *Mishnah* and the Talmud, which make up the oral Torah. The term, *revealed Torah*, also includes books pertaining to Jewish Law (*Halachah*).

These materials all deal with the practical application of Torah in the world. They are studied by Jews in traditional academies (*yeshivot*).

Secrets of Torah; Concealed Torah

This is the wisdom of the Kabbalah that deals with inner consciousness and the intimate connection between God and His creatures.

Torah and Mitzvot

The *mitzvot* in the Torah are called in the language of the *Zohar* by the term commandments [Heb. *pikudim*]. However they are also referred to as 613 pieces of advice. The difference between these two terms is that everything has a potential aspect and an actual aspect. This is also true for Torah and *mitzvot*. First comes the aspect of doing them without understanding, on the basis of faith alone. Then follows the aspect of doing them with full understanding. When they are done from faith alone without understanding, they are in potential and are considered as pieces of advice. When a person merits to understand their true meaning, they become commandments (*pikudim*).

But this term *pikudim* also means "deposits". There are 613 *mitzvot*. In each *mitzvah* is deposited a specific light. This light is specific to the particular limb of the soul and the body related to that particular *mitzvah*. When a person performs a *mitzvah*, he draws to himself the specific light for that particular limb of the body/soul entity.

Rabbi Ashlag uses the term, Torah and *mitzvot* to include:

a) The outer practice of good deeds, as, for example, giving charity to the poor. This also includes the performance of ritual *halachah*.

b) The inner consciousness—the connection of ourselves to our souls as part of God.

c) The study of Torah as a guide to this inner consciousness.

Movement, Time and Exchange

Kabbalah often uses expressions which seemingly refer to time and space. But Rabbi Ashlag teaches that in the spiritual worlds time, space or exchange as we know them in this physical world do not apply. So we need to ask what the expressions in Kabbalah relating to movement, space or time refer to?

Movement from place to place in the language of the branches refers to a new desire or a new change of form that has arisen in the vessel. Affinity of form, as we have learned, leads to unity. A change of form leads to a movement of a new entity away from the former. But this does not imply that the former vessel changes also. It remains as it was and the change of form is an addition to it. There is no *exchange* in the spiritual worlds but only additional forms that separate from the previous form. Those are referred to in terms of movement from the vessel.

A succession of changes of form leads to the Kabbalistic understanding of the concept of time. Just as in the physical world, if we and all around us were at total rest, we would have no concept of time. Time is conceived by us because a succession of movements has taken place, for example our breathing.

A succession of changes of form is also referred to as cause and effect; one form causing the next.

Cause and Effect, Before and After, Reward and Punishment

"Before and after" in Kabbalah, means cause and effect. The cause is termed "before," and the effect, "after." Cause and effect is often referred to in terms of reward and punishment. This follows from the fact that each of our acts is a cause that produces an effect, which may be positive (perceived as reward) or negative (perceived as punishment). But this is, of course, only from the viewpoint of the vessel. In actuality, the light of God is only good and God, all love, does not have any aspect of punishment.

Divine Providence

God is Good and does good to both those who are doing evil as well as to people who are doing good acts. This is the truth but it is not our usual perception. Our perception of how God deals with us is our perception of Divine Providence (see table 4).

The *Rasha* (the evil person), The *Benoni* (intermediate person) and the *Tzaddik* (righteous person),

A *rasha* or evil person, in Kabbalah, is one who is not in contact with his soul and his inner consciousness, and is thus liable to sin. He is considered to be a living dead-man.

The *benoni* or intermediate person is one who has a consciousness of the living God within him and is particularly aware of what separates him from God.

The *Tzaddik* has an abiding consciousness at all times of the love of God, both within himself and as the One manifests in the world.

These three aspects may refer to separate people or may be states of consciousness in the same person.

The End of the Time of Healing

We go through incarnation after incarnation, growing ever closer to God, transforming our vessels more and more. We cannot experience the work we have already achieved as this would remove the element of free choice. Each time we must make our choice anew. But when the vessels are transformed, all the world together will ascend in consciousness and the whole world will be filled with the direct experience of the Divine love. This time is extremely close, which is why the wisdom of the Kabbalah has never been so important. It is the need of our souls at this particular time.

Israel and the Nations

Our most Divine aspect is termed in Kabbalistic language the aspect of Israel within us. It comes from the term "*Isr-el*" meaning "straight to God." Our different wills to receive are referred to as *the nations of the world* or *the kings*. They are what are commonly called in modern psychology, sub-personalities. These terms *Israel* and *the nations* apply equally to the Jew and the non-Jew.

613 mitzvot; 248 positive commands/365 negative commands

Maimonides enumerated all the possible *mitzvot* as stated in the Torah. There are 613.

But as he himself states, 613 cannot possibly apply to one person in their life-time. Some only apply to a man, others only to a woman. Some could only be carried out during the time that the temple stood in Jerusalem. Others only apply to people living in the land of Israel.

For most people, the number of *mitzvot* they are ever likely to encounter in one lifetime is nearer sixty. Rabbi Ashlag uses the number 613 to imply the completion of a spiritual stage, which corresponds to the soul limbs of the spiritual entity. Basically, his meaning is that when the required work has been completed, the soul ascends.

The number 248 similarly refers to the maximum number of positive commandments. These correspond to the soul organs of the spiritual entity. The number 365 refers to the maximum number of possible negative commandments or actions to refrain from. These correspond to the sinews of the spiritual entity.

Light of Wisdom [Heb. Or d'Chochmah]
This is the light of the Infinite (*Ein Sof*) that God bestows on the creatures according to the Purpose of Creation.

Light of Lovingkindness [Heb. Or d'Chassadim], also called Returning Light
This is the light attracted to the vessel when it gives back the light to God or passes it on to someone else. It is the joy of giving. It is the light involved in the healing of creation.

Exploration of Fundamental Concepts
Sephirot
The Kabbalistic term *sephirot* or in the singular *sephirah* comes from the Hebrew *saphir* which is from the same root as the English "sapphire." This gives a strong clue as to its meaning which might be translated as "a shining emanation of God's light as reflected in one of its facets." There are ten *sephirot*. Not only do these ten *sephirot* describe the whole of spiritual reality from its beginning to its end, from the *Ein Sof* right down to the lowest aspect of this world, but

also every single separate detail in existence contains these ten aspects within itself. Furthermore, every single *sephirah* is itself composed of all ten.

The names of the ten *sephirot* are, *Keter, Chochmah, Binah, Chesed, Gevurah, Tipheret, Netzach, Hod, Yesod* and *Malchut*. Quite often, Rabbi Ashlag mentions only the five main *sephirot* which are *Keter, Chochmah, Binah, Tipheret* and *Malchut*. The remaining sephirot—*Chesed, Gevurah, Tipheret, Netzach, Hod,* and *Yesod*—are in fact aspects of *Tipheret* and are not always listed as independent *sephirot*.

Sometimes, Rabbi Ashlag mentions only four *sephirot*. *Keter* is the root of the subsequent *sephirot*. It is not separated from the *Ein Sof*. The four subsequent *sephirot* are identified with the four letter name of God which is made up of the four Hebrew letters, *Yud* [י], *Hay* [ה], *Vav* [ו] and *Hay* [ה]. The *Yud* represents *Chochmah*; the first *Hay*, *Binah*; the *Vav, Tipheret*; and the final *Hay, Malchut*. The *sephirot* exist in relationship to each other and each one is included in all the others.

The *sephirah* of *Malchut* is, in many respects, a special case. *Malchut* is the only *sephirah* which has the capacity to form a true vessel. The other *sephirot* act as transmitters or channels for the light. *Malchut* receives the light or chooses to reflect it. We belong to the *sephirah* of *Malchut* and the critical question is what we do with the light which comes down to us. We can receive it for our own egoistic enjoyment which is to take ourselves out of holiness and to place ourselves firmly in the realm of the framework of uncleanness, or we can decline to accept that which we would only use for our selfish indulgence and decide to take only that light which we can pass on with wisdom, love and compassion to others. In this case, we are in the realm of holiness and helping to fulfill the Divine plan. Once we have become whole beings, never functioning from our own egos but always with concern for others and their welfare, then we become channels for a huge amount of light to flow down through the *sephirot* and into *Malchut*. Then "the whole world is filled with His glory" and this is the end of the work of creation. At this point *Malchut* is united with the other *sephirot* and no longer separated from them. This is the great unification in which the final *Hay* of the four-letter name of God is brought together in unity with the other three, and this is the culmination of the creation process. At this point, creation is in affinity with Divinity. We are simultaneously receivers of the Divine light of which God is the giver and we are givers too. We have become one with God.

Torah

The narrow meaning of the term *Torah* refers to the five books of Moses that he received from God at Mount Sinai. However in Kabbalah, the appearance of these books in the world is seen as only the last stage of a process that reaches right back to the heart of Divinity. There is a principle in Kabbalah that "God and the Torah are one and the same." Of course this, as Rabbi Ashlag points out in the *Introductions*, is not at all apparent. He reminds us that the Torah mentions evil people such as Pharaoh, animals that are forbidden to eat, and it contains curses as well as blessings. There are plenty of deeds described in it that seem far from Divine!

The Torah originates in God and it descends downwards through a series of contractions, eventually becoming the revealed Torah; the five books of Moses and the other books of the Bible, also including the Oral Torah; the *Mishnah* and the Talmud. At this level it is entirely enclothed in garments which come from our physical world. For example, the Torah at this level tells us that a certain animal is permitted or forbidden to eat, clearly referring to a certain species of animal that exists in nature. However, at higher levels, the Torah is referring to spiritual rather than material entities. It tells us, for example, that the spiritual essence that is represented by such and such an animal in the physical world is or is not appropriate to associate with. As we move up through the worlds, the garments of the Torah become more and more pure and ethereal, until they fall away and the identity of the Torah with Divinity is fully apparent.

However it is important to understand that although the garments in which the Torah is cloaked become ever coarser as the Torah moves downwards through the worlds, the light of God which is contained within it is unchanged. God, Rabbi Ashlag teaches us, is as fully present in the Torah of this world as He is in the Torah of the higher worlds. It is just that He exists within the Torah of this world in a state of concealment.

There is an important principle in Kabbalah which tells us that there is no revelation except in a place where there is prior concealment. Another way of expressing the nature of the spiritual work is to say that we endeavor to find the light of God that is hidden in all of reality.

Worlds
Kabbalah explains that there are four principle divisions of worlds which are called, from above to below, 1) *Atzilut*, 2) *Briyah*, 3) *Yetsirah* and 4) *Assiyah*. Each world is an impression from the world above it and they are related to each other as a seal is to sealing wax. *Atzilut* imprints itself in *Briyah*, which in turn imprints itself in *Yetsirah* and so on. Our physical world is at the bottom of the chain of worlds but our consciousness can reach up to explore the higher worlds.

These worlds correspond to the four letter name of God, *Yud* [י], *Hay* [ה], *Vav* [ו], *Hay* [ה]. The *Yud* is *Atzilut*, the first *Hay* is *Briyah*, the *Vav* is *Yetsirah* and the final *Hay* is *Assiyah*. They also correspond to the *sephirot. Atzilut* corresponds to *Chochmah*, *Briyah* corresponds to *Binah*, *Yetsirah* corresponds to *Tipheret* and *Assiyah* corresponds to *Malchut*.

Whenever anything new comes into this world, it originates at the level of *Ein Sof*, the Infinite. It first manifests as a spiritual reality at the level of *Atzilut*. Then it filters down and, as the very last step in the whole process, it finally enters physical reality. All that has changed is that the garments with which the pure entity is enclothed have become increasingly coarse as it moves down from world to world. The framework of uncleanness has an increasing influence in the reality of this world as it becomes coarser and more material.

God

God as the One is changeless. The essence of the One is unknowable. Only through the light which emanates from Him/Her can we know the One. The different aspects of this light have many different names. Creation does not in the least affect God in the essence of the One. God is absolutely simple, one and changeless. Kabbalah does not deal with the essence of Divinity. There is an expression in Kabbalah, "God cannot be grasped with the mind at all" and another that says, "We can know nothing of God's essence. We can only know His deeds". Thus Kabbalah deals only with the emanations of God's light.

These emanations of light come to fill the various vessels that are formed. From the point of the view of the vessels, creation and its continued existence represent an incredibly complex dynamic of emanations of God's light coming and going and having cause and effect relationships on each other. The study of this dynamic is the main subject matter of Kabbalah, which tells the inner story of the universe, from the beginnings of creation through to its final redemption and complete healing.

Halachah

Halachah is usually translated as "Jewish Law" but its literal meaning is "going" or "treading the path," meaning the path back to God, to *D'vekut*, which means cleaving to God. In this way, Kabbalah tends to see *Halachah* less as a system of laws that have to be obeyed and more as a map for a journey of transformation to be undertaken. Rabbi Ashlag calls the *mitzvot* "pieces of advice." If you wish to return to the Source they contain good advice, but the choice is always yours.

Halachah comprises two categories of *mitzvot*; those that address the relationship between God and Man and those concerned with the relationship between Man and his or her fellow. Working with Torah and *mitzvot* purifies the different aspects of the will to receive for oneself alone.

The Framework of Uncleanness, also known as The Other Side or the Shells

The other side (Aramaic *Sitra Achra*) and the shells (*klipot*) are the Kabbalistic terms used to refer to the dark side of creation. There are four worlds of holiness, and opposing them are the four worlds of uncleanness. These two frameworks mirror each other. A person identifies with the framework of holiness when doing his or her spiritual work. When he or she is only interested in selfish self-love, then he or she is identified with the framework of the other side. A person can change from identifying with one or the other many times in the course of a day.

There are always two ways of responding to any situation. One is to act out of egoism, asking of the situation, "What can I personally get out of this? How can I exploit this situation to my own gain and advantage?" In asking this question, the feelings and needs of the other people involved may be irrelevant to me and I may be quite prepared to damage them in order for myself to profit. To act in this way would be to place oneself firmly in the realm of the other side and the shells.

On the other hand, we can always respond to any situation out of our own wholeness. The holy way of responding to any situation is to consider the true need, desires and aspirations of ourselves and others and respond to that. From this perspective the question we ask is, "What can I give to this situation? How can I use this situation to help all who are involved in it, so that all can fulfill their legitimate needs and aspirations?" "How can I help? How can I heal?" To ask these questions of any situation we encounter in life is to identify with the realm of holiness and to distance ourselves from the realm of the other side and the shells.

The question is asked in the *Introductions* as to why God created and sustains this realm of the other side and the shells. They seem to have exactly the opposite aims from those of God and it seems like the One is supporting the enemy!

The answer given is that although the shells are opposed to the realm of holiness, in the grander plan they have an important role. The purpose of creation is for God to bestow upon us the maximum good. In order for Him to do this, we must first want it. We must have the will to receive that which God wants to give us. Suppose, for example, a friend wants to take me out to an expensive restaurant and treat me to a large meal. Then, in order to enjoy the experience, I must first be hungry. I must have a real appetite. Otherwise I will either be unable to eat the meal at all, or I will force myself to eat it without gaining any pleasure from the experience. In just this way, God gives us a very large will to receive what He wants to give us. Otherwise we will either not enjoy it when it comes or we will refuse it altogether.

The purpose of the framework of uncleanness is to help us to enlarge our will to receive so that it will, in the end, be adequate to receive all that God wants to give us. The will to receive with which we are born needs a great deal of expansion and enlargement before it will be adequate to fulfil its ultimate task.

Another purpose of the shells and the other side is to enable the possibility of free choice. Light and goodness only exist as experiential phenomena when juxtaposed to their opposite, dark and evil. In such a case, a person can and often must choose between them. This enables the person to eventually develop into a fully-fledged conscious vessel for the light.

Shechinah

The *Shechinah* is the inner presence of God in the heart. God as immanent, God as receiver. The *Shechinah* is considered as feminine as opposed to God as giver, who is depicted as masculine. In Kabbalah, the *Shechinah* is depicted as being in a very sorry state, lying in the dust, unable to raise Herself without our active help and cooperation. The awareness of God within us increases as we work with Torah and *mitzvot* in order to give rather than to receive. As our inner purity increases, we become aware of the *Shechinah* and Her soft voice within us. This process is dependent on giving up listening to the strident demands of the will to receive for ourselves alone. That is why it is we who have to raise the *Shechinah* from the dust. When we value Her, respect Her and care for Her, and we give Her once more Her rightful place, the world becomes alive and vibrant again, and life assumes a meaning, purpose and joy that was previously absent from it.

Free Will

Free will is a fundamental principle of Judaism. It is so important a principle that the One hides from creation just in order to give us the free will to either come to our Source through our own choice or to choose not to do so.

However, free will has its place amongst a number of other principles, which limit it in various ways. Chief of these is the concept that

God is beyond time. In creating us, God made us in our full, perfected form. God created us as enlightened beings, fit to receive all the good that God has in store for us. We already exist in this form within the mind of God and so, within the realm of time, we have no choice but to come to our own enlightenment and perfection. Thus we are not at liberty to remain as we are. We have to become what we already are in the mind of God.

This, therefore, limits our freedom. Our goal is defined for us and we are not free to change it or ignore it. Our freedom lies only in how we get to this goal. Rabbi Ashlag teaches that there are two ways and that every moment we have a choice of which of the two ways to pursue. The first is called the way of Torah and *mitzvot*, which includes the idea of working consciously with all that life presents to us. This is a powerful way of moving away from our egoism and coming to our wholeness. The second way manifests if we do not consciously accept and work with the situations that life presents to us, then we will suffer and eventually that suffering will wear down our egoism and purify us.

Rabbi Ashlag often quotes the Biblical phrase, "In its time I will hasten it" (Isa. 60:22). Following the Talmud, he explains that "in its time" means that we will all come to our wholeness in due time through a great deal of suffering if we choose to go on the path of suffering. If, however, we chose the path of conscious work, then "I will hasten it" and the process proceeds much quicker and with much less suffering. There is no more powerful and effective way to follow the path of Torah and *mitzvot* than to study Kabbalah, whose light, Rabbi Ashlag repeatedly tells us, has exactly the transformative effect that we are looking for.

Cause and Effect (reward and punishment)
The notion of cause and effect is a fundamental concept in Judaism and

in Kabbalah. It is central to the religion and is one of those concepts whose meaning changes according to the level of consciousness of the person who is wrestling with it.

At its simplest level, it implies that the reality which a person brings forth through their actions, thoughts and feelings will be reflected back to them. "As you sow, so shall you reap."

At the lowest level of consciousness, cause and effect has the meaning it would have for a child. If a child is good, he will be given a reward, such as a piece of candy. If he is bad, then he will be given a punishment such as being sent to his bedroom or not being allowed to play with his toys.

Kabbalah, however, views cause and effect or reward and punishment from a much higher level of consciousness. It is fundamental to Kabbalah, and often quoted by Rabbi Ashlag, that God is Good and does good to good people and to evil-doers. At the highest level, the concept of cause and effect therefore means that God is always doing good to us through the universe reflecting back to ourselves whatever our concept of it is. As Rabbi Baruch Ashlag writes: by feeling blessed we attract blessings to ourselves. If we feel negative about our life, then we attract events that we perceive as negative.

This is the highest level of understanding of reward and punishment and this is its meaning in the Kabbalah. Rabbi Ashlag states in the *Introductions* that belief in reward and punishment is fundamental for anyone involved in the spiritual life. If we act on this belief in reward and punishment, we can use untoward happenings as stimuli to go into ourselves and discover our own motivations.

"Reward and punishment" is something which requires belief, since the results of our actions are not immediately obvious. We often see the wicked prospering and the good suffering. The justice of this is very far from apparent. The awareness that God is Good and does good to both the good and the evil requires faith. Yet the *tzaddik* dwells in this consciousness permanently.

Reincarnation and the Revival of the Dead

In Kabbalah, the notion of reincarnation and that of the revival of the dead, are two entirely separate ideas. It is understood in Kabbalah that we incarnate many times. The work of transformation of the will to receive is not easy and cannot be accomplished in one lifetime. What is more, in any one life we can only encounter certain aspects of the will to receive and not the total picture, which we need many incarnations to complete. So we have the whole of history in which to reincarnate many times and in many different situations and places in order to accomplish the necessary work of transformation.

When we have completed this work, and reached the stage of transformation from love, then there occurs the revival of the dead which is not another incarnation but, rather, something quite different. With coming into the consciousness of transformation from love, we complete the healing of our souls. We are now *complete tzaddikim*. However our bodies have not been healed. We are still physically born, and our bodies grow, only to decay and rot away. Physical death still occurs to all of us.

There is another stage of work, in which the task is to spiritualize our bodies so that they become bodies of light and are no longer physical and subject to degeneration and decay. When this happens, we no longer leave our bodies behind when we die, and death is swallowed up for ever. Rabbi Ashlag tells us that this will be the second great task for humanity to accomplish, after that of the perfection of our souls, but that there are already a few people who have begun this work.

A further explanation of *The Revival of the Dead* is as follows:

When a person reaches the end of his or her transformational journey and has attained all five lights of *Nefesh, Ruach, Neshamah, Chayah* and *Yechidah*, then he or she already knows that one does not use the will to receive, only the will to give. Therefore, the person now has the strength to *receive* in order to give. He or she may now receive everything, using their will to receive and yet, at the same time, remain in perfect unity with God because they are receiving only in order to give.

This state is known as *the Revival of the Dead*, as the will to receive which was previously "dead" because it was not in use, now reawakens to life.

Faith

Faith is one of the cornerstones of Rabbi Ashlag's teachings on how to do one's inner work. It is the antidote to the vessel's desire for information and knowledge. Metaphysically, faith belongs to the tree of life and thus represents unity as opposed to the tree of knowledge of good and evil; the world of logic and duality.

Faith is absolutely fundamental to the path of Kabbalah, whether it be faith in God, faith in the teacher and the teachings, or faith in oneself as a spark of God. The reason it is so important is that Kabbalah describes life and its processes from the point of view of an enlightened mind quite different from our regular, everyday consciousness. Its most fundamental idea, for example, is that God is Good and does good and that everything that happens to us is ultimately good. Kabbalah offers us a perspective that is not only radically different from our regular understanding of events, but also at times contradicts this understanding. Which of these two mutually incompatible views are we to accept? If we stick to our own perceptions, then we cannot move beyond them. Yet to abandon them in favor of another's understanding of reality requires an enormous leap of faith. We can choose to accept the *tzaddik* as our teacher and then regard his or her perception of reality as more correct than our own. This takes faith and is known in Judaism as *faith in the sages*.

Faith in God is yet a higher stage. It does not have anything to do with one's lifestyle, religious or secular. It is a personal relationship with the Divine. None of us know whether God is or is not. Belief is a choice. It is a choice that repeatedly presents itself in the challenges of everyday life. Do I choose to think, speak and act as if God is, or do I choose to think, speak and act as if God is not? Faith in God as a spiritual stage is a light which can only enter a vessel that is ready for it. It comes by grace. "I labored and I found – believe!"

Finally, in Kabbalah, one needs faith in oneself. Rabbi Ashlag tells us that we are the beloved children of God. God's whole purpose in creation was to give us all the good He has in store for us. To believe this is to value oneself to a very high degree, to really appreciate oneself as a beloved child of God. This is a perception of oneself which is very far from our usual one, which is so often filled with self-doubt, anger turned inwards against ourselves, guilt and shame.

Souls
Rabbi Ashlag tells us that souls are part of God, separated from the One by their association with particular combinations of will to receive. By these connections, the souls come under the influence of some of the qualities of that ego. When they do this, they separate themselves from God and from each other, as they now display differences of form that were quite absent before this. In this way, what was once one, now becomes many.

As people do their inner work and transform their wills to receive for themselves alone into wills to receive in order to give, their unique expressions of love come to the fore. Just as our outer appearances are different from each other, so is each soul a unique expression of God in the world.

Contraction

In the state of the *Ein Sof*, we were/are one with God existing together with the Divinity in a state of perfect unity. The vessel was filled with light. This might be compared to the state of the fetus inside the mother's womb.

However, within this sense of unity a thought arose. The wish arose to be more like God; as the branch desires to become like its root, so the vessel desired to become a giver like the light. The phrase used in Kabbalah is "*Le'kashet et atsmoh*", which means "to make oneself more beautiful, as does a lady who puts on her finest jewelry." Thus came the decision of the vessel to stop receiving.

As soon as this decision was made, the Divine light withdrew. This is called *tzimtzum* or contraction. It is a contraction of the will to receive leading to a withdrawal of the light. There is no compulsion in spirituality. So if the vessel says, "No" to the light, the light will not force itself upon it. As a result of the contraction, there is, for the first time, an aspect in existence in which there is no Divine light. Now, within this space, the entire drama of creation can take place, for there can only be creation where the Divine light has withdrawn.

This is the case because in the presence of the Divine light, the vessel is overwhelmed or submerged. It cannot establish its own identity. Rabbi Ashlag compares this situation to that of a candle flame submerged in the light of a bonfire. Only in the absence of light can the candle flame shine.

The Divine light limits the vessel's capacity as it fulfils the vessel's needs and desires before it has reached its fullest potential of longing. Thus the purpose of contraction is to allow the vessel to establish its own identity in full consciousness and with full freedom of choice.

Contraction is the vessel's perception of the absence of light. But in fact it is the vessel which has turned away from the light—which never ceases to shine—not even for a moment.

No Exchange in Kabbalah/Eternity

This new state of contraction does not replace the state of the *Ein Sof* in which the vessel was full, but is *in addition* to it. Each state that represents a new desire of the vessel, does not *replace* all its previous states, but is simply additional to it. Thus we, who originated in the *Ein Sof* and who have passed through all the four worlds of holiness before coming to our present state, exist simultaneously in all these states.

This illustrates an important principle in Kabbalah. Just as the vessel exists in the *Ein Sof*, filled with light, so it exists in the world of *tzimtzum*, empty of light, with both states existing simultaneously.

Chapter 6

One Person's Journey in Kabbalah

Mark and Yedidah Cohen

W e have now seen and studied the original texts that Rabbi Ashlag wrote setting out the basic ideas of Kabbalah. The question now is how to work with them and use them to promote the transformations within ourselves to which the texts refer.

These texts are amongst the most radical documents that exist in religious literature. They insist, for example, that we are simply not created the way we appear at present. The bodies that we have now, Rabbi Ashlag tells us, are not our true bodies, as they appear in the thought of Creation. They tell us that the sole purpose of creation is for us to receive all the good that God has reserved for us, like the inheritance a beloved child receives from his or her father. They declare that God's relationship to us is characterized by absolute love; that God is Good and does good to good people and evil doers alike.

These ideas are so different from those we normally carry around in our heads that although it may be relatively easy to grasp them intellectually, it often feels that it is next to impossible for us to absorb them into our hearts and to live them in practice. This is the difficult work of spiritual discipline and inner effort.

In order to do this, it is necessary to become intimate with this material to make it our own and to establish a personal connection with it. When these thoughts no longer come from the outside in, but, rather, they flow from the inside out, like an overflowing well, then we have truly grasped this material. It becomes us and we become it.

Becoming intimate with this material involves taking an inner journey, a voyage to the heart of our being, to meet whatever lies beyond and deeper than the myriad habits and the conditioning of decades that we regularly think of as ourselves. In coming to know our true selves, so we come to the heart of reality. The microcosm and the macrocosm are one. We are the universe and all of its countless constituents. This is a deeply personal adventure of consciousness which each of us must undertake for himself or herself alone. Other people can act as guides and supporters but no-one can do another's inner work. As an example of this work, Yedidah shares her story:

"It is true that everyone sees and interprets reality through the prism of his or her own experience and personality. That is as true of me as it is of you. So what I'm not going to do here is to write my own interpretation of Rabbi Ashlag's work. Each person can see for himself or herself how their life is mirrored within the work of Rabbi Ashlag. Nevertheless, I realize that one day you may be holding this book in your hands wanting to come closer to the practical work of self-transformation but without the benefit of the living presence of a guide or a teacher, such as I have had. So I would like to share with you some practical steps that have helped me along the path at different times.

"I came to the work of Rabbi Ashlag at a time of intense inner conflict. On the surface my life looked fine. I was married with two boys and a good relationship with my husband. But underneath I was not happy. My thirst for a real connection with God through a living truth had never been satisfied.

"I was brought up in a religious Jewish household that outwardly conformed to the rules and regulations, but an inner sense of the intimacy of Torah had been missing. I sensed, even as a child, that there had to be something more – but it had eluded me. I grew up and became a Doctor of Medicine. I specialized in anesthesia and became especially attuned to people's pain and their suffering. I learnt how to alleviate pain of different kinds, both physical and emotional. Yet I was never able to answer the question of why we suffer.

"I tried studying the *Tanya*, the classic work of the *Chabad* Chassidim and I felt that I was on the right track—but for me it still did not resonate. My inner distress continued within me, sometimes coming to the surface and at other times simply simmering underneath.

"A good and perceptive friend of mine who saw what lay beneath the surface and who was himself involved in the work of Rabbi Ashlag introduced me to this work. The note sounded. A chord had been struck. I knew that this material spoke to me in a way that no other material had.

"I started to study with my friend. Right from the start it was clear to me that this was no intellectual study. Used to learning, I nevertheless suddenly found myself unable to understand seemingly simple ideas. I found myself asking my friend again and again, "But what *is* the will to receive?" My difficulty did not lie in my inability to understand with my brain but, rather, in my inability to see that I also acted from a will to receive for myself alone.

"So my first exercise was simply to become an observer of myself. I began to try to see where I was acting from. What were the motives that lay behind my words and actions? This was hard for me. I had been so used to criticizing and judging myself and living up to high standards that simply asking myself the question, "Where am I acting from?" was not an easy task! What encouraged me was my knowledge, brought from the teaching of Rabbi Ashlag, that the ego is a necessary and precious part of God's creation. It is the raw material for the transformed vessel that will one day receive God's light. I no longer needed to judge myself or feel guilty. If I acted from my ego it was, after all, God who had placed the vessel within me! This helped relieve the difficult feelings of guilt and self-criticism with which I had always lived. The simple question, "Where am I acting from?" became more a matter of curiosity, interest and self-awareness. It was important at the beginning to ask this question without any hidden impulsion or compulsion to act differently; simply to grow in non-judgmental awareness.

"The months went by and I continued my studies. The yearly calendar with the High Holidays of *Rosh Hashanah* and *Yom Kippur* came around. They brought again the familiar hateful feelings of God sitting in judgement; sins, confession and repentance. I expressed my feelings to my friend. He looked at me in astonishment. "But God isn't like that at all! That is a projection on God that people have made over the centuries." I went back to the study of Rabbi Ashlag. My friend was right. I needed to correct my own inner image of God. I looked at the four stages of our perception of God's Providence as described in the *Introduction to the Study of the Ten Sephirot*. It did not matter to me which stage I was at—the very notion that I could change my concept of God—that it was possible to change—felt like a gift, a miracle. Whatever notion of God I had cobbled together within me from my background, culture and life experience could change! I did not have to be bound by it. I could move on. With that gift of inner freedom, I took on the affirmation, "God is Good and does good."

"It was not easy. I wanted more children and instead was suffering miscarriage after miscarriage. Sometimes I quarrelled with my husband. It was hard in those moments to say "God is Good and does good", let alone believe it! Yet I persevered. I did so much want a better and deeper connection with God than I had had previously.

"After about a year of studying the material, I decided that it was time to look inside myself and see in what ways I had changed. How had this hard work, this study, changed me? I looked within and found that it had not made any difference at all. I was astonished! How could that be? Extremely hesitantly, I shared this experience with my friend. To my surprise, a smile slowly spread across his face. The learning, he explained, had all been in the nature of surrounding light, the light which shines upon the vessel, awakening it to the need to transform. Now I was beginning to discover the true lack within me, the true need to give, the true need to act differently, to change my responses and my way of being in the world. Only when the vessel itself senses its lack of light can the real work begin of changing the vessel and bringing it into affinity of form with the light.

"That moment was eight years ago.

"Since then both the study of Rabbi Ashlag's works and my learning in the day-to-day endeavors of trying to put his teaching into practice continue, thank God. I often feel that I am going backwards instead of forwards. There are downs as well as ups. The question, "Where am I acting from?—Am I acting from my will to receive for myself alone?"—has become a constant one. I am helped enormously by the knowledge that I am not alone. All over the world, in so many different spheres, people are discovering these ancient yet simple truths. Living from our ego doesn't in the end give much joy, but living in order to give to others, and to our Creator, gives hope for us all and a deep and abiding pleasure within.

"My path is the path of Rabbi Ashlag. Each day I patiently build my faith anew, trying to put something of Torah and *Mitzvot* into practice with the consciousness of an inner intention of bringing benefit.

I know that any success is actually due to God anyhow, and I simply feel the privilege of being a Jew at this time for whom God has opened up this most intimate wisdom of the Kabbalah.

"I have found these same basic truths embodied in the work and lives of other people coming from different traditions and am encouraged by this. I acknowledge these teachers with much gratitude, as their writings illuminate and amplify aspects of my own path.

"I explore works which discuss anger and how to deal with it; compassion and how to bring it into manifestation. As my work on forgiveness deepens, I see my struggles to forgive mirrored in the work of others struggling with the same issues. I read articles on modern economics and see how man's greed and will to receive for himself alone underlie the globalization of the world's economy. The refusal of the industrialized nations to act conclusively to prevent global warming and the promotion of modern technological methods of food production of dubious safety, over traditional, sustainable agriculture are all fuelled by the same basic will to receive for oneself alone. Joanna Macy, the eco-activist, is right when she declares that ecology starts with ourselves.

"As I learn not to deny but to stay awake and present to my own suffering, I have found that my capacity to remain present to the suffering and pain of my friend, my neighbor and the people of the world, similarly grows. Likewise, my blessings and simple gratitude for what I have and my ability to be truly happy and content, deepens.

"Rabbi Ashlag wrote vast quantities of material, still available only in Hebrew. But looked at in depth, there are multitudes of levels combined within even relatively short pieces of writing.

"So I bless you, dear reader, that through these *Introductions* you will feel inspired to look within, both within the words and within yourself, at increasingly deeper levels, and may all beings benefit by your effort."

Notes

Introduction
Then the letter *bet* appeared—*Zohar, Perush HaSulam, Hakdamot l'Sepher HaZohar, paragraph 37.*

Chapter 1 Kabbalah in Context
Rabbi Abraham Isaac Kook (1865-1935) was the first Chief Rabbi of the Jewish community in the land of Israel. He saw the return of the Jews to Zion as an outer expression of the inner development of the human soul. His mystical writings and yearnings have created a new awareness of Kabbalah as the inner core of Judaism.

Joanna Macey (World as Lover, World as Self; Parallax Press 1991): A Western Buddhist eco-activist who sees the interconnection in the web of all life.

Vandana Shiva (Stolen Harvest; South End 1999): A dedicated eco-activist stemming from the Hindu tradition. Outspoken about the ravages of globalization and the patenting of life.

The metaphor of humanity as being chained inside a dark cave is taken from Plato's Republic, part 7, book 7.

William Wordsworth: "Trailing Clouds of Glory…"—from *"Ode: Intimations of Immortality from Recollections of Early Childhood."*

The Language of the Branches—Passage taken from *"The Study of the Ten Sephirot", part 1, Histaclut P'nimit.* Quoted by kind permission of Rabbi Y. Miller, the copyright holder.

The reward is according to the suffering—*Ethics of the Fathers, Chapter 5, end.*

Chapter 2. Rabbi Ashlag and his Predecessors.
"Rabbi Shimon Bar Yochai and his son…" —*Talmud, Shabbat 33b.*

The information on the biography of Rabbi Ashlag is derived from the book *HaSulam* by Rabbi Avraham Mordechai Gottleib. See Bibliography.

No one could have known of his inner work from the outside. This principle of inner work combined with outer modesty is part of Rabbi Ashlag's path. Otherwise there is a danger of appropriating levels of spiritual achievment for the ego.

Rabbi Ashlag's letter is printed in the first volume of the *Perush HaSulam*. It is reprinted here by kind permission of Rabbi Y. Miller.

Chapter 3. Introduction to the Zohar.

Paragraph 2
"From Your works we know you,"—*The Prayer book.*

Paragraph 3
If this is so, why do the dead need to be revived?—The revival of the dead is a fundamental idea in Judaism. See *Keywords, Definitions and Concepts* for a discussion of this topic.

Paragraph 4
…Rabbi Eliezer, the son of Rabbi Shimon, chanced to meet an extremely ugly man. —*Talmud, Ta'anit 20b.*

Paragraph 6
Our sages have taught us that God's only purpose in creating the world was in order to give pleasure to His creatures. —*Etz Chayim, Sha'ar HaClalim, Chapter 1.* See *Introduction* and *Keywords, Definitions and Concepts.*

Paragraph 8
…In spirituality, it is difference of form that divides one entity into two. See affinity of form, difference of form and antipathy of form in *Keywords, Definitions and Concepts.*

Paragraph 10
The four worlds, Atzilut, Briyah, Yetzirah and Assiyah. —See *Keywords, Definitions and Concepts.*
…The wicked in their lifetime are called 'dead'—*Talmud Berachot 18b.*

Paragraph 11
Receiving only for the purpose of giving to others or to God is considered as having exactly the same form as pure giving. —This idea is learnt from the *Talmud, Kiddushin 7a* in the discussion of a particular case of laws on marriage, in which a woman of poor status marries a man of high standing. She gives him a ring. (Normally, the man gives a ring to the woman.) His acceptance of the ring, although technically receiving, is actually giving to her because of the pleasure she receives in his acceptance of her gift.

Paragraph 12

This state is designated as the end of the healing process. —Also meaning a state when the world as a whole will rise up to a higher level of holiness. See *Keywords, Definitions and Concepts*.

Paragraph 13

…God does not require time. — *Zohar, Perush HaSulam, Mishpatim paragraph 51* and *Zohar Chadash, Bereshit paragraph 243*.

"Before the world was created, He and His name were One."—*Talmud Eser HaSephirot, part one*. "He" refers to the light, "His Name" refers to the vessel.

Paragraph 16

"If you reform, that is good, and if not I will set over you a king like Haman who will force you to reform."—*Talmud Sanhedrin 97b*.

Haman was the evil Prime Minister of King Ahashverosh, ruler of the Persian Empire. The biblical Book of Esther depicts how he plotted the destruction of the Jews but was undone by Mordechai and Esther through a series of "coincidences" which show the hidden hand of God. In Jewish thought, Haman is one of the archetypal figures of evil.

Paragraph 25

The blemishes that they acquired in their lifetimes so that no-one will be able to claim that this is someone else.—*Zohar, Perush HaSulam Emor, paragraph 51.3*.

Paragraph 27

The revival of the dead can only come about close to the end of the healing process —See *Keywords, Definitions and Concepts*.

Paragraph 30

…the *Nefesh* of holiness. (This is the smallest of the lights pertaining to the soul.) —See *soul* in *Keywords, Definitions and Concepts*.

Paragraph 31

…it is the step that brings the person to practise Torah and *mitzvot* for its own sake —meaning that we reach a level in which we act, not in order to gain something personally from our action, but out of service, love and compassion i.e. for God's sake.

As the sages taught, "A person should practise Torah and *mitzvot* even if it is not for its own sake, because through practising not for its own sake he will eventually come to practise for its own sake."—*Talmud, Pesachim 50*

…thus enabling him or her to merit the inspirational presence of the *Shechinah*.

The presence of God in the world and in us. See *Keywords, Definitions and Concepts.*

Paragraph 34

Every single world amongst all the higher worlds [and also our physical world] is divided into these four categories.—See the entry entitled *formation of the vessel* in *Keywords, Definitions and Concepts.*

The will to receive is revealed and developed gradually through the three previous levels before reaching its final completed form in the fourth level. —See *Talmud Eser HaSephirot, Part 1, Paragraph 50.*

Paragraph 37

...their fellow animal's happiness and suchlike.—Many of the higher animals can sense the misfortune or the happiness of other animals and humans. There are numerous stories of dogs concerned over their owners' welfare, or dolphins helping distressed people. The difference between this capacity and that of the speaking level is that they sense only the feelings of the other as it affects them. They cannot feel the other's feelings as if they were the other. They cannot put themselves in the other's shoes, so to speak.

Paragraph 44

...without any degree of love or awareness of serving God—Rabbi Baruch Ashlag comments here: At this point the person sees that he is unable to carry out Torah and *mitzvot* for its own sake (i.e. for God's sake) since his will to receive for himself alone does not permit it. Still he practises Torah and *mitzvot* in order that they will purify his will to receive. Then, indeed, the Torah and *mitzvot* are able to purify his will to receive at the level of the first aspect which is the aspect of the inanimate. This is not the case if he fulfills Torah and *mitzvot* for the sake of a reward and does not desire that the practice will lead him to the purification of his will. This is called an opposing action, i.e. he does in fact have an intention at the time of fulfilling Torah and *mitzvot* . His intention is that of receiving a reward.

...all the 613 commandments—See *Keywords, Definitions and Concepts.* The number 613 is used as a metaphor for completeness.

Paragraph 55

"When someone tries to purify themselves, they get help..."—*Zohar, Perush HaSulam, Noach, paragraph 63.*

Paragraph 59

...the holy *Tanna*—A *Tanna* is a Rabbi from the period of the *Mishnah*, roughly the first two centuries of the present era.

...doubts about its authorship. —See, for example, Gershom Scholem, *Fundamentals of Jewish Mysticism.*

Paragraph 61

...until the level of the chest—The term "chest" refers to the depiction of any spiritual entity based on the form of a man with a head, body and end (legs). The part down to the chest is the first third of the body.

Paragraph 63.

"Rav Papa said to Abaya..."—Teachers of the 4th and 5th generation of *Amoraim* (later teachers). They taught in Babylonia around the 4th century. Quotation is from *Talmud Brachot 20a.*

"...in the time of Rav Yehudah"—Rav Yehudah was head of the Academy at Pumpidita in Babylonia in the third century. He belonged to the second generation of *Amoraim.*

"If a woman presses vegetables in a pot"—*Uzkin* 2. Alt. Version, "Olives pressed with their leaves clean." *Uzkin* is the last of the *Mishnaot* and nowadays is placed at the end of the Tractate, *Tohorot.*

"...Rav and Shmuel"—Earlier teachers of the first generation of *Amoraim,* who taught in the early second century in Babylonia. Their discussions are found throughout the Talmud.

Paragraph 66

"Make your Torah your main occupation and your work secondary to it."—*Ethics of the Fathers Chapter 8, verse 1.*

Paragraph 69

"Come and wake up for the sake of the Holy *Shechinah*..."—*Tikunei HaZohar 30,* Column 2.

The Holy *Shechinah*—The presence of Divinity in the world, conceived of as female. See Introduction to *In the Shadow of the Ladder.*

Paragraph 70

"Sufferings only come to the world on account of Israel" —*Talmud, Yebamot 63a.*
"The Righteous are the first to suffer." —*Talmud Baba Kama 60a.*

Chapter 4. Introduction to the Study of the Ten Sephirot

Paragraph 1

The destruction of the Temple—took place in 70 CE. It was a pivotal point of

Jewish history marking the beginning of the Diaspora and the exile.

Paragraph 3

... The wicked in their lifetime are called 'dead'—*Talmud Berachot 18b.*

Torah and *Mitzvot* —See *Keywords, Definitions and Concepts*. Here Rabbi Ashlag is using the expression Torah and *mitzvot* to mean inner consciousness of the work—Torah and *mitzvot* for the sake of giving pleasure to God.

Paragraph 4

Torah for its own sake —See *Keywords, Definitions and Concepts*.

Paragraph 5

"This is the Way of Torah: You should eat bread with salt..." —*Ethics of the Fathers, Chap. 6.*

Other wisdoms of the world—Rabbi Ashlag is not discussing here the wisdom and practices of other religions. (It is doubtful whether in his day he would have known of them.) Buddhism, for example, does require certain aesthetic practices. Rather, he is referring to intellectual wisdom such as scientific knowledge and the like.

Paragraph 6

"Whoever labors in Torah..."—*Ethics of the Fathers, Chap 6 v.1.*

Paragraph 10

"Let there be light in this world and there was light in the world to come." —*Zohar, Perush HaSulam, Bereshit 1. para 351.*

Paragraph 11

The period of the *Mishnah* preceded that of the Talmud.

"A person should always practise Torah and *mitzvot*..."—*Talmud, Pesachim 50b*

Torah not for its own sake —i.e. impure motives. See *Keywords, Definitions and Concepts*.

"The light within the Torah will bring a person back to the good way." —*Midrash Raba Lamentations, paragraph 1.*

Paragraph 12

"Do not be like slaves..."—*Ethics of the Fathers, chap. 1 v.3.*

"For those who use it wrongly..."—*Talmud, Shabbat 88b.*

Paragraph 13

This is analogous to the rooster and the bat.—The analogy is from the *Talmud, Sanhedrin, 62b.*

Paragraph 16

"The Torah becomes the elixir of life..."—*Talmud, Ta'anit 7a.*

The commentators here raised the following objection —*Tosephot on Ta'anit 7a.* They juxtapose the quotation we learnt above *(Pesachim 50b)* that practice of Torah and *mitzvot* not for its own sake will lead to practice of Torah for its own sake with the idea that for those who practise Torah not for its own sake, the Torah becomes the drug of death.

Cause and effect is referred to in the text as reward and punishment. See *Keywords, Definitions and Concepts* for a discussion of this issue.

Paragraph 17

"The Master is faithful..."—*Ethics of the Fathers, Chap. 2 v. 21.*

"Habbakuk came and put faith at the very center of the religion..."— from the *Talmud Macot 24a,* which quotes the scripture (Hab. 2:4).

"Job sought to excuse all the world from judgment..." —*Talmud Baba Batra 16a.*

"If this knave attacks you, drag him to the **Beit HaMidrash**..."—*Talmud, Kiddushin, 30b.*

Paragraph 19

The quotation that Rabbi Chayim Vital brings from the Talmud, "If a student of Torah does not see a sign of blessing..."—is from *Chullin 24a.*

Paragraph 21

"The Holy One Blessed Be He said to Israel, 'By your life! All this wisdom...'" —*Midrash Raba, Zot HaBracha, section 6.*

Paragraph 24

"An ignorant person..." —*Ethics of the Fathers, chap. 2, v. 6.*

"An inadvertent error..." — *Ethics of the Fathers, chap. 4, v. 17.*

"Even an inadvertent error may nevertheless incur a loss of much benefit" —*Eccles. 9:18.*

Paragraph 27

Ma'aseh Merkavah is the esoteric explanation of Ezekiel's vision of the chariot *(Ezekiel chap. 1)* and **Ma'aseh Bereshit** is the esoteric explanation of the creation. They are, by tradition, only passed down privately between master and highly qualified student.

Paragraph 28

"It is quoted in the Book of Isaiah..." — *Talmud Pesachim 119a.*

Comment on verse *Exod. 3:15*, **"This is my name for concealment."** The word עלם
means "hidden" or "concealed" and also "forever."
"One does not expound..."—*Talmud, Chagiga 11b.*

Paragraph 29
There is some argument in the Talmud here.
The exact translation here is as follows:

"And the latter opinion does not conflict with the former. The two opinions only
differ concerning which principles are learnt from which expressions in the above
quotation from Isaiah [but they agree as to the principles themselves].

The first opinion understands the words, "stately clothing" as referring to the
great reward for concealing the *Sitrei Torah.* The second opinion understands the
previous phrase in this quotation, namely "to eat sufficiently," as referring to the
Ta'amei Torah, according to the phrase, "The palate tastes food." (Job 12:12) For the
lights of ta'amim (taste) are called "eating." Therefore the second opinion explains
the great reward of which Isaiah speaks, to refer to someone who reveals the
reasons of Torah. But both opinions hold that one is obligated to cover the secrets
of Torah and to reveal the reasons of Torah."

"When I remember Him, I just cannot sleep"—We have unfortunately been
unable to trace this reference (trans.).

Paragraph 33
The maidservant of the shells—The term "shells" is another expression for the
framework of evil or uncleanness.

Paragraph 34
Israel—refers to the highest aspect of consciousness within any man or woman.
See further note in *Keywords, Definitions and Concepts.*
The light of lovingkindness —is the light which a person attracts to himself
through his service or compassion to others. The light of wisdom is the light which
is a direct emanation from the infinite.

Paragraph 39
**"For the person who practises Torah not for its own sake the Torah becomes a
drug of death."** —*Talmud, Ta'anit 7a.*

Paragraph 40
If a person says, "I labored and subsequently I found..." —*Talmud Megillah 6b.*

Paragraph 45
Cause and effect —In the Hebrew this is written as *reward and punishment.* See

Keywords, Definitions and Concepts for a full discussion of this point.

Paragraph 48

"Then My anger will burn and I will conceal My face from them." —God in the essence of the One does not get angry! The light of the One is always at perfect rest. It is the perception of the vessel projected back onto God that perceives anger.

Paragraph 49

Such people have in fact turned to other gods.—As we have learnt, God is always within a person (in the form of the soul). The people referred to here have lost direct contact with that aspect of themselves.

Paragraph 57

At this level of **fear of sin**, which Rabbi Ashlag explains as fear of the consequences of the sin, namely suffering, one must understand that the sufferings referred to here are not those of bodily suffering or of punishment in this world or the next, which would be a low level of fear of sin. The sufferings referred to here are those suffered as a result of the spiritual anguish consequent on the sin causing us to be separate from the Source of all life.

Paragraph 59

The suffering that a person goes through has a purpose in helping him grow or spiritually heal and thus it is a consequence of Divine Providence. When a person views this as a punishment, it is because at this level of perception, he does not see that God is always Good and never punishes. This latter perception marks the stage of the complete *tzaddik*, as Rabbi Ashlag goes on to inform us.

Paragraph 66

612 mitzvot.—The total number of *mitzvot* is seen as being 613. The 612th is thus the penultimate *mitzvah*, the ultimate one being love for God.
See *Keywords, Definitions and Concepts* for a fuller discussion of the number 613.

Paragraph 76

The teaching of the Rabbis brought here, **"When the Rabbis…"** is from the *Talmud*, 17a.

Paragraph 78

"Even though the whole world were to say to you…"—*Talmud, Niddah 30b.*
"See yourself in your own eyes as a *rasha*."—The Hebrew word here is *rasha* which means "a wicked person" but it is clear that the intention is a person who may still come to sin and who still has free choice. A person who has reached the revelation of God's face as it really is, is no longer liable to sin, and is called a *tzaddik*.

Paragraph 81
"The reward is according to the suffering."—*Ethics of the Fathers*, end of chapter 5. The suffering involved in the performance of Torah and *mitzvot* are diametrically opposed to the will to receive for oneself alone which, as we have learned in the *Introduction to the Zohar*, is the nature we have within us.

Paragraph 86
"Raba said, 'A person should know...'"—*Talmud, Brachot 61b.*

Paragraph 92
"Do not believe one who says..."—*Talmud, Megillah 6b.* The full quote is found in paragraph 93.
"A person should always practise..."—*Talmud, Pesachim 50b.*
Rabbi Yitshak said, "If a person should say..."—*Talmud, Megillah 6b.*

Paragraph 97
"When a person occupies himself with Torah for its own sake, then the Torah becomes an elixir of life for him."—*Talmud, Ta'anit 7a.*

Paragraph 99
"One who practises Torah not for its own sake, his Torah becomes a drug of death for him."—*Talmud, Ta'anit 7a.*

Paragraph 110
The Talmudic passage is from *Kiddushin 40a.*
"The *Tanna* said..."—The *tanna* refers to a rabbi who taught at the time of the *Mishnah.* His name is not identified in the text.

Paragraph 129
"As a man perceives..."—*Talmud, Sotah 8b.*

Paragraph 133
"The world was created only for the sake of the complete *tzaddik*..."—*Talmud, Brachot 61b.*

Paragraph 137
"He and his life force and his vessels are One."—Preface to the *Tikunei HaZohar*, paragraph 69 in *Ma'alot HaSulam.*

Paragraph 139
"When Moses ascended on high..."—*Talmud, Shabbat 89a.*

Paragraph 141
"If only you would forsake Me..."—*Talmud, Yerushalmi, Chagiga Chapter 1.* Also, the opening of *Midrash Rabba* on Lamentations.

Paragraph 144

"There is not a single blade of grass..."—*Bereshit Raba, Chapter 10, section 6.*

"A man cannot even bang..."—*Talmud, Chullin 7b.*

Paragraph 148

The remarks of the *Vilna Gaon* are quoted from his prayer book in connection with the blessings on the Torah.

The revealed Torah of *Assiyah* is the five books of Moses (called *Peshat*, meaning "simple").

Remez refers to *Midrash* and *Aggadah*.

Derash refers to the commentaries and laws.

Sod refers to the hidden wisdom of the Kabbalah. Here Rabbi Ashlag explains that the *sod* is really the simplest level.

Paragraph 150

"Most of the world of Assiyah... —*Etz Chayim, Gate 48, paragraph 3.*

Paragraph 156

"You should not make any idol..."—The second of the ten commandments, (Exodus 20:3).

Glossary

Ari—An acronym for *Rabbi Yitshak Luria*, a major Kabbalist who lived in *Safed*, Israel in the sixteenth century. His chief work was "The Tree of Life" (*Etz Chayim*).

Assiyah—The lowest of the four spiritual worlds. Our world is a subdivision of *Assiyah*.

Atzilut—The highest of the four spiritual worlds.

Bet HaMidrash— A study hall.

Ben HaHa—A rabbi from the Talmudic period, quoted in *Ethics of the Fathers*.

Benoni—A person of advanced spiritual attainment who has not yet reached the stage of the complete *Tzaddik*.

Binah—One of the ten *sephirot*.

Briyah—The second of the four spiritual worlds.

Chayah—The spiritual light that pertains to the *sephirah* of Chochmah.

Chochmah—The second of the ten *sephirot*.

Chesed—The fourth of the ten *sephirot*.

Da'at—One of the ten *sephirot*.

Ein Sof—The level of the Infinite.

Gaon of Vilna—Great rabbi and kabbalist of the seventeenth century.

Gematriah—System of assigning numerals to the Hebrew letters of the alphabet which allows hidden connections between concepts to become apparent.

Gemarrah—The Talmud; part of the oral law.

Halachah—The body of Jewish law.

Hod—One of the ten *sephirot*.

Kabbalah—Literally, "received wisdom." The most intimate part of Torah.

Keter—The first and highest of the ten *sephirot*.

Ma'aseh Bereshit—literally, "The work of creation." This together with **Ma'aseh Merkavah**—the vision of Ezekiel's chariot—comprises two parts of Kabbalah which need to remain hidden and are only imparted from sage to advanced pupil.

Maimonides—Twelfth century Jewish sage, doctor and philosopher.

Malchut—the last and lowest of the ten *sephirot*.

Mishnah—the earliest part of the Talmud, also known as the oral law.

Mitzvot—literally, "commandments" Also includes good deeds. The practical part of the Torah.

Nefesh—The light pertaining to the *sephirah* of *Malchut*.

Neshamah—The light pertaining to the *sephirah* of *Binah*.

Netzach—One of the ten *sephirot*.

Perush HaSulam—Literally, "The commentary of the ladder." Rabbi Ashlag's translation and commentary on the *Zohar*.

Rasha—literally, "A wicked person." Rabbi Ashlag also uses the term for a person who experiences God's providence from the aspect of God being concealed. Such a person cannot help but stumble into sin.

Rashi—The major commentator on the Bible and the Talmud. Lived in the eleventh century in France.

Ruach—the light pertaining to the *sephirah* of *Tiferet*.

Sephirah—(plural *sephirot*). Literally, "The shining one." A means through which God's light is contained and transmitted throughout the worlds.

Sepher HaYetsirah—One of the earliest books of the Kabbalah. By tradition it is attributed to Abraham, but it was quite possibly composed by Rabbi Akiva, teacher of Rabbi Shimon Bar Yochai.

Shechinah—The indwelling presence of God. The female aspect of God; *Malchut*.

Talmud—The great compilation of oral law comprising the *Mishnah* and the *Gemarrah*. It contains discussions of the Rabbis, stories, laws and legends.

Tanna—Plural *Tannaim*. A teacher from the period of the *Mishnah*.

Tiferet—One of the ten *sephirot*.

Tikkunei haZohar—A later part of the *Zohar*.

Torah—literally "Instruction". The term has two meanings depending on context. One refers to the five books of Moses alone, but it is often used more broadly to refer to the totality of Jewish teaching.

Tzaddik—Literally "saint". Also meaning one who justifies the Creator. A person who has reached enlightenment.

Yechidah—The highest light, pertaining to the *sephirah* of *Keter*.

Yesod—One of the ten *sephirot*.

Yetzirah—One of the four spiritual worlds.

Zohar—Literally "shining." The main work of Kabbalah, by tradition composed by Rabbi Shimon Bar Yochai.

Bibliography, Sources and Resources

Hebrew Sources

Ashlag, Yehudah Lev. *Panim Meirot uMasbirot.*

———*Talmud Eser HaSephirot.* 16 vols. Jerusalem.

———*Talmud Eser HaSephirot* with commentary of Rav Baruch Ashlag, Jerusalem: Or Baruch Shalom 1997-2002. Vols. 1-5 published at present.

———*Beit Sha'ar HaKavanot.*

———*Perush 'HaSulam' al HaZohar.* 21 vols. Revised edition Bnei Brak, Kla'ar 1998.

Collections of essays by Rabbi Yehudah Lev Ashlag

Ashlag, Yehudah Lev. *Matan Torah.* Ed. A Brandwein, Jerusalem: Or Ganuz, 1995.

———*Pri Chacham.* 3 vols. Ed. Avraham Yehezkel Ashlag, B'nei Brak, 1999.

———*Hakdamot L'Chochmat HaEmet,* with commentaries *Or Baruch* and *Or Shalom,* B'nei Brak; Or Baruch Shalom, 2000.

——— *Peticha LeChochmat HaKabbalah* with commentaries *Or Baruch* and *Or Shalom,* B'nei Brak; Or Baruch Shalom, 1996.

Collections of essays by Rabbi Baruch Shalom Halevi Ashlag

Ashlag, Baruch Shalom. *Shamati* Ed. M. Leitman, B'nei Brak 1993.

——— *Sefer HaMa'amarim (Birchat Shalom)* 3 vols. Edited by A.M. Gottleib, B'nei Brak; Or Baruch Shalom 1998.

———*Birchat Shalom Al Parshat HaShavua,* 2 vols. Ed. S. Ashlag, B'nei Brak. Birchat Shalom Institute, 1997.

All the above books can be obtained from the publisher/distributor,
M Kla'ar,
Rechov Kehillot Ya'akov 58,
B'nei Brak 51645,
Israel,
Tel. 972-3-6772451.

Further Reading

Gottleib, Avraham Mordechai. *HaSulam*. Biographies of Rabbi Yehudah Lev Ashlag and Rabbi Baruch Ashlag and their pupils: Or Baruch Shalom 1997, Jerusalem. Also includes much valuable information on Rabbi Ashlag's thought and customs.

English Resources

Further Reading—Classical Kabbalah

Luzatto, Moshe Chayim. *Path of the Just (Mesilat Yesharim)*. Feldheim.

———— *The Way of God (Derech HaShem)*. Jerusalem/New York: Feldheim 1988.

Cordovero, Moshe. *The Palm Tree of Devorah (Tomer Devorah)*. Michigan: Targum Press (dist. Feldheim), 1993.

Zalman, Shneur. *Tanya*. New York: Kehot Publication Society, 1996.

Kaplan, Aryeh. *Sepher Yetsirah (Book of Creation)*. Translated by Aryeh Kaplan. Red Wheel/Weiser 1997.

———— *Rabbi Nachman's Stories*. Translated with a commentary by Rabbi Aryeh Kaplan. New York and Israel: Breslov Research Institute, 1983.

Contemporary Jewish Kabbalah

Steinzaltz, Adin. *The Thirteen Petalled Rose*. Translated by Yehudah Hanegbi. New York: Basic Books, 1980.

Kaplan, Aryeh. *Meditation and the Bible*. Red Wheel/Weiser 1988.

———— *Meditation and Kabbalah*. Red Wheel/Weiser 1989.

———— *Jewish Meditation, a Practical Guide*. Schocken Books, 1995.

———— *Inner Space, Introduction to Kabbalah, Meditation and Prophecy*. Ed. Abraham Sutton. Jerusalem: Moznaim Publishers, 1990.

Safran, Alexandre. *Wisdom of the Kabbalah*. Trans. by E.M. Sandle. Jerusalem/New York: Feldheim 1991.

Personal Growth in Jewish Sources.

Adahan, Miriam. *E.M.E.T.*

———— *It's All a Gift*. Feldheim 1992.

Twerski, Abraham. *I am I*. Mesorah Publications, 1999

Internet Resources of Rabbi Ashlag's work in English.

www.nehorapress.com Mark and Yedidah Cohen may be contacted through the website for information and for further study.

http//kabbalah-web.org. Bnei Baruch organization of Rabbi Leitman.

Index

Mark and Yedidah Cohen, the translators, have studied this work in its original. Mark has a doctorate in philosophy on the relationship between Kabbalah and psychotherapy; his interest lies in the support and growth of the individual with reference to the ancient wisdom. Yedidah is an anesthesiologist whose awareness of people's suffering has brought her to the study and application of inner as well as outer healing. Both are active teachers of Rabbi Ashlag's work and may be contacted through Nehora Press.